3/06

The American Revelation

Also by Neil Baldwin

National Book Award Classics:
Essays Celebrating Our Literary Heritage

Henry Ford and the Jews:
The Mass Production of Hate

Legends of the Plumed Serpent:
Biography of a Mexican God

Edison: Inventing the Century

Man Ray: American Artist

To All Gentleness:
William Carlos Williams, the Doctor-Poet

The Poetry Writing Handbook

The Writing Life (coeditor)

The
American Revelation

Ten Ideals That Shaped
Our Country from the Puritans
to the Cold War

———

Neil Baldwin

ST. MARTIN'S PRESS
NEW YORK

www.stmartins.com

Library of Congress Cataloging-in-Publication Data

Baldwin, Neil, 1947–
    The American revelation : ten ideals that shaped our country from the Puritans to the Cold War / Neil Baldwin.—1st ed.
        p. cm.
    Includes bibliographical references (p. 235).
    ISBN 0-312-32543-6
    EAN 978-0312-32543-5
       1. National characteristics, American. 2. Ideals (Philosophy) 3. United States—Biography. 4. United States—Civilization—Miscellanea. 5. United States—History—Miscellanea. I. Title.

E169.1.B217 2005
973—dc22   2004063288

First Edition: May 2005

10 9 8 7 6 5 4 3 2 1

For Roberta

Sometimes people call me an idealist. Well, that is the way I know I am an American. America, my fellow citizens—I do not say it in disparagement of any other great people—America is the only idealistic nation in the world.

—Woodrow Wilson, September 8, 1919

Am I embarrassed to speak for a less than perfect democracy? Not one bit. Find me a better one. Do I suppose there are societies which are free of sin? No, I don't. Do I think ours is, on balance, incomparably the most hopeful set of human relations the world has? Yes, I do.

—Daniel Patrick Moynihan, 1975

America isn't bound together by emotion. It's bound together by things that transcend emotion, by principles and laws, by ideals of freedom and justice that need constant articulation.

—Editorial, "America Enduring,"
The New York Times, September 11, 2002

Contents

The American Revelation

Introduction

I deals cannot exist without idealists. *The American Revelation* pays tribute to the people who engendered ten essential ideals in our history and illuminates the times in which they were first expressed. In our own twenty-first century, as I write these words, the pulse of the nation often sounds as if it is emanating from two separate heartbeats. We need to turn to galvanizing beliefs that will provide a unifying focus for our thoughts and our lives in an instructive mental conversation with the past. The ten ideals discussed in *The American Revelation* are the rightful patrimony of all Americans.

The first inspiration for this book came to me when the new issue of *The Economist* landed on my doorstep one day in early September 2002. A feature called "A Year On" caught my eye. A "special report" on the gargantuan struggles facing America twelve months after the cataclysm of 9/11, the piece endeavored to capture the powerful national theme "of America as a place apart . . . from George Washington's warning to the new republic against 'entangling alliances' to Ronald Reagan's summons to his fellow citizens to build an ideal 'shining city on a hill.'"

President Reagan was indeed fond of that popular image, which he used in his January 11, 1989, farewell address to the nation. But he did not create the concept. The English Puritan leader John Winthrop, governor of the Massachusetts Bay Colony, invoked the "city on a hill" in the spring of 1630 in a sermon delivered to his fellow passengers on the ship *Arbella* preparing to set sail from Yarmouth at the dawn of "the Great Migration" to the New World. Imagining the land across the sea, Governor Winthrop, in turn, took inspiration from Christ's words in the Sermon on the Mount in the fifth book of the Gospel according to St. Matthew: "Ye are the light of the world. A city that is set upon a hill cannot be hid."

President Reagan, like Winthrop before him, saw America as above all else a moral exemplar. "I've spoken of that shining city all my political life," he recalled from the Oval Office in a valedictory speech televised just after nine o'clock in the evening. "In my mind it was a tall, proud city built on rocks stronger than oceans, windswept, God-blessed, and teeming with people of all kinds living in harmony and peace; a city with free ports that hummed with commerce and creativity." Reagan's lofty remarks set my imagination spinning. What provoked John Winthrop's vision of an ideal community in a new Promised Land? How did he come to develop such a romantic image of our country as a world paradigm, a vantage point for vigilance, likewise willingly exposed, open to be judged—and emulated—from afar?

John Winthrop's vivid metaphor is the natural beginning for the book you hold in your hands. He was a lawyer, scholar, and religious man, devoted to family and church. His colleagues on the governing Board of the Massachusetts Bay Company selected him as their leader to shepherd them across the ocean and make a new home in the wilderness. Winthrop employed his knowledge of scripture to inspire, not intimidate. He accepted his responsibility to set the tone for a fledgling pioneer community far from England. Winthrop conceived of this uncharted land as a place of promise where worldly fulfillment was possible through good works. His lay sermon, "A Model of Christian Charity," entered our national discourse precisely 375 years ago.

A century later another Englishman, Thomas Paine of Norfolk, came to America with the single-minded intent to start anew. From his earliest career as an excise collector in Lewes, Paine was an adamant champion of the rights of the workingman. Once on these shores, he sensed the undercurrent of desire for self-determination in the character of the American colonies as emblematic of "the cause of all mankind." In Philadelphia in January 1776, encouraged by Benjamin Franklin, Paine wrote and published *Common Sense,* the most influential and politically engaged pamphlet of its time, perhaps of all time. It was a hymn to America as a republic meant to survive for posterity. Paine's inflammatory rhetoric stands as a landmark in the American tradition of the free press.

The source for the ideal examined in the third chapter—our national motto, *E Pluribus Unum*, which means, "Out of many, one"—was likewise an immigrant, by way of Geneva and the West Indies. His name was Pierre Eugène Du Simitière, and he lived in Philadelphia during the Revolutionary War. Among his talents were heraldry and graphic design. During the momentous summer of 1776, Du Simitière was asked to serve as consultant to the Great Seal Committee of the Second Continental Congress. He labored closely with Benjamin Franklin, John Adams, and Thomas Jefferson to create an enduring coat of arms and a symbolic slogan for the thirteen United States of America. After trying various phrases and sketches, Du Simitière selected three words that have come to express the nation's multifaceted identity.

I turned next to Boston-raised, Harvard-educated Ralph Waldo Emerson, the most eloquent practitioner of nineteenth-century American individualism. Trained for the clergy, as a young man he abandoned the conventions and restraints of the church, preferring to make a living as an itinerant lecturer, preaching the gospel of the inexhaustible self. To "see into the life of things," Emerson dared to be different. He believed it was necessary to go against the grain in order to improve the society at large. Emerson's philosophy advocated truthful introspection as the foundation for integrity in the wider world. In 1841, living with his family in the quiet sanctuary of the Concord woods, he published the essay "Self-Reliance," a hymn to the singular American spirit.

Four years later two words expressing the inexorable progress of the nation entered the national vocabulary. John Louis O'Sullivan was a thirty-two-year-old lawyer, Jacksonian Democrat, and editor of the *New York Morning News* and the *United States Magazine and Democratic Review*. His passionate daily editorials added momentum to the expansionist fervor sweeping America, "to make the wilderness blossom as a rose" in the drive ever westward from sea to shining sea. "The fulfillment of our Manifest Destiny," he wrote, "[is] to overspread the continent alotted by Providence for the great experiment of liberty." For John O'Sullivan, manifest destiny heeded a higher purpose.

Chapter 6 is about a neglected supporting player in American history. To Henry George, land was also sacred property, but in a different way, as the basis for a worldwide "single-tax" movement, inspired by the publication of his best-selling work, *Progress and Poverty*, in 1879. Dropping out of school in Philadelphia at thirteen, George spent most of his adult life working as a typesetter and printer in San Francisco. Even when he founded his own newspaper and launched a career as a self-taught writer, he never lost sight of the sufferings of the "proletarian laborers" who bore the preponderant economic burden of an industrializing nation. In *Progress and Poverty*, Henry George proposed a leveling revision in the nation's unfair tax structure as the only way to remedy the grievous gap between "monstrous luxury and debasing want."

Long before the women's movement, a singular "modern woman" lived in perpetual motion, seeking to transcend the limitations imposed upon her sex. Jane Addams of rural Cedarville, Illinois, believed that "truest womanhood can yet transform the world." Committed to the obligation to serve those less fortunate, Addams established Hull-House, the first major social settlement in America. Located in the poorest immigrant ghetto of Chicago, Hull-House combined school, daycare and community center, gymnasium, soup kitchen, and library. Addams was the charismatic presiding spirit. Her 1902 essay, "Political Reform," appealed to every thoughtful American to do well by doing good: "The sphere of morals," she wrote, "is the sphere of action."

Three generations of a Jewish immigrant family living in a brownstone tenement in a shabby neighborhood of Staten Island within view of the statue of *Liberty Enlightening the World* were the protagonists of *The Melting-Pot*, a drama by Israel Zangwill. The son of an impoverished London East End old clothes trader, the playwright was enthralled by America as "God's crucible" for "all the races of Europe . . . to unite to build the Republic of Man and the Kingdom of God." The show premiered on October 5, 1908, in Washington, D.C. Pres. Theodore Roosevelt was so aroused by the final curtain that he shouted to the author across the crowded theater, "That's a great play, Mr. Zangwill!" *The Melting-Pot* idealized America as the epitome of egalitarian opportunity.

Carter Godwin Woodson, the first child of former slaves to attend Harvard, came north by way of the coal mines of West Virginia. Studying for the Ph.D. he earned in 1912, Woodson was told by his professor, Edward Channing, that "the Negro had no history." The dismissive remark inspired Woodson to correct that misconception during a life of lecturing, teaching, and exhaustive documentary research. He published dozens of books by himself and other Negro scholars and amassed "an arsenal of facts" on the saga of his race. With his own savings, he founded the Association for the Study of Negro Life and History. During the Harlem Renaissance in 1926, he created the February celebration of Negro History Week, now Black History Month. Carter Woodson's stubborn insistence on the legitimacy of black heritage laid down a path for all disenfranchised Americans.

The tenth and final chapter of *The American Revelation* turns around the global perspective begun when we followed John Winthrop westward on a voyage of hopeful renewal to foreign shores. In 1948 the Marshall Plan extended America's helping hand for the urgent cause of European recovery in the wake of a devastating war, harsh winters, and sparse harvests. Former general of the army George C. Marshall, Pres. Harry S. Truman's secretary of state, shepherded through Congress the largest voluntary transfer of economic resources in history—billions of dollars in development loans and outright grants, as well as raw materials, food, fuel, and machinery. On December 10, 1953, in ceremonies at Oslo, Marshall became the first professional military man ever to receive the Nobel Peace Prize, accepting it "on behalf of the American people" and telling the world of his conviction that America was a compassionate country, mindful of its great riches, and cherishing "a creed which comes to us from the deep roots of the past."

The American Revelation sheds light upon the human nature of our country. When we read the words of these ten patriots, we may well wonder if history has diminished their idealism. However, it is my belief that just because we have lost sight of a principle does not mean it no longer exists. "Patriotism" is not a one-dimensional abstraction, and the definition of national character does not come exclusively from the top down. Its legitimate meaning needs to be developed one citizen at a time—one reader at a time.

GOV. JOHN WINTHROP
1588 - 1649   SCHOOL OF VAN DYKE

JOHN WINTHROP

1

City on a Hill

The central problem of Puritanism as it affected John Winthrop and
New England has concerned men of principle in every age, not least of
all our own.

It was the question of what responsibility a righteous man owes to
society.

—Edmund S. Morgan, *The Puritan Dilemma:*
The Story of John Winthrop (*Preface* to First Edition, 1958)

Sunday, the Lord's Day, June 6, 1630, dawned at sea with raw wind,
rain, fog, and cold, six leagues west of the southern tip of Cape
Sable, Nova Scotia. Toward early afternoon the mist lifted. Capt.
Peter Milborne spotted land—for the first time in the two long months
since the 350-ton *Arbella* pulled away from Yarmouth on the Isle of Wight,
stemmed the tide with a slight wind, and slipped past the Needles into the
English Channel, beyond Plymouth and Cornwall into the choppy Atlantic.

Following a routine begun as a teenager that he would adhere to for two
more decades, the Right Worshipful John Winthrop, Esquire, Governor-
elect of the Massachusetts Bay Colony, sat at his desk in the small cabin he
shared with his two young sons, Stephen and Adam, and in "devilishly difficult," crabbed penmanship made note of the occasion in his notebook—
he did not call it a journal, considering his writing to be "history" or
"annals." This was as good an occasion as any to drop anchor at thirty
fathoms and try some cod fishing, the sea being "somewhat calm" and the
boxes of dried salt fish provisions depleted by the many travelers cramped
below decks. Within two hours and "with a few hooks," more than sixty

"very great" cod were triumphantly pulled from the water, "some a yard and ½ long and a yard in compass."[1]

Two days later, continuing south and west into warmer climes, Winthrop sighted Mount Desert Island. "We had now fair sunshine weather," he wrote, "and so pleasant a sweet ether as did much refresh us, and there came a smell off the shore like the smell of a garden." With the wind behind her, the *Arbella* passed Camden Hills and Penobscot Bay. A wild pigeon alighted on the deck. As Mount Agamenticus, near York, Maine, loomed into view, Winthrop discerned trees along the shore lowlands. Inspired, he drew a sketch of the coast.[2]

The mackerel were plentiful off Cape Ann, harbingers of a safe arrival. Firing two celebratory cannon shots at four o'clock Saturday morning, the *Arbella* passed between Little Misery Island and Baker's Island, dropping anchor in the harbor of Salem, "peaceful" in Hebrew, called Naumkeag by the Indians.

John Endecott, provisional leader of the advance settlement in Massachusetts Bay, came aboard in greeting. One-fourth of his people had died during the hard winter just past. Endecott, who had left his home in Devon two years previously, eagerly welcomed the promised transfer of authority to his successor, Governor Winthrop. Venison pasty, beer, and fresh strawberries were served. Weary passengers of the *Arbella*, women and children and some babies born on the voyage, made their way ashore, joined within the coming days by compatriots from sister ships *Jewel, Talbot,* and *Ambrose,* last seen veering away near Georges Bank, south of the Bay of Maine.

John Winthrop knew that before autumn he would have to find—in all practicality, construct—another community, beyond Salem, to accommodate his growing congregation. During the summer they moved up Mystic River to build a church at a new village later called Charlestown. By the end of the first year of the Great Migration to America, seventeen ships delivered to these shores more than one thousand English Protestants, called Puritans because they were determined to reform and "purify" the Church of England while remaining part of it—on their own land and subject to the will of their membership. Winthrop's Trading Company of Massachusetts moved its headquarters to the mouth of the Charles River where Boston was established. By the end of its first decade of life, the Massachusetts colony held fifteen thousand souls within "two days' march" or "a fair day's sail" of each other.[3]

The Puritan pioneer John Winthrop is known as the "most extraordi-nary, representative man" in the history of the Atlantic world, and the "first citizen of early New England." His grandfather, Adam, was a "wealthy clothier" providing capital for the purchase of wool from Stour Valley sheep farmers. In 1544 Adam Winthrop (the elder), the duly-elected master of the Clothworkers, acquired the manor house of Groton, set on more than five hundred acres in the rolling, rural Suffolk hills and meadows and "quiet horizons" eighty miles from London at the heart of East Anglia. The only son of lawyer-farmer Adam Winthrop (the younger), and his wife, Anne Browne, John Winthrop was born at Edward-stone in Suffolk on January 22, 1588, seven months before the defeat of the Spanish Armada by the British navy.[4]

As children, John and his sisters—Anne, the oldest child; Jane and Lucy, younger than John—enjoyed the unfettered pleasures of country life. The lad developed a bookish, spiritual side. He "caught the fever" of an en-during Calvinist faith in God as the determining force for all mankind. Raised in a devout household, John recalled with humble irony that "from about ten years of age I had some notions of God . . . the remembrance whereof many years after made me think that God *did* love me, but it made me no whit the better."[5]

At fourteen, John was sent up to Trinity, largest of the Cambridge col-leges, where he began every day with compulsory 5:00 a.m. prayers. In 1605 he left abruptly to marry a girl four years his elder, Mary Forth of Great Stambridge in Essex. On the birth of their first child, John Jr., in February of the following year, Winthrop the joyous teenaged father started a private "spiritual diary" titled "Experiencia." Written partly in code and now lost, the original manuscript was disparaged by nineteenth-century scholars as "imperfect . . . stained and torn in many places, and quite illegible in oth-ers . . . plainly intended for no eye but his own."[6]

Winthrop's diary was an unsparing, cumulative list of his "many sinnes . . . an account-current" against himself. The goal of the harsh soul-searching was to present the author as a spiritual example to his children and grandchildren. In the gradual religious development of a Puritan, the pilgrimage to understanding was lifelong and intensely private. Winthrop monitored his worldly transgressions closely. They ranged from staying up too late at night to overeating and ignoring exercise, from using tobacco to neglecting his wife by spending too many hours tramping through the fields shooting pheasants. These liabilities would have to be overcome if he was ever to reach what his friend John Cotton of Derby—a Puritan preacher whom Winthrop met in Emmanuel College when they were both Cambridge undergraduates—called the "essentiall wisdome."[7]

In 1610, at the age of twenty-two, Winthrop purchased the family property at Groton from his uncle. Following his father's path into the legal profession, Winthrop conducted court sessions at the manor as justice of the peace for Suffolk, settling disputes between farmers. He continued with law education and reading at Gray's Inn, one of the four Inns of Court in central London, where he studied the biblical precedents for judges' rulings. In addition to a focused "habit of command," Winthrop knew that it was customary for a gentleman magistrate judge to bring a sense of spirituality to bear upon his position. After all, his sage friend John Cotton once cautioned, "Zeale is but a wilde-fire without knowledge."[8]

John Winthrop believed that political engagement was a calling equal to ascending to the Christian pulpit. His aspirations as a soldier of the court were to protect the "weale publick," and as a soldier of the Lord to "advance the gospell." This faith in the word of law and the revealed holy "Word" found its roots in the English Puritan tradition. Puritans, thus named beginning in the 1560s, were Protestants who believed that the newly established Church of England should be cleansed of all hierarchical strictures, ceremonies, and polluting rituals remaining from the "smoky fornace of poperie," the Catholic Church of Rome.[9]

The earliest Protestants were also known as Precisians. Prefiguring the Fundamentalist movement born in America in the years leading up to World War I, the Precisians believed that they were guardians of the text of the Bible as the wellspring for all truths, and that familiarity with its literal message was the natural right of all free-willed people. The Scriptures were God's direct way of communicating to mankind. As such, they should no longer be subjected to the intermediating and arcane interpretations of the priesthood; bishops were resented and condemned by outspoken early Puritans for their arbitrary and unwarranted authority.[10]

The Puritan of John Winthrop's time lived by a succession of moral ideals. First of all he should read the Bible daily and depend upon it as the only guidebook needed along the path toward salvation. He should listen quietly to the "awful and gracious voice of God." He and his family should hope for election to membership in a close-knit community gathered with "one Unitie of Spirite that [will] strengthen and comforte one another, daylie growinge and increasinge in true faythe." Such choices would eventually bring a self-scrutinizing, disciplined man or woman of good character—with hard work and constant attention to the blessed burden of free will—to illumination by the redemptive light of God's grace. Then he would meet his maker face to face in "the perfect beawtie of Sion."[11]

By 1618 John Winthrop had suffered the loss of his first wife, Mary, who had borne him three living sons and a daughter; and his second wife, Tomasine Clopton of Groton, who died in childbirth a year after their marriage. He wedded Margaret Tyndal, daughter of a judge in the nearby town of Great Maplestead. Margaret would be his "sweet spouse" and devoted soul mate, loving her husband with "an unfeigned heart" for thirty years. By 1627 they had four sons. Winthrop was once again settled as the resident squire of Groton Manor, convening the daily morning, evening, and Sabbath "exercises" of prayer with his wife and brood of children, setting tasks for the farm workers, serving on the sewer commission, and hearing petitions from victims of small crimes and disputes in the village.[12]

In 1627 the family considered setting up an additional household in London when Winthrop was named to a prestigious position as an attorney in the Court of Wards and Liveries and admitted to practice in the Honourable Society of the Inner Temple, between Fleet Street and the river Thames. He worked there for the next two years and kept a special notebook composed of phrases he heard in noteworthy sermons.

On March 10, 1629, Charles I dismissed Parliament. This imperial action removed the people's ability to petition for legislative recourse for their grievances, and Winthrop was deprived of his attorneyship. Charles's royalist ally, Bishop of London William Laud, chancellor of Oxford and a watchful anti-Puritan with little patience for unorthodox and nonconformist clergymen, ascended to greater power as archbishop of Canterbury. Laud's desire to strengthen established High Church rituals, government, and canon enjoyed the encouragement of the king.

". . . [M]y Office is gone, and my Chamber [in London] . . . so as I hope, we shall now enjoy each other againe as we desire," John gloomily and wistfully confided to Margaret in one of the many letters he sent while professional affairs kept him in town during court sessions and she remained at Groton. "I am veryly persuaded, God will bringe some heavye Affliction upon this lande, & that speedylye."[13]

In the early summer of 1629, Winthrop departed the Temple and London for the quiet countryside. During July and August, with heaviness in his heart, but in accordance with the Puritan commitment to scholarly writing and publishing of all manner of papers and pamphlets, Winthrop began to compose and codify his first labored thoughts and "grevances" on a "propounded Course" to leave England. He submitted the drafts for critique and commentary to his fellow corporate investors in the Massachusetts Bay Company when they gathered at Bury St. Edmunds near Winthrop's Suffolk homestead, and also at Tattershall in Lincolnshire, on the estate of Winthrop's colleague, the wealthy landowner Isaac Johnson and his wife, the Lady Arbella Fiennes. Winthrop's goal in encouraging the debates was to emerge with an agreed upon template for a principled "removal" from England. At one time Winthrop called the proposal in progress "Arguments and Generall Considerations for the Plantation of New England" and at another, more personally, "Perticular Considerations in the Case of J. W." "Why should any of us go?" melded with "Why should I go?" Winthrop wanted the company's governing partners to understand that the flexible mandate in the charter establishing the "rights and privileges" of their joint-stock commercial trading business made its jurisdiction just as feasible on the soil of the New World as anywhere in England.[14]

In the proposal Winthrop first staked out where he stood on the ideological spectrum of religious dissent. He was not a radical. Those were the other Puritans—called Separatists then, and now known to us as the Pilgrims of the *Mayflower*—who first fled to Leyden, Holland, then headed from Delfts-Haven across "a sea of troubles before them in expectation" toward Virginia in 1620. Under William Brewster's leadership as their ruling elder, the first 150 Pilgrims landed by navigational accident at Cape Cod and settled in Plymouth Plantation, finding "easiness, plainness, and plentifulness in living."

John Winthrop made it clear from the outset of his exhaustively reasoned petition for withdrawal from England that he did not view himself or the members of the company in the same light as Brewster's followers, nor like the Scottish Presbyterians, treasonous zealots whose "wicked myndes" could not accept the idea of remaining within a national church. Separatists even descended to the claim that the churches of England were not legitimate houses of worship, to which Winthrop mildly countered that "the corruption of a thing doth not nullify the thing."[15]

That said, as a sensitive Puritan, John Winthrop was mindful of the buildup of social prejudice against the continuing observance of his type of Protestantism. More and more Puritan preachers were arbitrarily suspended by the Anglican hierarchy, as centralized ecclesiastical courts at Westminster superceded the authority of local congregations that had always served as models for correct Puritan practice.

Winthrop read these disturbing trends as signals that in order for the Protestant Church he cherished to remain strong, it was necessary, if frightening, to "rayse a bullwarke" against the harassments by King Charles and Bishop Laud, and take a dramatic, life-changing risk—"runne the hazard" of seeking refuge and renewal elsewhere in the world. Winthrop waxed enthusiastic, imagining the fresh rewards of engendering new parishes in a faraway church "in the infancye . . . as by timely assistance may growe stronge and prosper."

Winthrop wrote with ambivalence and melancholy of his beloved green and pleasant England, "this lande growes wearye of her Inhabitants." A Stour Valley countryman for his whole life and the descendant of country gentlemen, he was depressed by the depletion of natural resources through overcrowding, overbuilding, and speculation. Such economic conditions were the root causes for "Intemperance" and "excesse of Ryot." It was sadly no longer worth "striving heere for places of habitation" when "the whole earthe is the Lordes garden and he hath given it to the sons of men to be till'd and improved by them." Winthrop's own "Meenes here are shortned," he wrote, "[and] I shall not be able to continue in this place and imployment . . . many of our owne people do perish for want of sustenance."[16]

Winthrop's own brother-in-law, Deane Tyndal, had written him to express "lament when I think of your journey." Was it not, Tyndal asked, a "great wronge to our owne Churche and Countrye to take away the good people?" Once one embraced the universality of the concept of the true church, Winthrop replied, this objection dissipated. The true church needed to be everywhere. A particular good example of the church in one place would by nature bolster all the others.

What about the possibility that Winthrop's concerns for the future of his native country were exaggerated? Although for many years he had "feared Judgement," he could not have known, of course, that civil war in England would break out a dozen years later. Was it sensible—or just willful—to depart from his "fruitfull Lande" aware of the overwhelming odds that whole families might "perish by the way" or meet unforeseen dangers when, or if, they reached the fatal shores ahead? To these speculations John Winthrop responded that faithful emigrants will "trust God's Providence" and accept that the imperative of the Gospel was that it be preached "to all Nations."[17]

The eleven other presiding members of the company board were won over, signing a pledge at Cambridge to move themselves and their families the following spring to Massachusetts, where their corporate provenance would be transferred and reestablished. And the majority of the Massachusetts Bay Company shareholders believed that forty-one-year-old John Winthrop possessed the stuff of leadership and was "Godly enough" to take command. On October 20, 1629, his colleagues of the landed gentry elected Winthrop as governor and charged him from that very day with the mission to "superintend the tumultuous work of their departure."[18]

He was a hands-on manager during the ensuing half year, authorizing the purchase of the leading ship, *Eagle*, for 750 pounds and ordering provisions for the voyage, ranging from seeds for planting and domestic farm animals, including turkeys and rabbits; to weaponry and musical instruments; to beer and wine; candles and soap; beef and pork. Winthrop also supervised the recruitment of clergy for the trip and wrote dozens of solicitation letters to relatives and neighbors asking them to join the core group of Massachusetts Bay Company members and their families. Residents of the counties of Essex and Suffolk made up one-third of the first wave of voyagers, swelling to thousands more in the ensuing surges of the Great Migration.[19]

Winthrop had complex financial agreements to negotiate with cautious company partners who decided, at least in the first year, not to make the journey. He had to attend to the sale of his own house and lands, a drawn-out process that kept Margaret from joining him on the trip. To soften the pain of a two-year-long separation, husband and wife agreed that every

Monday and Friday evening between five and six o'clock, during the many weeks John was obligated to remain in London, during his journey to Massachusetts, and after his arrival there, they would take a pause to hold one another in their private thoughts, "meeting before the Lord in a dialogue of the spirit. . . . It refresheth my heart," Winthrop wrote in one rapturous letter, "to think that I shall yet againe . . . see that lovely countenance that I have so much delighted in."[20]

Since 1612, having completed clerical training at Cambridge's Emmanuel College, Winthrop's friend John Cotton had presided as vicar of St. Botolph's Church in Boston, Lincolnshire. Cotton did not embark upon the maiden voyage to Massachusetts. Within two years, however, he was summoned to appear before the High Court of Commission in London because of increasingly critical statements against the Anglican Church. Cotton fled to Massachusetts, settled in the Bay Colony, and became a leading Congregational figure and beloved "Teacher" in the First Church of Boston.

In mid-March 1630 Cotton accompanied a contingent of parishioners to Southampton, the port of departure. On Sunday the twenty-first he conducted the morning service in the Holy Rood Church. Winthrop's ship—its name changed from the *Eagle* to the *Arbella* in honor of Isaac Johnson's wife—was at the dock awaiting favorable winds. A blessing was needed on this day before casting off into the channel to calm the fears of the migrants to North America, many of whom had made their wills and were preparing for a tempest-tossed and terrifying ordeal to test their faith as Christians on a sea of sin. "The safety of mariners' and passengers' lives," said Cotton, "lieth not on ropes and cables, but in the name and the hand of the Lord," as written reassuringly in Psalm 107: "They that go down to the sea in ships . . . see the works of the Lord and His wonders in the deep."[21]

In the course of his sermon, urging the assembly to "goe forth, every man that goeth, with a publick spirit," John Cotton reinforced many of the ideals Winthrop proposed in his "Arguments and Considerations." Originally called "God's Promise to His Plantations," Cotton's sermon was published in London soon after its delivery under the more explicit title, *The Divine Right to Occupy the Land*. Cotton chose the primary text for the day's lesson from 2 Samuel 7:10: "Moreover I will appoint a place for my people Israel, and will plant them, that they may dwell in a place of their own, and move no more; neither shall the children of wickedness afflict them anymore, as beforetime."

Cotton's selection surely was intended to strike a personal chord with John Winthrop, appointed to depart from his country farm and guide his followers to New England, even as in 2 Samuel the Lord had taken David "from the sheepcote, from following thy sheep, to be ruler . . . over Israel," and "commanded judges to be over [His] people." Magistrate of the court John Winthrop would also proceed to build a new church, "a house for [God's] name . . . to be blessed forever" in Massachusetts. The Lord found "a vacant place for the sons of Adam and Noah to come and inhabit," and now, Cotton said, he was providing for the sons of Albion to do the very same: "He hath placed thee in Rehoboth, in a peaceable place."[22]

Toward evening the same Sabbath day, the flagship *Arbella* raised anchor, left Southampton Water estuary, and crossed the Solent to the Isle of Wight, stopping at Cowes. At the end of March, Winthrop's ship and her three sister vessels set forth again, managing to proceed westward as far as Yarmouth before being forced by foul weather to drop anchor again. On April 7 Winthrop and six colleagues signed a parting letter. Its respectful tone made a final statement distancing the Puritans from the extreme doctrines of Separatism, imploring the king and his church not to despise the emigrants, but to pray for these nonseparating Puritans as they began their "solemn enterprise. . . . We cannot depart from our native Country," the unknown writer, thought to be Rev. George Phillips, one of the signatories, declared, "without much sadness of heart and many tears in our eyes."[23]

During the preceding ten days, John Winthrop had been composing a sermon to express publicly his own sentiments about the hazardous and momentous journey ahead. In a practice common to the times, he delivered "A Model of Christian Charity" to crew and passengers in conjunction with the taking of holy communion, before the *Arbella* left Yarmouth. The original manuscript has not survived. A transcription in scrivener's handwriting on twenty leaves of Amsterdam watermark paper is preserved in the manuscript collection of The New-York Historical Society.[24]

The first section of the speech was only four lines, laying out the "Model

Hereof" in the title. Winthrop used the word "Model" in the sense of being an example or design for action meant to be imitated. His own life was also a "Model" of striving toward correct behavior. Winthrop held a hierarchical view of the way society was structured that conformed to accepted Puritan doctrine, believing that man in society did not automatically start with rights: "Some must be rich, some poor, some high and eminent in power and dignity, others mean and in subjection." And all classes of people—nobles and servants, middle-class burghers, wives and children—were represented on the passenger manifest for the *Arbella*.[25]

Differences of wealth and power encouraged mutual dependencies among the ranks of a perfect society. This interdependence was a positive, cohesive force (the "Sement") bonding the layers of humanity together. In Winthrop's opinion "meere Democracy among most Civil nations" was tantamount to anarchy. He argued that "there was no warrant in scripture for it, and no such Government in Israel." The unequal "condition of mankind" was ordained by God out of His benevolent love. God's scheme of variety required the presence of both the good and the wicked, the saved and the damned.

Standing before the multitude assembled on the deck of the *Arbella*, those who had made the commitment to come with him despite the perils ahead, Winthrop revealed honest self-consciousness of the weight of his responsibility. He understood that authority did not automatically confer superiority. Politics was subservient to religion. The requirement that a magistrate answer to God made him more humble toward the constituency he served. His actions emanated from the sheer will to believe in the ideal "love that flows from regeneration in Christ." Encouraging others to live by this special kind of love and true liberty united the body politic in the same way that ligaments knitted the bones and sinews of the human body—and in the same way that "Christ and his Church make one body."[26]

This extended social concord is what the governor meant by "Christian Charity" and what he desired for Massachusetts. He hoped that the plantation would fulfill this ideal and become a community. It would not be Paradise, but it would be a natural terrain upon which to enact a new life. The anticipation of such a reconstructed commonwealth, he said, inspired him to put pen to paper and "gave [me] the occasion to write . . . the present discourse."[27]

———

The long remainder of the tract following the brief "Model hereof" was headed "The Reason hereof," and began as an extended meditation rich with biblical citations on the interpenetration of the Law of Nature and the Law of Grace. In Winthrop's thinking, the moral law drawn up by man necessarily coexisted with the law as put forth in the Scripture in order to establish "a form of Government both civil and ecclesiastical." He conducted the arguments of his sermon in lawyerly fashion in the same rhetorical way he had built up his reasons for leaving England by raising questions and then proceeding to answer them. How can a man be expected to promise his all to the collective society and at the same time continue to provide for his own family? How can a man live fully in the demands of the present while also remaining on guard against evil times ahead? The solution to these quandaries resided in what Winthrop called "the exercise of Mercy."

Ever since the Fall of Adam, who as a consequence, Winthrop said, was "rent"—separated—from his Creator, man had never ceased to define himself by trying to reconstruct that original divine connection, "the Cause between God and us." The Puritans on the brink of their voyage were part of the same tradition. "Whatsoever we did or ought to have done when we lived in England," Winthrop said, "the same must we do and more also where we go." Reciprocal actions and works of mercy among "brethren," no matter how distant they might become from one another in different towns and villages, would maintain and strengthen the social "Covenant," as written in Galicians 6.2: "Bear ye one another's burdens and so fulfill the law of Christ."[28]

In Congregationalist practice, any seven or more "elect" persons could come together and make a church of their own. Winthrop defined the Covenent in his sermon as more than "an holy Confederacy" that governed the members of a church and more than a relationship that regulated the common daily life among residents of a neighborhood or a town. It was therefore a given, he said, that the community "must delight in each other, mourn together, labor and suffer together." The further challenge of the Covenant of living together was to include God, by means of all the implicit agreements an individual made with Him in prayer or in practice. In the end man was fallible, and God determined the structure of his moral life in pursuit of perfection.[29]

Having provided the dramatic buildup for his closing message, Winthrop turned to the Scriptures for the finale. The Sermon on the Mount in Matthew, the first and most widely read Gospel of the New Testament, provided the perfect basis for Winthrop's enumeration of the components of the ideal community. Mercifulness, purity of heart, respect for those who mourn, tranquility—these human qualities were the very same as Christ's demands upon those who would enter the Kingdom of Heaven.

Matthew 5: 14–16 provided familiar inspiration to Winthrop's audience: "Ye are the light of the world. A city that is set upon a hill cannot be hid. Neither do men light a candle, and put it under a bushel, but on a candlestick; and it giveth light to all that are in the house. Let your light so shine before men, that they may see your good works, and glorify your Father which is in heaven."

Winthrop played thus upon the theme: ". . . [M]en shall say of succeeding plantations: the Lord make it like that of New England. For we must consider that we shall be as a City on a Hill, the eyes of all people are upon us." Here was the "Model" and core rationale for the entire sermon. The people of the Massachusetts Bay Colony were exceptional. They were chosen to enact God's will on earth in an historic, human example that—if it proved to be successful—would reignite the dulled fires of Reformation from the sanctity of a safe and separate land, "help to rid Europe of the Antichrist . . . [and become] a spearhead of world Protestantism."[30]

What if their communal citadel should fail in this "divine opportunity"? What if the "lamp of saving light," the beacon of faith the Massachusetts Puritans held proudly upward for the world to see and follow were extinguished? The consequences would be wrathful, harsh, and enduring: "If we shall deal falsely with our God in this work we have undertaken," Winthrop warned, "we shall be made a story and a by-word through the world . . . we shall cause the prayers of God's worthy servants to be turned into Curses upon us."[31]

Winthrop, a skillful orator, did not want to leave his audience on a negative note. He moved smoothly into the Old Testament for the concluding lesson, drawing from Deuteronomy 30–31, Moses' famous *Teshuvah* speech, his Code or "Conditions for Restoration and Blessing," the last exhortation before his followers crossed over the river Jordan into Canaan. "And the Lord thy God will bring thee into the land which thy fathers possessed, and thou shalt possess it; and he will do thee good. . . . And the Lord thy God will make thee plenteous in every work of thine hand, in the fruit of thy body, and in the fruit of thy cattle, and in the fruit of thy land, for good: for the Lord will again rejoice over thee for good, as he rejoiced over thy fathers."

The Chosen People of God crossed the river to enter their Promised Land flowing with milk and honey. The latter-day Chosen People of Massachusetts were on the brink of crossing the ocean to find their New Israel between the Merrimack and the Charles. The Puritans, like the Israelites of old, Winthrop said, were "commanded this day to love the Lord our God, and to love one another, to walk in His ways and to keep His Commandments and His Ordinance and His laws, and the Articles of our Covenant with Him."

There was one significant difference between the exodus of the biblical Moses and John Winthrop of the *Arbella*. In book 31 of Deuteronomy, Moses' speech was a valedictory. God did not permit the old patriarch to cross over Jordan. Moses summoned Joshua, the son of Nun, and gave him his blessing with words of strong encouragement, ordering the elders of Israel to bear the Ark of the Covenant alongside their sacred laws. Then God appeared in a pillar of cloud and predicted darkly to Moses that eventually the people of Israel would "act corruptly . . . and turn to other gods and serve them, and despise Me and break My Covenant."

Winthrop framed God's wrathful and dire prognosis for the people of Israel as an hypothesis within the final phrases of his sermon, emphasizing: "If our hearts turn away so that we will not obey . . . but shall be seduced and worship other gods . . . we shall surely perish out of the good land whither we pass over this vast Sea to possess it."

He then invoked for a soaring conclusion book 30 of Deuteronomy, verses 19 and 20, reciting a lyrical, uplifting exhortation to the English travelers before him—and to the unknown Americans after him:

Therefore let us choose life,
that we, and our seed,
may live; by obeying His
voice, and cleaving to Him,
for He is our life, and
our prosperity.

At six o'clock on the morning of Thursday, April 8, 1630, the winds blew east and north "with a merry gale," the brooding clouds parted, and the *Arbella* slipped into the English Channel within sight of the chalk white peaks of the Needles. Her voyage at last began.[32]

John Winthrop spoke in a mood of extreme anticipation on a day filled with religious significance. He used the idiom and the familiar references he knew would be readily grasped by his audience, hungry for encouragement on the verge of moving from a known to an unknown world. From our situation in twenty-first-century America, although those circumstances may appear distant and different, we should remain mindful of John Winthrop's point of view on the correct values of the ideal citizen. Winthrop teaches us that the degree to which we feel naturally obligated to "give back" for the amelioration of our society is predicated upon the belief that we have been tangibly improved by the privilege of living in the society. We do not have to be biblical constructionist scholars to understand and accept the moral basis of that transaction. Winthrop asked the seven hundred people following him to New England to draw upon the reservoir of their abiding faith in order to carry them forward. He did not shy away from depicting the New World as a place where individual reward would arrive only if the considerable burden of risk were collectively assumed. Winthrop's sermon teaches us that even a city upon on a hill, imagined with the most inspirational language and settled with the highest intentions, has no inherent guarantee of survival. The perseverance of its inhabitants will determine whether the city will stand or fall, stagnate or prevail. It would become the responsibility of every succeeding generation to reinvigorate the city on a hill.

Thomas Paine

2

Common Sense

It's time that we realize that our so-called Founding is not the source of our political and constitutional achievement. We owe our success to the common sense of the American people throughout our entire history, and our continued success will depend upon that common sense and not upon the creative moment of the Founding.

—Gordon S. Wood, *The New York Review of Books*, February 13, 2003

When introduced, he did not ask, "How do you do?" but rather, with a soft-spoken, rural Norfolk inflection, "What news?" If you did not come forth with any, he willingly provided his, doffing his hat, bowing graciously, grasping your hand in his own, slim and well formed. He held your attention with a knowing look: brilliant, deep blue eyes, a raised eyebrow, and a bemused half smile. He stood five feet, nine inches; his face full, clean-shaven, and oblong; brow lofty; complexion ruddy; nose prominently hooked; mouth firm; dark brown hair pulled back into a ponytail.

In conversation he invariably took the lead, brushing off impertinent questions. His comic timing was impeccable, like an actor reciting well-practiced lines. His language was frank and direct, refreshing in freedom from pomposity, witty, and chockful of anecdotes—vocabulary simple, never two words when one would do. He began each day with a perusal of all the local newspapers and imported English magazines he could find and was never at a loss for timely gossip on politics, his favorite topic.

He loved to be out in the open air. After a late and hearty breakfast, long, introspective strolls along the bustling, cobblestoned tree-lined thoroughfares of downtown Philadelphia helped invigorate his mind and prepare him for the day's writing.

He never carried a sword or used a cane, preferring to walk with his hat in one hand, the other clasped behind his back, unless he wanted to drive a point home, in which instance Tom Paine stopped in his tracks, tilted his head to one side in a posture of rapt attendance, and enjoined you to smile or frown along with him.[1]

Thomas "Pain," as it was occasionally spelled until he arrived in America, was born on January 29, 1737, to Joseph and Frances Cocke Pain—written "Paine" on their marriage license and "Payne" on their daughter's birth record—of Bridge Street in the eighth-century village of Thetford ("the People's Ford") on the river Ouse in Norfolk, England. Joseph, a stay maker and freeman, managed a small farm and was a practicing Quaker; Frances, the daughter of a respected attorney, was a member of the Anglican Church.[2]

Tom was raised with two competing faiths. He tagged along with his father to the small, drab Friends Meeting House on Cage Lane and also dutifully recited Anglican daily prayers at Thetford Grammar School. He favored classes in history, mathematics, and science. In poetry Tom possessed some talent, but admitted to feeling "repressed rather than encouraged." Against his father's wishes, he secretly tried to teach himself to read Latin.

At the age of twelve, Tom left school to apprentice with his father, assembling ladies' corsets. At Joseph's side for seven years, Tom learned the delicate, repetitive task of sliding steel rods and whittled whalebone ribs into the stitched fabric channels of intimate garments. At the age of nineteen, "heated with false heroism" and desperate to get out of the shop and taste adventure, Tom ran off to London with the fantasy of shipping out on the privateer *Terrible* under the supervision of Capt. William Death. Tom's father pursued him to the Thames dock and, in the nick of time, "happily prevented" his son from going aboard.

The young man fell back reluctantly upon the field of his training and assisted a stay maker in Covent Garden for less than a year before he found a berth for six months during the Seven Years' War on the *King of Prussia,* another privateer out of London in need of a crew. The ship's mission, patrolling the English Channel under Capt. Edward Menzies, was a success, seizing half a dozen French ships in rapid succession.

At twenty-one, established as a "Master Staymaker" in Sandwich, on the coast southeast of London, Tom met and married Mary Lambert, an orphaned, young woman working as a maidservant for a prominent woolen drapery merchant in town. They moved to Margate in Kent. Within the year Mary died in childbirth. Neither did the baby survive. Disconsolate, Tom moved back to Thetford to live with his parents, deciding to train for a new career in the excise (customs) service as his late wife's father had done. He passed the exams and was assigned as a supernumerary officer in Grantham, Lincolnshire. His job was to measure the contents of brewers' casks, assess pub owners and purveyors of coffee and tea, collect duties and taxes, and also—at great risk to life and limb—patrol the marshes on the lookout for smugglers. He moved to Alford, in coastal Lincoln, as a permanent excise officer at a salary of fifty pounds a year.

In late summer 1765, Tom was dismissed from the Alford post, falsely accused by a resentful supervisor of "stamping"—favoring shopkeepers by approving their merchandise consignments without being present to check the contents of the shipments. Although the document has never been found, he is thought to have sent a confession to the Board of Excise asking to be reinstated if a proper vacancy came up. The distasteful experience was sufficient to send Tom back to London. He was somehow able to persuade the headmasters of schools in the Goodman's Fields and Kensington neighborhoods to hire him in subsistence-level positions teaching reading and writing to working-class children for "twenty pounds a year, with five pounds for finding his own lodgings." According to one questionable account of the period, he also may have spent some time as an itinerant lay preacher.[3]

In February 1768, at the age of thirty-one, apologetic Tom Pain was given one more chance to work in the excise service, at Lewes, a town of five thousand citizens nestled in the Sussex Downs ten miles from the health resort of Brighton by the Sea. He took lodging in modest rooms on the second floor above the shop of Samuel Ollive, a tobacconist and snuff merchant. Ollive also performed his civic duty as a local constable, responsible for maintaining order in his parish. His business establishment was situated at the corner of Bull Lane, next door to the Quaker Meeting House and within shouting distance of the home of relatives of the poet Percy Bysshe Shelley.

Mr. Ollive passed away the following year. Continuing to work for the excise, Tom helped the widow, Esther, expand and manage her husband's store. In the spring of 1771, at St. Michael's Church, Tom married twenty-two-year-old Elizabeth, youngest of the Ollive's four children.

Tom's political stance was characterized by a friend at the time as "strong Whig," meaning that he was an advocate for popular rights with a tolerance for dissenters, "notorious for that quality which has been defined [as] perseverance in a good cause, and obstinacy in a bad one." As was his habit, he became involved in the social fabric of Lewes. Samuel Ollive had managed to insinuate Tom into the "Society of Twelve," a governing cadre of town movers and shakers who convened twice a year to vote on issues deemed important to the common weal. He also frequented a group that liked to call itself "the Headstrong Club." This "respectable, sensible and convivial set of acquaintants" got together once a week at the White Hart Tavern, across the High Street and downhill from the tobacco shop. Over mugs of ale around a communal oak table in the spacious, high-windowed, ground-floor assembly room, Tom Pain engaged in "warm and high disputes" and regaled his comrades—according to one who was often present—with "witty sallies . . . and tenacious opinions . . . maintained with ardour, elegance and argument."

The club circulated a well-worn volume of the works of Homer as an impromptu trophy for "the most obstinate haranguer" of the group the morning after a particularly intense debate. Praised as "General of the Headstrong War," Tom Pain was the most frequent recipient of the book. "Thy soul of fire must sure ascend the sky," fellow members inscribed it, "thy fame can never die." Although all records of the Headstrong Club, notes from meetings as well as occasional papers written by the members, have been lost, it is difficult to imagine that these politically obsessed gentlemen did not devote time to discussing the crises developing throughout the British Empire and especially in northern America. A number of dramatic incidents had occurred across the Atlantic, including the widespread nonimportation boycotts of British goods in New England, the Boston Massacre in March 1770, the burning of the British schooner *Gaspee* in Narragansett Bay off Rhode Island in the summer of 1772, followed that fall by publication in Boston of *The Votes and Proceedings*, a systematic account of British violations of American rights.[4]

In the summer of 1772, Tom Pain began a twenty-one-page tract regarding a cause close to his heart and his pocketbook that was to become his first published pamphlet, *The Case of the Officers of Excise, With Remarks on the Qualifications of Officers, and on the Numerous Evils Arising to the Revenue, from the Insufficiency of the Present Salary: Humbly Addressed to the Members of both Houses of Parliament.*

The immediate reason for writing the *Case* was economic. The gross annual pay for excise officers of Pain's rank was fifty pounds. The net was closer to thirty-two because at least eighteen pounds a year had to be spent on "the excessive dearness of horse-rent." The take-home pay for a countryside excise officer dependent upon his horse was a paltry one shilling and nine-pence farthing per day. Excisemen in London made out much better because they, unlike their country brethren, performed their duties on foot. "There is," Pain wrote, quoting Abraham of the Scriptures, "a great gulf fixed," in the far more burdensome transportation situation among the rural excisemen for whom he spoke. The stress and strain of maintaining professional resistance to bribery offered at every turn, constant travel over long distances, and "frequent removal" for stretches of time—these "numberless evils" and pressures took their toll on family life.

Seduced by the appeal of greater issues, Pain pushed the argument onto higher ground, implying that the excise officer was trapped by planned obsolescence. "Perhaps it may be said," he challenged, "why do the excise officers complain; they are not pressed into the service, and may relinquish it when they please; if they can mend themselves, why don't they? Alas! What mockery of pity would it be to give such an answer to an honest, faithful old officer in the excise, who had spent the prime of his life in the service, and was become unfit for anything else. . . . Every year's experience gained in the excise is a year's experience lost in trade; and by the time they become wise officers they become foolish workmen."

These social inequities laid the groundwork for Pain to sound a poignant warning signal. "Poverty, like grief, has an incurable deafness, which never hears. . . . There is a powerful rhetoric in necessity," he went on. "No argument can satisfy the feelings of hunger, or abate the edge of appetite. . . . The excitements to pleasure, grandeur, or riches, are mere 'shadows of a shade' compared to the irresistible necessities of nature." He could not resist turning provocative and contentious, even at the risk of alienating the landowning legislators he was attempting to win over. "The rich, in ease and affluence, may think I have drawn an unnatural portrait; but could they descend to the cold regions of want, the circle of polar poverty, they would find their opinions changing with the climate. . . . Eloquence may strike the ear," he observed with poetic cadence, "but the language of poverty strikes the heart; the first may charm like music, but the second alarms like a knell."[5]

Four thousand copies of the pamphlet were printed in Lewes, subsidized by five hundred pounds raised through small donations from excisemen throughout England. In the winter of 1772–73, Pain traveled to London where, assisted by a few bold colleagues, he presumptuously sought out meetings with individual MPs in the House of Commons. He sought fruitlessly to identify just one "representative of the people" willing to deliberate upon the merits of the appeal and send it up to King George's Cabinet Council for action. Pain's lobbying was for naught. Neglected by Parliament, the petition languished and died. On April 8, 1774, Tom Pain was summarily again dismissed from excise service. Pain's London sojourn did not endear him to the tax-levying bureaucracy. The condemning citation referred to his having "quit his Sussex Collection Business without leave" for six months. One week after he lost the excise job, Pain shut down Ollive's old tobacco and grocery shop in order to pay his debts and auctioned off the inventory as well as his household possessions ("Rings, Plate, Cloathes, Linen, Goods . . . and two unopened Crates of Cream-Colour Stone Ware").

In early June he signed a formal deed of separation from his wife. "It is nobody's business but my own," Pain told his first biographer, Thomas "Clio" Rickman, in sharp response to the question of why the marriage failed, "I had cause for it, but I will name it to no one." Elizabeth moved "as if she were a Feme Sole," to live in Cranbrook, Kent, with her brother, Thomas, a watchmaker.

There was nothing to keep Pain in Lewes any longer. At the beginning of September, with no job, no property, and no family, he went to London and found temporary lodging "in Ailiffe-Street, an obscure part of the City . . . without fortune or friends."[6]

In London Pain immediately sought out one of his allies, George Lewis Scott, a member of the Board of Excise who remained sympathetic to him. Scott, an educated man and in Pain's estimation "one of the most amiable characters I know of," had been a tutor and, like Pain, possessed an interest in mathematics and the sciences. Eager to help a friend in dire need, Scott seized the opportunity to "put twin planets in conjunction." He obtained Pain an appointment with Benjamin Franklin.[7]

At the time of the meeting in his rooms on Craven Street, off the Strand near Charing Cross, the sixty-eight-year-old Franklin was attempting to put off the conclusion of his decade-long tenure in London as agent general for Pennsylvania. Franklin "hated conflict" and hoped that by continuing to be "industriously engaged in [his] little measures" advocating for moderation on both sides, he could help improve the deteriorating situation between England and her American colonies. He confessed to being in "a perpetual anxiety [about] a people whose minds are in such a state of irritation [as] may produce a tumult . . . [and] such a carnage may ensue as to make a breach that can never afterwards be healed."[8]

The week Pain arrived in town, Franklin's essay, "Causes of the American Discontents Before 1768," was republished serially in The London Chronicle. The past half year had seen an acceleration of such causes—starting during the preceding spring with Parliamentary passage under King George III of the Coercive Acts, called the Intolerable Acts by the colonists. The acts dictated that the port of Boston be closed to general commerce until the East India Company was reimbursed for the fifteen thousand pounds' worth of merchandise destroyed in the infamous December 16 "Tea Party." Disenfranchising the legislature of Massachusetts, the acts provided new legal rights and privileges for royal officials in that recalcitrant colony, making them free of prosecution there.[9]

The First Continental Congress gathered for eight weeks in Philadelphia starting in early September 1774. Fifty-five delegates came from twelve of the thirteen colonies. A resolution vowing to maintain resistance to the imperialistic behavior of Parliament and the repression of the Intolerable Acts was one of the first matters placed on the table through the outspoken efforts of Samuel and John Adams, Patrick Henry, and Richard

Henry Lee. "I suppose," an apprehensive Franklin wrote to his friend
Thomas Cushing in Boston, where there was one British soldier for every
five residents, "we have never had since we were a people so few friends in
Britain . . . a breach with America, hazarded by the late harsh measures,
may be ruinous to the general welfare of the British Empire."[10]

Troubles abroad did not deter Pain from confiding in Franklin his wish
to emigrate. On September 30, 1774, the older man gave Pain two letters of
personal recommendation, one addressed to Franklin's daughter Sarah,
who lived in Philadelphia with her Lancashire-born merchant husband,
Richard Bache, and the other to Franklin's son, William, the Oxford-
educated Royal Governor of New Jersey. "The bearer, Mr. Thomas Paine,"
Franklin wrote—adding the loop of a final "e," and in that stroke of
spelling perhaps providing the stimulus for Thomas to adapt the change he
kept henceforth—"is very well recommended to me as an ingenious worthy
young man," Franklin wrote. "He goes to Pennsylvania with a view of settling there. I request you to give him your best advice and countenance as
he is quite a stranger there. If you can put him in a way of obtaining employment as a clerk, or assistant tutor in a school, or assistant surveyor, all
of which I think him very capable, so that he may procure a subsistence at
least, till he can make acquaintance and obtain a knowledge of the country, you will do well, and much oblige your affectionate father."

Within the next few days, Paine found a berth as one of five cabin passengers on the *London Packet* bound for America.[11]

I t was my fate to come to America a few months before the breaking out
of hostilities," Paine wrote fourteen years later, recalling his first impressions. "I came [to Philadelphia] some months before Dr. Franklin, and
waited here for his arrival." After a hard voyage, Paine disembarked from
Jeremiah Warder's ship on November 30. Franklin's wife, Deborah, died in
Philadelphia on December 19, 1774. The following March Franklin sailed
for home, his final moderate proposal for reconciliation with the colonies
rejected by the ministers in the House of Lords. He had already received a
grateful letter from Paine, informing him that "your countenancing me has
obtained for me many friends and much reputation."[12]

"I found the disposition of the people such, that they might have been
led by a thread and governed by a reed," Paine remembered of his early days

in America, capturing with a hint of criticism the reigning ambivalent atmosphere as well as "an excess of tenderness. . . . Their suspicion was quick and penetrating, but their attachment to Britain was obstinate; and it was, at that time, a kind of treason to speak against it." Playing upon this metaphor, Paine was paying homage to his sponsor and friend Franklin. During his first sojourn in England in 1766, Franklin had pleaded with members of Parliament to repeal the Stamp Act because there was no imperative for further taxation. Content with British control, he said then, the Americans "were led by a thread."[13]

Self-determination rather than fate impelled Tom Paine to the premier commercial center and political capital of British America. Philadelphia was also the acknowledged nexus of literary America. By 1775 there were thirty-eight newspapers in the colonies, the majority published in Philadelphia along with pamphlets, single-sheet broadsides, chapbooks, and magazines. Philadelphia boasted more than thirty bookshops and "twice the number of taverns and coffeehouses." Across the street from the London Coffee House, the most crowded and popular of them all, Paine sought the center of all this ferment. The "lone wayfaring man" in the City of Brotherly Love rented a room in a three-story house at the southeast corner of Market and Front streets, near the library and next door to the bookstore and print shop of Scotsman Robert Aitken, born in Dalkeith in 1734.[14]

Paine was a regular visitor to Aitken's shop, standing many hours in the aisles between overflowing shelves, pulling, reading, and replacing book after book. Aitken's longtime dream was to start his own publication of "original American productions," and he engaged Paine to write a column for the inaugural issue of January 24, 1775. *The Pennsylvania Magazine, or, American Monthly Museum* was a handy size, about three by six inches. The striking logo on the title page depicted "the sun rising behind an olive-twined shield upon which were emblazoned a globe, a book, a flower, a lyre and an anchor, all tied together with the motto in the pastoral spirit of Rousseau endorsing the blessed state of nature, *Juvat in sylvis habitare* (Happy it is to live in the woods)."[15]

Paine's essay, "The Magazine in America," sounded like a nationalistic manifesto, couched in language far more engaged and worldly than the journal's bucolic slogan. "America has now outgrown the state of infancy," he announced at the outset. Perhaps thinking of writings soon to be addressed to the people of his newly adopted country, Paine continued,

"There is nothing which obtains so general an *influence* over the manners and moral of a people as the Press; from that, as from a fountain, the streams of vice or virtue are poured forth over a country. . . . *We* are not exceeded in abilities, have a more extensive field for enquiry, and, whatever may be our political state, *Our* happiness will always depend upon ourselves." Paine had been residing in Philadelphia for less than two months and already felt comfortable and hopeful enough to consider himself at home in America during "the present enlarged and improved state of things [when] change of times adds propriety to new measures."[16]

The piece was well received, and Aitken appointed Paine editor of *The Pennsylvania Magazine* at the same salary he had drawn as an exciseman— fifty pounds a year. Paine held the post for the next eighteen months, during which he dramatically increased the circulation of the magazine from six hundred to over fifteen hundred and wrote "at least seventeen and perhaps as many as twenty-six" articles on current issues. These included a piece sharply criticizing the widespread British and American practice of slavery, under the byline "Humanus," and "An Occasional Letter to the Female Sex," appealing for broader rights for women in the colonies, where they were "robbed of freedom and will by the laws." The precise number of Paine's appearances in print is impossible to determine because he employed a variety of pseudonyms or left articles unsigned.[17]

Paine set forth to reinvent himself through the medium of print. When his new essays began to proliferate in *The Pennsylvania Magazine*, Paine compared them to "the early snowdrop, coming forth in a barren season, contenting itself with modestly foretelling that choicer flowers are preparing to appear." Insisting that "the cause of America made me an author," he was secretive about the personal details of his "first life" in England, because it was so unhappy and filled with misfortune. Willfully misrepresenting his past, Paine wrote that he had "never troubled others with my notions until very lately . . . [and] never published a syllable in England in my life." The message of a text should be foremost, he believed, not publicity for the author. "Measures" were "the thing in question," not men.[18]

On April 18 and 19, 1775, with tensions in the colonies continuing to rise, Gen. Thomas Gage, the British commander in Boston, dispatched Maj. John Pitcairn to take hold of rebel headquarters and military storehouses in nearby Concord. Crossing the Charles River and advancing through the Lexington village green toward Concord North Bridge, Pitcairn's light infantry and grenadiers were surrounded by the local militia and opened fire. Eight Americans were killed. Routed on the roads back to Boston, the British troops suffered heavy losses. The following month, in defiance of British constitutional authority, the Second Continental Congress assembled in Philadelphia and appointed "the modest and virtuous, amiable, generous and brave" Col. George Washington of the Virginia militia to be commander of the newly established Continental army.[19]

Tom Paine took to his bully pulpit in the magazine. His rhetoric escalated to match the temper of the times. From this moment onward, his attacks on England became more acerbic. No longer was America merely growing up out of childhood to make steady, benign progress in the world. The country was in the midst of a veritable "tempest," from which, Paine prophesied, "She will rise with new glories from the conflict, and her fame will be established in every corner of the globe." At the Battle of Bunker Hill in Charlestown, Massachusetts, on June 17, 1775, the British sustained more than a thousand casualties. Paine wrote an article immediately thereafter on the nature of war, which concluded that "arms preserve order in the world as well as property." On August 23 King George III rejected the conciliatory Olive Branch Petition and declared the colonies to be in open rebellion. Tom Paine replied through one of his last contributions to *The Pennsylvania Magazine*, a song called "The Liberty Tree," that "Kings, Commons and Lords" were the "tyrannical powers" conspiring to "cut down this guardian of ours. . . . From the east to the west," he wrote, "blow the trumpet to arms, / Thro' the land let the sound of it flee."[20]

The idea of writing *Common Sense* did not hit Tom Paine in a flash of inspiration. There was a gestation period—as transpires before most historical moments. Paine said that the seed of necessity was planted in his mind with the pity for the sufferers he felt keenly in the days following "the April massacre at Lexington." Benjamin Franklin landed at Philadelphia from London in early May 1775 to attend the Second Continental Congress and reconnect with Paine. His old mentor suggested that Paine draw up an informal history of the circumstances building toward the current conflict. Some "contemporaries" said that Franklin provided "a large share of the materials" for the document. Paine insisted that by autumn he had already "formed the outline" for three essays in the pamphlet. Paine told

Henry Laurens, president of the Second Continental Congress, that when the Olive Branch Petition was turned down, "I determined with myself to write the pamphlet." Another friend, the physician, philosopher, and patriot, Benjamin Rush, claimed it was at his suggestion that Paine embarked upon the project, telling Paine that "he had nothing to fear from the popular odium to which such a publication might expose him."[21]

Although Rush also took unsubstantiated credit for the title of the pamphlet, Paine may well have been familiar with the tradition of "common sense" philosophy. This popular eighteenth-century school—also known as "Scottish Enlightenment philosophy" because of its articulation in the writings of Thomas Reid and Dugald Stewart—endorsed the dependability and importance of "ordinary language and everyday thought." As opposed to dilatory intellectualizing and skepticism, these thinkers favored man's innate and dominant capacity to feel "virtuous and natural judgement . . . those essential tenets that we cannot help but believe." The common sense philosophers said that man was born with a practical "strength of motive," a powerful, emotional predisposition to action. This species of common sense, emanating from the realm of sensation, was the highest and most benevolent characteristic of human nature. The ideal is reinforced in Paine's essay by the pervasive tone of inevitability and endorsement of free will. Let us remember that bookseller Robert Aitken as well as the first printer of Common Sense, the proud "Republican" Robert Bell, were both Scotsmen.[22]

Paine said that he read excerpts of the work in progress to Franklin and Rush as well as to Samuel Adams and David Rittenhouse along the way. Ultimately "the changes made were few." Paine characteristically took pride in the originality of his ideas, saying that he "succeeded without any help from anybody."[23]

In the fall of 1775, Paine resigned from the editorship of The Pennsylvania Magazine in order to devote himself full time to the intense, quick composition of his most important and influential work. On October 18 he published a brief editorial in The Pennsylvania Journal titled, "A Serious Thought," concluding with a preview of what was soon to come: "I hesitate not for a moment to believe," he wrote, "that the Almighty will finally separate America from Britain. Call it Independancy or what you will, if it is the cause of God and humanity it will go on."[24]

A n announcement ran in *The Pennsylvania Journal* of January 10, 1776. "This day was published, and is now selling by Robert Bell, next door to St. Paul's Church in Third-Street, Philadelphia, price two shillings, 'Common Sense,' addressed to the inhabitants of North America." Actually, the title page read "INHABITANTS of AMERICA." Paine timed the piece to appear on the same day that "the royal brute" King George's "bloody minded" speech of "finished villainy . . . [and] Monarchical tyranny" for the opening of Parliament was published in America.[25]

"In a great affair, where the good of man is at stake, I love to work for nothing," Paine wrote. True to form he gave the job to the "courageous Typographer" Robert Bell with the guarantee that the printer would receive half the profits, the other half to be allocated for the purchase of mittens for the American invasion force headed into Quebec. Any loss arising from the production would be paid for by Paine out of his own pocket. Within weeks of publication, Paine accused Bell of cheating the soldiers in Canada out of the proceeds. For a second printing, Paine excised the byline "written by an Englishman," wrote an expanded but still anonymous version of the essay, and offered it for sale for one British shilling—a bargain in bulk, ten pence for a dozen—at the London Coffee House.[26]

The beauty of *Common Sense* resides in its transparently fresh, emotional tone and directness. At times it reads like a Shakespearean soliloquy, at others it feels reminiscent of a confessional poetic monologue by Robert Browning. From the opening dogmatic phrases, Paine, ever the "philosophic lover of humanity," addresses his reader face-to-face, fixing his impassioned, compelling gaze upon us to the very end. The relentless momentum of the eighty pages (seventy-nine of text, one advertisement for Bell's other publications) is sustained so impeccably that by the time the inspirational, crescendolike conclusion is reached, the claim to the "FREE AND INDEPENDANT [sic] STATES OF AMERICA" seems inevitable.[27]

Paine accomplishes this forward energy in three major ways. He expands and contracts, from the broadest historical and philosophical perspective down to the particular crisis at hand, and then outward again—from "the cause of America" to "the cause of all mankind," from the "local" to the "universal"—so the paragraphs seem to breathe in and out as we read. The consummate propagandist, he sets up a sustaining rhythm of opposites from the outset but never strays from the argument. And he is a master of repetition, weaving reiterating, hypnotic word patterns to make the themes resonate like music.[28]

Absolute government, Paine writes, represented by the self-perpetuating, "debasing" monarchy of England, is an aberration defying the ideal liberal society. America, in thrall to outworn loyalties, has lost sight of her mission in the world. She has ceded authority to the "evil"—and complex—institution of monarchy. She has forgotten her simpler obligation to guide herself via the "moral virtue" of a Republican system. Americans have long since forgotten their egalitarian origins in the order of creation. God made the world, Paine says, and then the kings came along and robbed Him of it. The bracing antidote of common sense tells us now the time is "ripe" to reclaim our origins, by means of what Paine calls the compact of "continental union," the required alternative to "reconciliation" with the mother country. "Can ye give to prostitution its former innocence? Neither can ye reconcile Britain and America." The debate over the future is at an end. Our destiny lies in our mutual agreement to be "Americans" not "subjects of Great Britain."[29]

This is not abstract theorizing. Paine claimed with pride never to have read the works of John Locke, but the assertion that rebellion is permissible when the people decide their government has abused its given role by acting "contrary to their trust" sounds like Locke's classic *The Second Treatise of Civil Government* (1690) seasoned with a healthy dash of radicalism. Americans in 1776, Paine says, are blessed with the opportunity to create a new and favored world where "the Almighty . . . has opened an asylum and a sanctuary for the persecuted lovers of civil and religious liberty from every part of Europe." Living in America brings with it the responsibility to look with dispassionate vision upon the ulterior motives of England. Once the common people cast a cold eye toward the all-encompassing empire that would continue to hold them in its sway for antiquated, exploitative, self-interested, and commercial reasons deriving no benefit to the colonies, disconnection leaps to mind, and " 'TIS TIME TO PART." Paine builds further upon this theme by making reference to King George as a "sullen-tempered Pharaoh," reminding the reader that the Hebrews found self-reliant legitimacy only after their separation from Egypt.[30]

Common Sense calls upon the resolution of the American people to abandon their passivity once and for all, to take responsibility for their own affairs, and to advocate rupture from England "on a secure, firm and honorable basis." Despite acknowledging an ongoing succession of "quarrels" and conflicts, some of them bloody, Paine's Quaker roots come into play. He stops short of a clarion call for the extreme response of violent revolution and issues a summons to seek universal peace. Once the polarizing "names of Whig and Tory" have been dissolved—liberal-minded citizens who believe in independence, pitted against conservatives who would remain loyal to the Crown—and the colonies confederate in friendship with one another to turn their backs on England's false system of government, the result will be an economically healthy, lasting, emancipated republic for posterity. "It was to bring forward and establish the representative system of government," Paine wrote in later years, "that was the leading principle with me in writing [Common Sense]."[31]

Paine's wry observation that the pamphlet's appearance "gave a turn to the politics of America" was quite an understatement. With pride and gratitude, he sent Dr. Franklin the first copy of Common Sense off the press. Franklin pronounced it to be "prodigious." Read aloud and passed from hand to hand among the delegates to the Second Continental Congress in Philadelphia, the pamphlet was a crystallizing force at a crucial moment in the new year of 1776 when they were still reluctant and divided over the right course to take. George Washington supported Paine consistently throughout his life, despite their later disputes, and correctly predicted to Joseph Reed, a Pennsylvania delegate to the Congress, that the author's words would "work a powerful change in the minds of men" and awaken the public imagination. Washington further approved of Paine's "sound doctrine and unanswerable reasoning." The general's aide-de-camp, Edmund Randolph, made perceptive note of Paine's simple writing style and the egalitarian "ease with which [it] insinuated itself into the hearts of the people who were unlearned or learned. . . . The public sentiment . . . over-leaped every barrier." Benjamin Rush applauded the "celebrated author" for the "effect which has rarely been produced by types and papers in any age or country." Joseph Hawley, distinguished judge of the General Court of Massachusetts, spoke for many colonists when he avowed that "every sentiment sunk into my well-prepared heart."[32]

"Perhaps there never was a pamphlet, since the use of letters were known, about which so little pains were taken, and of which so great a number went off in so short a time," wrote the author, preferring to downplay the extent of his promotional involvement. To publicize the second, substantially enlarged edition of *Common Sense* printed in Philadelphia by William and Thomas Bradford, Paine set off by coach to New York in February for a round of dinners and salons, where he met General Washington's second in command, Maj. Gen. Charles Lee, who saw "the genius in his eyes." The metropolitan Whig press was likewise intoxicated by his wit and "sparks of original genius." It seemed that the influence of Paine's propaganda might be taking hold. During the spring, delegates from Massachusetts, North Carolina, and Virginia fell into line as the balance in the Second Continental Congress began slowly to tip from late December's tally of one-third against independence to two-thirds toward it. Despite sliding again into debt with waning care about collecting royalties, Paine freely ceded the right of publication to printers throughout the thirteen colonies. Translations soon appeared in Europe. By the end of the year 1776, *Common Sense* had gone through twenty-five editions and more than 120,000 copies were estimated to be in circulation in America.[33]

Paine's feisty affection for controversy fueled debate. Vehement and malicious voices instantly attacking the iconoclastic tract only served to extend the immense, rapid reach of *Common Sense*. The first public antagonism came in the form of a series of acerbic letters in the *Pennsylvania Gazette* under the pseudonym "Cato," criticizing Paine's inflammatory style, the heat of his writing, its lack of restraint, shameless "anger and fury," and deficiency of "calm command over passions and feelings." The substance and the manner of Paine's argument were deemed unseemly.

These letters were composed by Dr. William Smith, an Anglican clergyman, provost of the College of Philadelphia, and an outspoken Tory. The Reverend Smith's choice of a pen name was appropriate: Marcus Portius Cato (234–149 BC) was a wealthy Roman statesman, orator, and defender of conservative Roman ideas. He was known as "Cato the Censor" because of his conscientious monitoring of public officials, his outspoken campaigns to remove members of the Senate whom he deemed too liberal or

open to foreign ideas, and especially his crusade to expunge Greek influence from traditional Roman society.

Smith guessed correctly at the identity of the "Englishman" who wrote
Common Sense, scorning Paine as "[a] stranger intermeddling in our affairs."
Smith's letters began to appear while Paine was in New York. In response to
an urgent appeal by Franklin and Rittenhouse, he returned to Philadelphia
in March 1776 in order to engage in a proper journalistic battle—just as
armed American privateers were launched to seek and destroy enemy ships,
British troops were ordered to evacuate Boston, and the Second Continental Congress opened American ports to trade with all foreign nations except England. After all, Paine wrote in early April, "To be *nobly wrong* is
more manly than to be *meanly right*." Although his name had been exposed,
Paine issued the replies to "Cato" under his own evocative pseudonym, "the
Forester," perhaps a nostalgic reference to the masthead motto of *The Pennsylvania Magazine* where he had served his first American editorship. Or it
might have been an acknowledgment of Jean-Jacques Rousseau's conviction that even if we cannot literally return to the woods from whence we
came, we can at least restore moral contact with ourselves.[34]

Paine's four "Forester's Letters" defending *Common Sense* appeared in
the *Pennsylvania Journal* and the *Pennsylvania Packet* during April and May
1776, while the Continental Congress issued stern resolutions telling the
colonies that the time had come for them to create new governments "under the authority of the people." The letters served as postscript and ampli-
fication to *Common Sense*. Paine deliberately reached for the broader
audience beyond his immediate adversary. He addressed sections of the letters "To the People," indulging his penchant for reprising important themes
and variations as a way to "detect and expose the falsehoods and fallacious
reasonings" of his ideological opponents. Paine said that Cato's plea for
"reconciliation of differences" with England, as if the mother country and
her colonies had engaged in nothing more serious than a "lover's quarrel,"
was "a meer [sic] bug-bear," coming far too late in the game—"'Tis gone!
'Tis past!" Cato's insistence upon addressing only the people of Pennsylvania betrayed his ignorance of the power of the consolidated colonies. His
criticism of the "restraint" of the liberty of the press was unfounded, the argument possessing "as much order in it as the motion of a squirrel . . .
jump[ing] about because he cannot stand still." And, Paine pointed out
with special bitterness, Cato, the chronic revisionist, misconstrued the rea-

sons why Europe was looking with more attention than ever to the colonies—not as ungrateful transgressors but rather as potential economic and political allies.[35]

The esteemed lawyer John Adams also joined the chorus as one of the most opinionated early critics of *Common Sense*. Riding through New York at the end of January on his way to Philadelphia and Congress, Adams picked up two copies of the pamphlet. He kept one and sent the other home to his wife, Abigail, in Braintree, Massachusetts, commenting to her—and to friends William Tudor and James Warren—that the author "has a better hand at pulling down than at building. . . . I believe every [argument for independence] that is in it has been hackneyed. . . . He is a keen writer, but very ignorant of the science of government."[36]

Adams shared Paine's inclination toward independence but feared his antipathy toward the British constitutional model and the precipitous effect such radicalism or, worse, anarchy might have upon the people at large at such a volatile moment. To the conservative Adams, Paine's zealous vision for America was too "democratical," and he wrote his own epistolary pamphlet in response, called "Thoughts on Government." Contrary to Paine's insistence that monarchy was downright unlawful, Adams argued that men require the security of structure in their institutions. Adams referred to Paine in later years variously as a "star of disaster" and a "disastrous meteor" with respect to this fundamental point of disagreement. To Adams balanced government was symptomatic of society's essential need for "a frame, a scheme, a system . . . an empire of laws and not of men."[37]

To Thomas Paine, the less government the better. The colonies, he said, should follow their faith toward self-definition. On July 2, 1776, they did so, when Richard Henry Lee put forth a motion at the Continental Congress, that "these United Colonies are, and, of right ought to be, Free and Independent States." The thirteen-hundred-word Declaration of Independence was adopted two days later.

On July 9 Thomas Paine volunteered his services as secretary for the Associators, one thousand men under the command of Gen. Daniel Roberdeau of the Pennsylvania militia. He took up his musket and left Philadelphia for Perth Amboy, New Jersey, where the British were massing in Raritan Bay to launch the invasion of New York.[38]

L ike John Winthrop before him, Thomas Paine saw America as the ideal testing ground upon which to realize all that was inherently right about the human condition. However Paine differed from Winthrop in a major way: he was emphatically not a religious person. Man's sovereignty was conferred upon him by God, but beyond that legitimate blessing, society and government parted ways. The laws defining the political institutions created by man were his to modify or, if need be, reject through the gift of free will. Of all the political institutions on the face of the earth, Paine said, monarchy was the most dispensable. Now was the time and America was the place to get rid of that antiquated practice. What the colonies needed instead was unity through separation from the "parent" England or, better still, a model for national unity that would be accomplished through the force of separation. The doctrine of common sense required that decisive action be taken, not only because "resolution" was the defining characteristic of human nature, but also because America's latent identity would rise to the surface as a result.

It is important to bear in mind when reading *Common Sense* that Paine's insistent dwelling upon "rupture," while a preponderant and influential part of his overall argument and a polarizing lightning rod for public opinion and reaction, represented only the first step. The ordeal of war followed and, in the process, as we shall now examine, created more questions that needed to be answered about the vocabulary of national self-definition.

DESIGN FOR THE GREAT SEAL OF THE UNITED STATES

3

E Pluribus Unum

Resolved. That it be recommended to the respective Assemblies and Conventions of the United Colonies, where no Government sufficient to the exigencies of their affairs has been hitherto established, to adopt such government as shall in the opinion of the Representatives of the People best conduce to the happiness and safety of their Constituents in particular, and America in general.

—Resolution of the Continental Congress, Philadelphia, May 10–15, 1776[1]

O n July 4, 1776, the distinguished gentlemen of the Second Continental Congress gathered in the Pennsylvania State House assembly room to adopt and date the revised Declaration of Independence. The document would not be signed by the members until August 2. Only one other piece of business remained in the late afternoon before the agenda was completed: "Resolved, that Dr. Franklin, Mr. J. Adams and Mr. Jefferson, be a committee, to bring in a device for a seal for the United States of America." At seventy, Franklin was the elder statesman of Congress. An energetic participant in collective decision making, he was already involved with the Committee of Secret Correspondence and the Committee on Maintenance and Supervision of the Continental Army, among several other groups. With Adams, Franklin had been working for the previous three weeks on a committee to prepare a list of protocols for treaties with foreign powers, while at the same time the two men had been suggesting minor modifications to Jefferson's draft for the Declaration.[2]

There was some urgency to complete the mission of the Great Seal Committee as soon as possible. Within a week of the committee's establishment, John Adams proposed that the seal be ready in time to attach to the fully executed ("subscribed") Declaration of Independence. Since none of the three statesmen possessed specialist talents in heraldry, they needed to find someone "creatively involved in the art" to "apply himself with gusto" to the task. To assist in the creation of the Great Seal they required a consultant. They called upon the talents of an eccentric son of the Enlightenment, a Swiss draftsman, artifact collector, numismatist, cartographer, historical researcher, and sometime silhouette cutter, a solitary bachelor who lived in two disorderly and cluttered rooms rented from a Mrs. Robinson on Chestnut Street opposite the Fountain Inn in Philadelphia. His name was Pierre Eugène Du Simitière.[3]

The unlikely protagonist of our story was a driven man who made many elegant "portraits of notables," but of whom no reliable, authenticated likeness survives. He was born on September 18, 1737, in Geneva, the son of French Protestant parents, Jean-Henri Ducimitière, a merchant broker, and Judith-Ulrique Cunégonde Delorme. For the first two decades of his life, there remains no documentation. By age twenty, inspired by the writings of the founder of the British Museum, Sir Hans Sloane's *The Natural History of Jamaica* and *Voyage to Jamaica*, Pierre had "embarked upon an odyssey" from Amsterdam to Saint-Eustache in the West Indies. In Jamaica and Santo Domingo, he gathered specimens from nature, made watercolor drawings in the field, and kept notes on indigenous life, with the idea of publishing a natural history of the islands upon returning to his homeland. But he never went back to Switzerland.

By 1763 Pierre was in New York. For the ensuing decade, infatuated by America, he lived itinerantly, with brief sojourns in Burlington, New Jersey; Charleston, South Carolina; Philadelphia; Boston; and Newport, Rhode Island. He became a naturalized citizen of New York State in 1769. He revisited the West Indies for a short stay and in the fall of 1774 returned to Philadelphia, having decided that his projected natural and civil history would become a detailed, copiously illustrated epic of the American colonies' "Revolution in North America." Du Simitière remained in Philadelphia until his premature, depressed, and impoverished death in October of 1784, precise day unknown.[4]

Why did he choose Philadelphia? Most assuredly for the qualities that attracted Tom Paine, who arrived at the same time. It was "a world of living and active men," "the Paris of the New World," and as Du Simitière happily discovered soon after his arrival, the liveliness of the city kept his hopes kindled. In his eyes it was a central, seminal place where "Ingenious Men of all Societies" came together for "Mutual Harmony. . . . I expect something New from your New World, our Old World as it were exhausted." To the delight of this amateur historian, Philadelphia was a city of superb libraries—to name but a few, those of Ben Franklin, David James Dove, Francis Alison, and James Logan. "Their use [was] confined to the masculine citizenry," and Du Simitière took full advantage.

Du Simitière barely eked out a modest living as a professional artist and miniaturist painter, using what little extra money he made to support his insatiable compulsion to collect. He owned a fully documented international coin and paper money display album filled with examples picked up during his journeys through the Caribbean and the colonies. He had a library of books and broadsides and complete runs of periodicals and political pamphlets, with a focus upon those that documented the developing American struggle for independence and "the disputes between Great Britain and the American Colonies." He accumulated a large assortment of colored prints and etchings. With diverse items of historical and archaeological value acquired in his travels—commemorative medals, fossils, preserved animals, potsherds, bones, the occasional arrowhead, autographed manuscripts—as well as gifts sent from sympathetic donors in response to Du Simitière's cascade of appeal letters, this polymath "natural philosopher" laid the foundation for a massive, mahogany encyclopedic "cabinet of curiosities . . . and objects of Natural History," which he advertised and revealed for the price of admission to a curious public after the revolution.[5]

Although Du Simitière was something of a loner, within a year of his arrival in Philadelphia, he was nevertheless becoming known in certain intellectual and political circles. He was elected a member of the American Philosophical Society, became a part-time curator there, and must have crossed paths with its founder, Benjamin Franklin, although Franklin does not mention Du Simitière in his writings. He was acquainted with at least one other delegate to the Continental Congress, Richard Smith, who came to Du Simitière's rooms during a recess at the end of September 1775 and spent an "amusing morning" viewing Du Simitière's encyclopedic hoard. From his earliest days in town, he frequented Robert Aitken's bookstore. In the late fall of 1774 Aitken commissioned him to create an "allegorical" engraving for the frontispiece of the new *Pennsylvania Magazine, or, Ameri-*

can Monthly Museum, as well as the "vignette" design for the table of contents page. The two men remained colleagues for ten years.[6]

During the eighteen months of the magazine's short run, Du Simitière contributed several "Indian ink" drawings as feature illustrations, including a new type of "fire place and Stove" invented by one Ebenezer Robinson, as well as a picture of "a New Electrical machine." For the April 1776 issue, Du Simitière collaborated with Aitken on a detailed map of "the maratime [sic] parts of Virginia from Tangiers Island in the Chesapeake Bay in the North to below Cape Henry in the South, and from City County in the West to the Atlantic Ocean in the East," recognized as the first separate map of Virginia to be published in the colonies. Neither Aitken, the *Pennsylvania Magazine* publisher, nor Thomas Paine, the celebrated editor, make any reference to Du Simitière in their writings.[7]

Of the three august members of the Great Seal Committee, John Adams most likely sought out Du Simitière for the most important assignment of his career. Adams had approached the Swiss artist four months earlier, with the request to design a gold medal for George Washington in tribute to his siege and victory at Boston on March 17, 1776, over the British admiral Lord Richard Howe. The proposed Washington medal became the prototype for the Great Seal. The face of the design for the medal showed—in Adams's words—the female figure of "Liberty with her spear and *pileus* [cap of liberty, hanging from the tip of her spear] leaning on General Washington." Looking admiringly at the general, Lady Liberty extends her left arm in an elegant gesture toward "the British fleet in Boston Harbour, with all their Sterns towards the town, the American troops marching in." Du Simitière's sketch for the reverse of the medal portrayed the all-seeing eye of Providence in a triangle, with rays of glory emanating from it. Underneath the eye was a muscular right arm, sword in hand. These motifs were enclosed within a circle. Around the circle was a ring of shields, one for each of the thirteen colonies. Congress voted to pay Du Simitière thirty-two dollars for this design.

On the recommendation of John Jay, General Washington visited Du Simitière in his home on February 1, 1779, and sat "with great good nature" for a pencil portrait in profile, which took nearly an hour. The sketch was subsequently made into a fine engraving, and Washington later recalled the "good likeness" with admiration.[8]

The final commemorative medal of "Washington Before Boston" was not struck until the new year of 1790, six years after Du Simitière's death. It was engraved by the French artist Pierre Simon Duvivier, based upon a profile view of Washington taken from the classic bust done at Mount Vernon in 1785 by Jean-Antoine Houdon. Du Simitière's intimate image of the general and the lady was superceded by a more militaristic, comradely tableau: Washington astride a rearing steed accompanied by his military staff and aide-de-camp on a bluff overlooking Boston harbor. Washington points over a foreground mass of armory and cannonballs to the retreating British in the background. Above him, arranged in a triumphant arc, are the words, Hostibus Primo Fugatus (The Enemy for the First Time Put to Flight). The medal was presented to the first president of the United States by Thomas Jefferson.[9]

During the summer of the Great Seal project, Jefferson visited Du Simitière's apartment on two occasions to borrow books from the artist's eclectic collection, "[Basil] Kennett's American Library" (ca. 1696) and "Memoirs sur l'Arcadie [Nova Scotia]" by Joseph Robineau de Villebon (1690). Like Adams before him, Jefferson sought Du Simitière's expertise. He wanted a coat of arms for his native state of Virginia. Toward the end of July, Jefferson referred to Du Simitière as an "excellent drawer here [in Philadelphia, who] did great seals for Jamaica and Barbadoes both of which are said to have been well done, and a seal for the Philosophical society here which we are told is excellent. But they are expensive [sic]. The drawing . . . will cost about 50 dollars."

The concept for Jefferson captured what Du Simitière believed to be the spirit of Virginia. To symbolize the juxtaposition of newfound Indian lore upon old English tradition, his sketch showed the Cross of St. George pierced at its center by a knife. A tobacco plant, wheat sheaves, a stalk of Indian corn, and the four great rivers of the state rounded out the crowded iconography.

The entire escutcheon, or "shield," was supported in the artist's detailed formal proposal "by a figure dressed, as in the time of Queen Elizabeth, representing Sir Walter Raleigh, planting with his right hand the standard of liberty, with the words of the Magna Charta written on it." On the left side of the finished design, Du Simitière proposed "a Virginia rifleman of the present times completely accoutred." This ambitious visual history lesson was too dense and retrospective for Jefferson, who decided to go with something more pertinent—simply: "Virtue with her foot on a prostrated tyrant."[10]

After receiving the assignment to develop the design for the Great Seal, Adams and Jefferson met with Du Simitière on at least two occasions without Franklin to discuss their individual projects, the Washington medal and the Virginia coat of arms. During the same six-week span, a contentious debate continued in Congress about the structure and content of Franklin's draft "Articles of Confederation and Perpetual Union," which would bring the colonies together. Despite the tension of these confidential deliberations, all three committee members found time to share preliminary ideas for the Great Seal among themselves. On Tuesday, August 13, 1776, Adams visited Du Simitière to hear what he had to say about their various notions and to examine what the artist consultant offered in return.

As was customary throughout his life, Adams took pen in hand the next day and diligently reviewed and reported the details of the excursion to Abigail, his wife and "absent friend" at home in distant Braintree. "This Mr. Du Simitière is a very curious man," he wrote. "He has begun a Collection of Materials for an History of this Revolution. He begins with the first Advices of the Tea Ships [i.e., the Townshend duties of April, 1770]. He cutts out of the Newspapers, every scrap of Intelligence, and every Piece of Speculation, and pastes it upon clean Paper, arranging them under the Head[line] of the State to which they belong and binds them up in Volumes. He has a list of every Speculation and Pamphlet concerning Independence."[11]

Adams laid out his version of Franklin's idea first. "Dr. F. proposes a Device for a Seal," Adams wrote, "Moses lifting up his Wand, and dividing the Red Sea, and Pharaoh, in his Chariot overwhelmed with the Waters—[and engraved at the bottom of the design] this Motto: "Rebellion to Tyrants is Obedience to God.""

Jefferson admired this ringing phrase so much that he suggested it as an appropriate motto for the state of Virginia and added it to his personal seal. He did not know at the time—and the good doctor did not correct him—

that the sentence had been appropriated by Franklin from the epitaph engraved upon the tombstone in Martha's Bay, Jamaica, of John Bradshaw (1602–59), British lawyer and president of the Parliamentary Commission that tried and sentenced King Charles I to death. In an 1823 letter to Edward Everett, Jefferson attributed the motto accurately to "one, I believe, of the regicides of Charles I. . . . Correct its syntax, 'Rebellion *against* tyrants is obedience to God,' [and] it has lost all the strength and beauty of its antithesis."[12]

According to his handwritten notes, Franklin envisioned Moses "in the Dress of a High Priest," and Pharaoh with a crown upon his head and a sword in his hand. "Rays from a Pillar of Fire in the Clouds" reached down to Moses, "to express that he acts by Command of the Deity." Even as the Children of Israel were chosen by God to leave their oppressor, cross the great divide, and establish a sanctioned new land, so were the beleaguered and estranged children of Britain in the eighteenth century destined—and blessed—to do the same by turning their backs on George III.[13]

In addition to Dr. Franklin's slogan, Thomas Jefferson also favored his imagery, opting, with slight variants of language, for the powerful biblical metaphor of "the Children of Israel in the Wilderness, led by a Cloud by day, and a Pillar of Fire by night." For the other side of the Great Seal, Jefferson turned to an altogether different tradition. There, Adams recalled to Abigail, his colleague wanted a picture of "Hengist and Horsa, the Saxon Chiefs, from whom we claim the Honour of being descended and whose Political Principles and Form of Government We have assumed."

The brothers Hengist and Horsa were leaders of the Jutes, a continental Germanic tribe that helped the Britons stave off an invasion of Picts and Scots in the middle of the fifth century AD. Jefferson had studied Anglo-Saxon "dialect" and history in his youth, and it remained a lifelong "hobby" that he admitted "too often runs away with me where I meant not to give up the rein." It was Jefferson's firm belief that Anglo-Saxon common law, "the happy system of our ancestors," was infused with awareness of the natural rights of man. And, he pointed out, this early ethos was introduced into England two hundred years before Christianity.[14]

For his Great Seal idea, Adams told Abigail he was "profoundly" moved by a picture in a volume on the shelves of his household library. "I proposed the Choice [Judgement] of Hercules, as engraved by [Simon] Gribelin in some Editions of Lord Shaftesbury's *Works*." He continued, "The Hero is resting on his Clubb, [looking at] Virtue pointing to her rugged Mountain, on one Hand, and perswading him to ascend. Sloth [a diaphanously clad maiden], glancing at her flowery Paths of Pleasure, wantonly reclin[es] on the Ground, displaying the Charms both of her Eloquence and Person, to seduce him into Vice."[15]

Anthony Ashley Cooper, the third earl of Shaftesbury, commissioned Paolo de Matteis to paint this allegorical scene in 1712 and the following year asked Gribelin to engrave it for the book, *Characteristicks of Men, Manners, Opinions, Times.* The fifth edition was published in 1773 by John Baskerville in Birmingham, England, and acquired by Adams that same year. The book is catalogued in Adams's personal library, housed at the Boston Public Library. Matteis's sensuous canvas now hangs in the Ashmolean Museum at Oxford.[16]

Adams's choice is in keeping with the "neoclassical dreams" of the founders and the model sources of antiquity they searched for inspiration. The ancient story of Hercules was recounted by Xenophon in his *Memoir of Socrates*, recalled as a poem composed by Prodicus, a sophist of Ceos. Hercules appears "on the verge of manhood and contemplating his future." Two women come to him, one offering a "flowery," easy path to a life of pleasure. Her name is Vice. The second woman, Virtue, "tall and austerely beautiful," tells Hercules that "what is truly good can only be obtained through hard effort" along the steep and rugged path of life. Hercules's choice is not shown, but one can tell from the body language of Gribelin's tableau where the hero's judgment will take him.[17]

Conceding that it was "too complicated . . . and not original" enough for a coat of arms, Adams did not reveal to Abigail what train of thought had led him to the parable in the first place. Perhaps Hercules entering manhood represented the American nation, young and strong, coming to terms with the painful challenge of revolution as necessary separation from the familiar, outworn "seductions" of the mother country.[18]

Finally it was Du Simitière's turn. He showed Adams a small pencil sketch and a comprehensive heraldic description for the Great Seal entitled "The Coat of Arms of the States of America." The design was composed of a central shield with two "supporters," or figures, one on either side, a crest at the top, and a motto at the bottom. The shield was divided into six parts, each representing a "principal" European country from which settlers came to America: England, Scotland, Ireland, France, Germany, and Holland. Arranged around the shield were thirteen *escutcheons* representing the "Independent States of America."

The figure standing to the right of the central shield was the Goddess Liberty, appropriated from Du Simitière's design for the Washington medal. She was garbed "in a corslet of armour (alluding to the present times [war])." In her right hand was the familiar "Spear and Cap." In her left hand was an anchor, "emblem of Hope." To the left of the shield was an American soldier, sibling to the rifleman Du Simitière had suggested to Jefferson for the Seal of Virginia. This gentleman was more heavily armed, "completely accoutred in his hunting Shirt and trowsers, with his tomahawk, powder horn, pouch &c., holding with his left hand his rifle gun."[19]

For the Great Seal crest, Du Simitière also abstracted from his earlier idea for the Washington medal, placing "the Eye of Providence in a radiant Triangle whose Glory [rays of light] extend over the Shield and beyond the Supporters." Du Simitière was familiar with this iconography from his studies in the art of the occult; his library contained half a dozen titles on the subject. The shape he refers to as a triangle is better known as the Pyramid (or *mastaba*) of Progress, derived from the arcane belief—popular in eighteenth-century America—in Egypt as the birthplace of civilization.

The "all-seeing" eye of an omniscient, ubiquitous deity represents the supremacy of the spiritual over the material world and is an assertion of the primacy of "the American cause." Benjamin Franklin was the only member of the Great Seal Committee who was a Freemason, and the symbol of the Eye of God, "The Great Architect of the Universe" was integral to that radical Enlightenment society. For this reason the design has been erroneously attributed to him.[20]

The words **E PLURIBUS UNUM** appeared at the bottom of Du Simitière's sketch inscribed in bold face and all capital letters within a scroll unfurling at the feet of Lady Liberty.

Tracking down the origin of **"Out of Many, One"** as the motto of the United States of America leads to London at the end of the seventeenth century and a short-lived publication called *The Gentleman's Journal: or the Monthly Miscellany*, edited by Pierre Antoine Motteux, a Huguenot *émigré*. On the title page of this periodical, which ran from January 1691 to November 1694, there was a picture of a hand holding a nosegay of flowers, accompanied by Motteux's explanation, "That which is prefixed to this *Miscellany*, among other things, implies that tho' only one of the many Pieces in it were acceptable, it might gratify every reader. So I may venture to crowd in what follows, as a Cowslip and a Dazy among the Lillies and the Roses." The motto beneath the picture was printed with a comma, E pluribus, unum—in other words, "one *selected from* among many."[21]

To reflect upon where Motteux, in turn, might have unearthed the motto, classicists debated the matter inconclusively for decades at the turn of the late-nineteenth and early twentieth centuries, considering Virgil's poem, *Moretum*; Horace's Second Book of *Epistles*; *De Amicitia* by Cicero; the Fourth Book of St. Augustine's *Confessions*; and Aristotle's *Politics*.[22]

A chronic collector of periodicals, Du Simitière may or may not have been aware of the *Gentleman's Journal*, but he certainly was a compulsive reader of its long-lived, immensely popular successor, *The Gentleman's Magazine; or, Trader's Monthly Intelligencer*, founded in London in 1731 by Edward Cave Jr. under the pseudonym "Sylvanus Urban, Gent. of Aldermanbury." Edited by Cave until his death in 1754, the venerable magazine went on for another 175 years thereafter.

This "uniquely rich and compendious record of eighteenth-century life" declared itself to be "A Collection of all Matters of Information and Amusement . . . whatever is worth quoting from the numerous Papers of News & Entertainment, British and Foreign, viz., Publick Affairs, Foreign and Domestick." *The Gentleman's Magazine* enjoyed greater fame and wider circulation than any other journal of its time, extending by subscription as far as the homes, clubs, and pubs of the colonial intelligentsia. By 1741 its "leading staff writer," the renowned Dr. Samuel Johnson, claimed that "it is read as far as the English Language extends, and we [even] see it reprinted . . . in the Plantations."[23]

Beginning in 1732 annual December retrospective "anthology" volumes of the *Gentleman's Magazine* contained fully indexed collections of articles, news, and poetry covering the preceding twelve months. Displayed at the bottom of the title page of the anthology issues was the familiar image of the hand grasping a bouquet, and the motto—this time, without the comma—"E pluribus unum"—in other words, *one composed of many.*

In the event any erudite readers might have missed the visual cue, Cave concluded an introductory poem for the 1734 compendium as follows, "To your motto most true, for our monthly inspection. You mix various rich sweets in *one* fragrant collection."[24]

In the summer of 1775, as one of several historical research projects in which he was involved during the decade he sojourned in Philadelphia, Du Simitière set forth to assemble a year-by-year chronology of the history of Pennsylvania, beginning with the royal charter of William Penn and ending with Benjamin Franklin's return from London the preceding May. His primary sources for noteworthy events were back issues of the *Gentleman's Magazine* dating to the early 1740s. There is a complete set of the *Gentleman's Magazine* in the Du Simitière collection of the Historical Society of Pennsylvania.[25]

Well versed in the protocols of heraldry—that was why the committee approached him in the first place—Du Simitière understood that it was the traditional privilege of the artist who designed a coat of arms to select the underlying motto. This he did with reference to the *Gentleman's Magazine*. The phrase is a veritable caption for the image of the diversity of the thirteen independent states circumscribing the European origins of the American people, and this realm within a realm is further pulled together inside the shield: E Pluribus Unum.[26]

On August 20, 1776, Thomas Jefferson, on behalf of the Great Seal Committee, presented its report to Congress. In the nature of all good committees, the members had reached a compromise. The seal was described as a "pendant." The reverse synthesized the cautionary allegorical image set forth by Franklin and Jefferson—Pharoah in the middle of the parted waters of the Red Sea, approaching Moses, who stands dominant on the shore, "extending his hand over the Sea caus[ing] it to overwhelm Pharoah." The Chosen People will again prevail, as they did in an era long past. "Rebellion to tyrants is Obedience to God" was the dramatic motto.

The front of the Seal showed Du Simitière's concept nearly verbatim, except that Lady Liberty's anchor was removed, her left hand resting directly on the shield of the states; and the elaborately "accoutred" American soldier was replaced by a more moderate persona, "the Goddess Justice bearing a Sword in her right hand, and in her left a Balance."

We can only surmise about the discussion following the presentation of the design. No record has been found of the debate, save a rather discouraging procedural note: "Ordered, To lie on the table." E Pluribus Unum failed to capture the imagination of the Continental Congress in the momentous summer of 1776.[27]

The motto was rejected because its expression was six years premature. Debate in the Continental Congress was fueled by two definitions of America as a democracy: Was it a "confederacy of sovereign states or a single unified nation?" Should the individuality of each colony be preserved—what James Madison later identified as "the spirit of locality"—or should thirteen separate identities be subsumed? Should the power of the central government hold sway over the separate states, as Benjamin Franklin first advocated, or should sovereignty be dispersed? Should voting in Congress be allocated proportionately, according to the population of each state, or should representation be equal across the board, regardless of size? John Adams came up with an alchemical prophecy. According to Thomas Jefferson's notes during the heated summer days of 1776, Adams referred to the individuality of the colonies as "a mere sound . . . [rather] The confederacy is to make us one individual only; it is to form us, like separate parcels of metal, into one common mass."[28]

In the midst of the struggle in Congress, the states were encouraged by formal resolution to search for "alternative structures of authority" by drafting and ratifying their own provisional constitutions, loosely proscribed by the Congress as aiming to be "sufficient to the exigencies of their affairs." Between January and December 1776, New Hampshire, South Carolina, Rhode Island, Virginia, New Jersey, Delaware, Pennsylvania, Connecticut, Maryland, and North Carolina fell into place, in that order. Georgia, New York, and Vermont followed suit by July 1777.

In accordance with the ideal character of the slowly and stubbornly coalescing republic, the constitutions of the thirteen "free and independent states" varied. Some legislative committees acted behind closed doors without any referendum. Others opened the deliberative process to the public. Separation of powers was weighted toward both ends of the spectrum. Some states placed decision making squarely within the province of a bicameral legislature, while others vested greater authority in a chief executive. Pennsylvania did neither, focusing all governmental power in a unicameral, popularly elected General Assembly.[29]

An "extralegal" entity, the Continental-Confederation Congress had been created out of sheer necessity in 1774. Now an official instrument of government for "the United States of America" needed to be presented to and approved by the constituent states in order to legitimize congressional authority and clarify the boundaries of its power. The Articles of Confederation were drafted to begin to define "a firm League of Friendship" among the states. Under the Articles, a majority of nine states would be required to ratify such major decisions as making war, signing treaties, and coining money. In the last analysis, each state retained any "power, jurisdiction [or] right" not explicitly delegated to the "United States." On March 1, 1781, with the final approval of the Maryland state legislature, the Articles of Confederation were unanimously ratified.[30]

Five months following ratification, on August 23 Congress rejected the drawings for a new Great Seal submitted by Francis Hopkinson, the well-known designer of the first official U.S. flag, deciding that his red, white, and blue "fancy-work . . . ought not to be acted upon." Another year went by. In the spring of 1782, Congress appointed a third Great Seal Committee to take up the matter. Three activist members were selected: Arthur Middleton, the committee chairman, hailed from Charleston, South Carolina; Elias Boudinot of New Jersey, president of the Continental Congress, went on to become first president of the American Bible Society; and John Rutledge was the former governor of South Carolina. They were joined in an unofficial capacity by Arthur Lee of Westmoreland County, Virginia, one of the delegates sent to the court of George III to present the Olive Branch Petition. Just as the first committee had done with Du Simitière, this group hired a consultant, a young and artistic Philadelphia lawyer with knowledge in heraldry named William Barton.[31]

Barton set to work instantly and hastily. In less than one week, between May 4 or 5, and May 9, 1782, he produced a number of complicated designs. The important elements in his first so-called "Armorial Atchievement" [sic] for the Great Seal of the United States came down to a striking echo of Du Simitière's thoughts—a shield with thirteen horizontal stripes pulled together by a one strong vertical bar down the center. The shield was supported on its right side by Lady Liberty (called by Barton "The Genius of America") holding a dove of peace in her right hand and a knight in complete armor standing on the left.

In a second drawing, for the reverse of the Seal, Barton added another idea reminiscent of Du Simitière's. He proposed a shield with a border composed of thirteen smaller shields surmounted by an eagle. The lovely "Maiden with flowing Auburn tresses" remained in place. The new supporting figure on the left was transformed into an American soldier decked out in the regalia of the Continental army. A golden pyramid of thirteen steps topped by an all-seeing eye completed the design.

Barton put forth a selection of patriotic and weighty Latin mottos for the United States of America, preferring *Virtus sola invicta* ("Only virtue unconquered"), *Deo favente* ("With God's favor"), *In vindiciam libertatis* ("In defense of liberty"), and *Perennis* ("Enduring through the years").[32]

The cumulative dossier was then placed into the "fine organizing hands" of the permanent, unanimously elected secretary of Congress, a man who had been present from its creation in 1774, signed the original Declaration of Independence on July 4, 1776, and would continue on until the federal government came to power in 1789. Charles Thomson (1729–1824) was given a thick portfolio containing proposals, sketches, and notes generated by six years' worth of Great Seal Committees. He was charged "to take Order" of the situation and make a decision. There was no better man for a responsibility of such a moment. Approaching six feet in height, with "furrowed countenance and sparkling eyes," the sober, thoughtful, and honest Derry-born Irish Quaker was affectionately regarded by his colleagues as the "soul" of Congress. When Thomson retired from public life, this former schoolmaster, Latin teacher, and devoted amateur historian took on as his "extremely zealous" twenty-year mission the project of translating the Old and New Testaments from Greek into English. The four-volume opus was published in 1808 to great admiration.[33]

For the final design, Thomson plunged fearlessly into the "intellectual forest of classical and Biblical themes" and pruned with care the many elements put forth by the three committees. He then created a rudimentary sketch of his own for a design which—with minor modifications—still remains in use today. The hand of Pierre Eugène Du Simitière is predominant. "The Secretary of the United States in Congress assembled," Thomson began, in the report submitted on June 20 1782, "to whom were referred the several reports of committees on the device for a great seal," presented as the strong, central figure for the obverse (front), the native American bald eagle with widespread wings and fanned-out tail as if in flight, "on the wing and rising." For it was written in Exodus 19:4, as God spoke to the pilgrims of Israel, "Ye have seen what I did unto the Egyptians, and how I bore you on eagles' wings, and brought you unto myself." In the book of Revelation 12, "the two wings of the great eagle" represent the "special providence and agency of the Almighty God in conquering the enemies of His people." The savior eagle carried a shield on his breast "without any other supporters," Thomson specified, "to denote that the United States of America ought to rely on their own Virtue."

The shield bore a chevron of thirteen alternating red ("hardiness and valor") and white ("purity and innocence") stripes representing "the several States." The stripes were on a blue field ("the color of the Chief, signifying vigilance, perseverance and justice"), uniting the whole and representing Congress. Gripped in the eagle's right claw was an olive branch with thirteen leaves (peace), and in its left, a bundle of thirteen arrows (war). Above its distinctive if erroneously crested head hovered a constellation of thirteen six-pointed stars of David, arranged in a circle surrounded with bright rays ("a new nation taking its place among other sovereign states"), and an array of puffy clouds. The eagle's proud head was facing right, the traditional direction of honor in heraldry, so that its left eye glared out. Gripped in the eagle's beak was a ribbonlike, undulating pennant with Du Simitière's original motto once more in thirteen capital letters, **E PLURIBUS UNUM.**

For the reverse (back), Thomson wanted—the descriptive language is, again, familiar—an unfinished pyramid ("strength and duration"), at its zenith an eye in a triangle "surrounded with a glory." Thomson heeded Barton's message but superceded the attorney's various popular Latin choices with two from Virgil of his own preference. Over the eye Thomson specified the words ANNUIT COEPTIS. At the base of the pyramid were the numerical letters MDCCLXXVI (1776), and below them the words NOVUS ORDO SECLORUM.

Annuit coeptis is an allusion to line 625 of the ninth book of the *Aeneid.* The words also are present in somewhat different form in the *Georgics,* Book 40, line 1. In both cases, Thomson was no doubt after the connotation of beseeching the Eye of Providence to be "favorable to America's undertakings." Later interpretations led toward translating *Annuit coeptis* into the perfect tense, as, "God has favored our undertakings." *Novus ordo seclo-rum* is adapted from Virgil's *Eclogues*, Book 4, line 5, which may be read as "the great series of ages begins anew," or, more recently, "A new order of the ages."

The prominence of Virgil (70–19 BC) in the Great Seal comes as no surprise. Thomson was a Latin scholar, and the year 1782 was the eigh-teenth centenary of the poet's death. To round off the Virgilian theme, Thomson would have been familiar with *E pluribus unum* from his reading of the "Moretum," line 104, but, as noted, Du Simitière appropriated those words from *The Gentleman's Magazine*.[34]

The brass die for the Great Seal, just under two and one-half inches in diameter, was most probably engraved by Robert Scot in his shop on Front Street in Philadelphia. The die and a small, screw-action engraving press were deposited in Thomson's office in the Philadelphia State House during the summer of 1782. On September 16 the Seal was placed into use for the first time to execute a document giving Gen. George Washington the power to negotiate an agreement with the British for better treatment of American prisoners of war. On March 4, 1789, the effective beginning of the American government under the new Constitution, the Great Seal was declared to be the Seal of the United States and *E Pluribus Unum* became the "national motto." It has appeared continuously since, on the seals, among others, of the president, the United States Supreme Court, and the Department of State.[35]

As for Pierre-Eugène Du Simitière, he had designed his own coat of arms, a head of armor and two crossed swords within a shield, with the motto *J'espère* ("I hope") written on a pennant below, but hope was insuffi-cient to sustain him. The income from public viewings "at half a dollar each ticket" on Tuesdays, Thursdays, and Saturdays in his domestic "Mu-seum" on Arch Street did not help to cover mounting bills. He sold an oc-casional print for ten shillings but could not bring himself to sell the entire cabinet collection despite the fact that in the fall of 1784 he was dying of starvation and too ill to achieve his dream to produce an illustrated history of "our glorious Revolution." As Du Simitière wrote toward the sad end of his life in America, ". . . none will ever surpass me in the zeal and the desire I had in being really useful to the people among whom I have lived so many years and for whom I entertain a real esteem."[36]

The expressive beauty of E Pluribus Unum as an American ideal arrived with the slow resolution of the founders' essential tension. The members of the Continental Congress acted out the drama of autonomy versus community on a personal level, one with another. They grappled with the configuration of the American colonies, independently and in relation to each other, more like the sovereign countries of Europe than the states they eventually became. That is why it took so long for E Pluribus Unum to be approved.

That hard-won cohesiveness was lost with the Civil War. After the division of the Union, and with prolonged agony, came a surge of immigration that forced another change in the definition of nationhood. E Pluribus Unum became an image of the nucleus of democracy. No matter how the varied ingredients that went into the makeup of the country were categorized—ideologies or races, neighborhoods, or rural townships—they could be resolved to a kernel of meaning. The identity of American culture existed to be discovered within each citizen, in his or her own fashion. The definition of America became the sum total of its constituent parts. As Ralph Waldo Emerson will now demonstrate, as long as the life of the mind was well and thriving, "America" would continue to evolve and expand.

Ralph Waldo Emerson

4

Self-Reliance

Mr. Emerson is the most American of our writers. The Idea of America, which lies at the bottom of our original institutions, appears in him with great prominence. We mean the idea of personal freedom, of the dignity and value of human nature, the superiority of a man to the accidents of a man. Emerson is the most republican of republicans, the most protestant of the dissenters.

—Theodore Parker, "The Writings of Ralph Waldo Emerson," *The Massachusetts Quarterly Review* III (March 1850).[1]

It is impossible to extricate oneself from the questions in which your age is involved. You can no more keep out of politics than you can keep out of the frost.

—Ralph Waldo Emerson, 1862

He was born in Boston, "new England's metropolis, then as now," on May 25, 1803, the fourth of eight children of the Reverend William and Ruth Haskins Emerson. Waldo, as he preferred to be called, was the descendant of generations of ministers stretching back to the seventeenth-century Puritans. His father, pastor of the city's First Unitarian Church, died of a stomach tumor when Waldo was eight years old. To make ends meet, Mother Ruth, daughter of a distiller, sold the family library, rented rooms in their home to boarders, and took on work as a domestic. Although the Emerson family lived poorly, reverence for education and pride of self-culture ran deep. With the encouragement of his erudite, pious, and opinionated maiden aunt, Mary Moody Emerson, Waldo enrolled in Boston Public Latin School.

At fourteen the boy entered Harvard, working as a servant in the president's lodgings and tutoring classmates during term breaks. Chosen by fifty-eight fellow students to be class poet, young Waldo's professed desire was to become a painter. In January 1820, the pivot point of junior year, he began to keep a careful journal of his "reckless ragamuffin ideas." Within its early pages, Emerson entitled the projected boundaries of his mental universe as envisioning "The Wide World." He proudly scribbled that his words were "dedicated to the Spirit of America." The journal, he vowed, would serve as his "savings bank," "storehouse and retreat," and "consoler." It went on for decades and became a multivolume epic. Thus began the pulse-taking documentation of Emerson's omnivorous life of the mind, really a life in the mind. His multileveled, restless, and contradictory inner life was propelled forward by the ambitious moral obligation to see all, feel all—and eventually redefine all.[2]

But first things first. The adolescent daydreamer had to graduate from college, and he did so, in the middle of the class. He moved to Waltham and taught in a young ladies' finishing school founded by his brother, William. Impatiently fearing a fate of "quiet mediocrity of talents and condition," he enrolled in the middle class at Harvard Divinity School, again at the urging of Aunt Mary, reminding him of the family tradition. His studies were disturbed by eye troubles, lung ailments, and rheumatism.

In the fall of 1826, Emerson received a license from the Middlesex Association of Ministers and was approbated to preach. Three years later he became junior minister under Henry Ware Jr. in the Second Church of Boston, where Cotton Mather had once presided. He was appointed chaplain of the Massachusetts State Senate, and when Ware left his post to join the Harvard Divinity School faculty, Emerson rose to the senior position. He married his eighteen-year-old sweetheart, Ellen Louisa Tucker. She died a year and half later, succumbing to tuberculosis in the winter of 1831. "Ellen went to heaven to see, to know, to worship, to love, to intercede. . . . God be merciful to me a sinner," the distraught husband wrote, "& repair this miserable debility in which her death has left my soul."[3]

Within grief brewed a conflict between vocation and faith. Never an idle conversationalist, not given to social superfluities, Emerson was cordial rather than warm. He shied away from the required neighborhood "calling" visits of parish work, preferring the mental challenges of public speaking.

Six feet tall, black suited, with erect bearing—he found rigid posture neces-sary because of persistent back pain—and a pleasing, sonorous voice, he presented a dramatic oratorical figure on the pulpit. Reverend Ware cau-tioned Emerson that audiences were perplexed by his preference for em-ploying biblical texts as metaphorical illustrations to substantiate his spiritual lessons rather than preaching explicitly from them, to which Emerson responded that he did not believe in miracles.

The ostensible reason Emerson presented in his dramatic offer of resig-nation from the ministry in September 1832 was that he could no longer in good conscience serve Communion. "In an altered age, we worship in the dead forms of our forefathers," he told the Second Church governing coun-cil. Members of the congregation were reluctant to let the gentle and re-spected "Mr. Emerson" go. As a compromise measure, they proposed that he be spared from taking the Lord's Supper. Emerson's objection to the rite of the Eucharist was the result of a lonely, introspective search for an au-thentic life purpose. Wondering "where & how I ought to live . . . God will show me," he wrote, hoping to reach beyond the constraints of an inher-ited career. "I would be free. I cannot be while I take things as others please to rate them."

His religious crisis accompanied by nervous exhaustion and chronic stomach pains, Emerson was advised by his physician to seek warmer weather. On Christmas Day 1832 he sailed out of Boston on the brigantine *Jasper*, headed for Malta, vowing "to lay out my own road" and hoping that the Mediterranean climate would prove "sanative" to his exhausted body and mind.[4]

For three months Emerson meandered through the "European school-room." One night at an Easter Week dinner party given in Rome by a former Harvard classmate, Emerson fell into a conversation with Gustave d'Eichthal, French sociologist, scholar of Greek history, and friend of the English economist John Stuart Mill. Emerson told d'Eichthal he was making his way northward to London and from there to Scotland in hopes of meeting the philosopher Thomas Carlyle, whose work he so ad-mired. D'Eichthal kindly provided Emerson with a letter of introduction to Carlyle's friend Mill. Sightseeing in Florence, café hopping in crowded

Paris, and visits to museums and scientific lectures in cacophonous London followed. In early August Emerson sent a note to Dr. James Gillman, north of the city in Highgate, at whose home the poet Samuel Taylor Coleridge had been lodging in declining health for many years. Coleridge's critical works interested Emerson greatly, especially the essays meditating "on politics, morals and religion" found in *The Friend* (1818) and *Aids to Reflection* (1829), aimed at "direct[ing] the reader's attention to the Science of Words." Through Dr. Gillman's good will, Emerson, like many young disciples before him, was able to spend an hour of copious conversation with the elderly man of letters, who died one year later.[5]

The fruition of Emerson's therapeutic travels came on a Sunday morning in late August, ten days before his journey's end. Bearing a letter provided by Mill, not knowing that Mill had already written to Thomas Carlyle directly, Emerson made the much-anticipated pilgrimage to an isolated farm in the "blasted Paradise" of lower Craigenputtock, in southwestern Scotland, thirty miles south of Edinburgh and sixteen miles from Dumfries, to meet the outspoken critic and social philosopher, and "hide myself in the dens of the hills, in the thickets of an obscure country town." Within hours of Emerson's arrival at Carlyle's two-story stone estate house, the two men went out for a long walk through the heathered, rocky fields and hills, "looked down upon Wordsworth's country," then paused to sit upon a mossy stone and "talked and talked" to their "heart's content" of the immortality of the soul.[6]

Carlyle's beautiful and brilliant wife, Jane Baillie Welsh, recalled Emerson's arrival as "the visit of an Angel." The first encounter launched a thirty-eight-year correspondence knitting together an historic friendship. The Scotsman's distant and puritanical father, James, a stonemason, shared with Carlyle's mother, Margaret, an abiding belief in education. Thomas walked from his farm home in the village of Ecclefechan to attend classes at the University of Edinburgh. He spent desultory years as a tutor and schoolmaster, having abandoned a half-hearted year of training for the ministry. In his mid-twenties Carlyle passed through a spiritual awakening and alienation from organized religion. He devoted more time to magazine writing and independent scholarship. He wrote a magisterial *Life of Schiller* and became immersed in the pioneering study and translation of Johann Wolfgang von Goethe, embarking upon a steady exchange of letters with him.[7]

Carlyle's grounding in German language and literature provided the key that opened a major intellectual portal for Emerson. During the year prior to their meeting, Emerson borrowed from the Boston Athenaeum, read, and admired Carlyle's three-volume translation of Goethe's *Wilhelm Meister's Apprenticeship*. Emerson also followed Carlyle's provocative essays in the *Edinburgh Review* including "Characteristics," "State of German Literature," and "Taylor's *Historic Survey of German Poetry*." Earlier, Emerson read Carlyle's fresh observations on German metaphysics in an 1829 essay in the *Foreign Review* on Novalis, the pseudonym of Georg Friedrich Philipp von Hardenberg. Novalis, a Romantic Prussian poet popularly known as "the prophet of Romanticism," believed that knowledge of the symbolic "remote blue flower of the Absolute" would always be beyond man's grasp, yet he continued to long for it and was compelled to seek a redemptive glimpse.[8]

Carlyle took this premise a step further with meticulous exegetical readings of Immanuel Kant's monumental *Critique of Pure Reason* (1781, 1787) and *Critique of Practical Reason* (1788). In his Novalis piece, Carlyle expanded upon Kant's depiction of the self-made "idealist" as a man of strong will espousing a "higher faculty of understanding." Kant's "high-minded" idealist lived by the philosophy of "Transcendentalism," in other words, "ascending beyond the senses." The goal of the "transcendental idealist" was to harness the energy of his intelligence toward a spiritual end, cultivate knowledge, and strengthen his mind to habits of heightened perception, looking "fixedly upon Existence, till, one after the other, its earthly hulls and garnitures have all melted away." Emerging from the underbrush of distraction, the pure phenomenal world appeared as a revelation in a dew-drenched clearing, just as it did to Adam in the Garden.[9]

Through Carlyle, Emerson arrived at an understanding of the Kantian insistence on intense subjectivity as the means to achieve wisdom, and Kant's emphasis on the mutuality of reason and sense perception. In the very first letter he wrote to Carlyle, in May, 1834, Emerson noted that the "Truth-speaker" had to be above all else a "Thinker." When Emerson's *First Series of Essays* was published in the spring of 1841, he reprised this analogy, equating idealism with transcendentalism in an address delivered at the Masonic Temple in Boston and later reprinted in the *Dial Magazine*.[10]

N ewly refreshed by drinking avidly from the intoxicating wellsprings of British Romanticism and Continental European philosophy,

Emerson arrived in Boston in early October energized and primed to apply the lessons he had learned. The following month he delivered his first lecture before the Natural History Society at the Masonic Temple. Over the following several years, Emerson broadened the range of his secular subject matter, speaking at schools and adult education societies. For a fee and travel expenses, Emerson discoursed on history, human culture, ethics, and English literature, with decisive emphasis against the empirical strictures of John Locke and for the radical, "primary" poetic imagination of Coleridge, representative of "the Infinite *I Am*." The fact that he had no permanent pastorate did not deter Emerson from continuing his free-range contract preaching every Sunday at a variety of pulpits close to home and as far afield as Maine and New York.[11]

He married Lydia (whom he preferred to call "Lidian") Jackson of Plymouth and moved with her to a house on two acres of meadows and woods near the Cambridge Turnpike, a half mile outside the village of Concord, purchased for thirty-five hundred dollars with proceeds from the estate of his late wife. These additional inherited funds provided Emerson with the wherewithal to pursue independent study.[12]

In September 1836 Boston's James Munroe and Company published one thousand copies of Emerson's first book, "a 95-page azure-colored pamphlet" of brief, ardent essays collectively entitled *Nature*. In conjunction with this occasion, some loosely associated, like-minded scholars, Unitarian ministers, social reformers, naturalists, educators, artists, and radical writers from Boston and Cambridge began to convene weekly for tea and Socratic conversation. One of their early number was Emerson's friend two years his junior, the Reverend Frederic Henry Hedge. A Coleridge scholar and Swedenborgian trained in Germany, Hedge recalled the atmosphere at the first "Symposium" in the Boston home of George Ripley as characterized by "general agreement that the state of public opinion in theology and philosophy was . . . very unsatisfactory."

During the ensuing seven years, the group grew to include Amos Bronson Alcott, Elizabeth Palmer Peabody, William Ellery Channing, Orestes Brownson, Jones Very, Margaret Fuller, William Henry Furness, James Marsh, Theodore Parker, and later, Henry David Thoreau. Each one valued by all the others for his or her unique personality, they came together in response to Emerson's exuberant invocation at the beginning of *Nature* call-

ing for innovative thought and transforming ways to negotiate the sanctuary of the "inner temple."[13]

Drawing upon another inspirational Romantic concept, this time from
William Wordsworth, Emerson warned his admiring colleagues that
painful, introspective effort was required to "see into the life of things."
Their sustained thinking had the potential to become a "perturbing and
enriching" stimulus toward a new American culture and, eventually, a new
American language and literature. "The foregoing generations beheld God
and nature face to face; we, through their eyes," Emerson wrote in the
opening passages of *Nature*, seeking to express the birthright for his generation. "Why should not we also enjoy an original relation to the universe?
Why should not we have a poetry and philosophy of insight and not of tradition, and a religion by revelation to us, and not the history of theirs?"[14]

Toward the conclusion of *Nature*, Emerson announced that he was going to devote himself to "an entire and devout attention to truth." He resolved to undertake a wholesale revision of his personality by means of
"untaught sallies of the spirit, a continual self-recovery, and entire humility." Only then would he be able to feel the immanent presence of God.
Emerson had resolved in his *Journal* while still a teenager that he would follow the example of the community of ancient Greek Orphic poets and mu-
sicians, who sought spiritual purification, not in the confines of the temple,
but in personal rituals of ecstasy.[15]

In 1880 forty-four years after *Nature*, Emerson presented his one hundredth lecture in the Concord Lyceum, a center of education and a lively
forum for social reform. He reflected upon the "little pamphlet" of essays
that first announced the flowerings of the Transcendental "Club."
Throughout his life, and even at this commemorative celebratory occasion
just two years before he died, Emerson denied that the opportune coalescing of friends under his reluctant leadership constituted any kind of institution or formal movement. There was "no external organization, no badge,
no creed, no name" to the transcendentalists. Rather, Emerson recalled
simply, that period "appeared to be that the mind had become aware of itself . . . there was a new consciousness," with one major distinction: "This
idea, roughly written in revolutions and [other] national movements, in the
mind of the [American] philosopher had far more precision: the individual
is the world."[16]

After the publication of *Nature*, the opposing rhythms of Emerson's life were manifested to him like the diastole and systole of a heartbeat. The intensifying pressures of public demand for his speeches alternated with the comfortable seductions of domesticity. The death in New York the preceding May of Emerson's beloved brother Charles from tuberculosis was counterbalanced by the birth of his son, Waldo, at the end of October. Emerson doted upon the child, noting with delight every new "irresistible warble" and movement. Thursday evenings by the hearth, Emerson rehearsed his weekend text with Lydia, before sallying forth to Roxbury or Framingham or Lowell or Salem or Plymouth or Providence or wherever his presence was required.[17]

On August 31, 1837, he pushed the ambitious "world-building" doctrine developed during the preceding decade with an impassioned Phi Beta Kappa oration at Harvard, afterward titled "The American Scholar." Oliver Wendell Holmes affectionately called it "our intellectual Declaration of Independence." In the lecture Emerson endorsed the "speculative man" as the true leader and hero of his time, responsible for giving voice to and defining the current age. Applied, disciplined thought was a legitimate, ennobling "action."[18]

"No man could be better occupied," Emerson wrote, "than in making his own bible by harkening to all those sentences which, now here, now there, now in nursery rhymes, now in Hebrew, now in English bards, thrill him like the sound of a trumpet." In order to build one's own world, one had to build one's own language. More than any other expression—conversation, lecture, or polished essay—Emerson's journals were the organic proving ground for the extremity of daily introspection he believed was the only true path to illumination. For good reason he referred to his journals as a vast, dangerous, inexhaustible "quarry" from which he extracted the raw material of Emerson the private man to be refined into Emerson the public man.[19]

Emerson's "meteorology of thought" did not acknowledge adverse weather. Rain or shine, delving into the deepest self was the thinking man's "Duty and Discipline." The deeper he excavated in search of language with which to construct his moral constitution, the more disengaged he became from the received and claustrophobic "old worships" and "secondary knowledge" of Unitarianism. Its trappings had no use for him. "Take away then thy pulpit & psalmbook & table; it is dead," he wrote to himself, "&

like [that] yonder tall dead tree intrudes into living nature & affronts the world." He was far more connected to the transcendental visionary's "natural motions of the Soul." In March 1838 an opportunity arose for Emerson to bridge the chasm opening up between the two realms and articulate the terms of his moral transition.[20]

A committee of three "friendly Youths" from the Harvard Divinity School—George F. Simmons, Harrison Grey Otis Blake, and W. D. Wilson—wrote to "the Sage of Concord" asking him to deliver the annual address before their senior graduating class in the chapel "on occasion of [their] entering upon the active Christian ministry." The talk was scheduled for Sunday evening, July 15. Emerson had almost four months to prepare, building on an indignant head of steam that had been percolating for some years. The discourse would be "rammed with life." What better place to deliver the lesson than on its spawning-ground, the stronghold of establishment New England Unitarianism?

Emerson began to chip through many veins in his stratified mental quarry in the early spring of 1838. Characteristic of his layered mode of thought, he extracted ingredients and ideas for the "Divinity School Address" embedded in a mixture of other subject matter, including many thoughts and idealizations he would revisit and elaborate upon as themes for his pivotal 1841 essay, "Self-Reliance." For example, when Emerson was preparing to begin work on the Harvard "Address," he resolved "to go upright & vital & say the truth in all ways." This phrase appeared three years later in "Self-Reliance." Sitting by his pond in the Concord woods preparing for the "Address," Emerson copied down in his journal an anecdote from Volume IV of the *Memoires* of Emmanuel Augustin Dieudonné, comte de Las Cases, about the Emperor Napoleon's conviction that to make his army stronger he would follow the example of the ancient Romans, ordering his men to hand mill their own corn and bake their own bread for sustenance. The citation was used in the final paragraphs of "Self-Reliance." Writing notes for the "Address" in late April, aware that his speech was going to give rise to a certain amount of "commotion," as Henry James delicately put it in 1883, Emerson reminded himself that "What I do, be sure, is all that concerns my majesty & not what men great or small think of it"—a self-exhortation he reproduced in "Self-Reliance." By June, his deadline fast approaching, Emerson turned for encouragement to *Paradise Lost*, spurring himself in Milton's words to "advance & advance

& advance into [the] Chaos & the Dark." This very language also found a home in "Self-Reliance."[21]

"[T]he discourse now growing under [his] eye to the Divinity School" was almost ready. From his solitary quarry, Emerson mined final encouragement five days before he traveled to Cambridge. "A true man can never feel rivalry," he wrote, preaching to an audience of one. "All men are ministers to him[,] servants to bring him materials, but none or all can possibly do what he must do. He alone is privy[,] nor even is he yet privy to his own secret."[22]

The crowded second-floor chapel in Divinity Hall was hushed in anticipation. There were six graduates, all in the front row. The rest of the "hundred or so listeners who could find seats" included Emerson's friends, members of his occasional discussion group, and senior members of the present and past Divinity School faculty.

"Like a cat bringing home to the feet of his mistress a dead field mouse," Emerson presented to the college a report of his investigations into the importance of a direct, unmediated relationship between man and his personal God. Rather than launching that volatile subject directly, he eased into the lecture with benign, pastoral language designed to comfort his audience. Then Emerson led his listeners to the threshold of the vast territory where he felt most comfortable, the spacious, opened mind, and the cosmic "Truth . . . within and without." Inspired by his favorite biblical passage, from John 17, "The Kingdom of God is within you," he invoked "intrinsic energy" as the source for legitimate "religious sentiment" in every man. Interpersonal—one might say inter-mind—connectedness was the key to fulfillment, not the "Cultus," the "second hand" interpretations of ritual emanating from the depleted sanctuaries of the "public Church."[23]

With that revolutionary concept expressed, his talk segued into darker modalities. Two defects of historical Christianity entered Emerson's sights, which he enumerated systematically. First, the person of Jesus as the representative of God's will had become obscured by centuries of church rhetoric. The true Christ was hidden within a protective shell of myths and legends. Second, spiritual revelation had been relegated to the historical past, implying that transformative moral insight was no longer available to modern man on his own terms and only possible within the confines of the church proper. These problems were manifested every Sunday from the pulpit. According to Emerson, this platform of influence had been usurped by "formalists" whose conservative, unchanging methods and static prayers deprived the seeker of faith of the incentive to make the journey by himself.

Every classic commencement speech winds down with advice for the graduates. Emerson's was no exception. His final words to the six men in the front row were delivered not as a reassuring benediction but as if throwing down a gauntlet. "[G]o alone," he challenged them and himself simultaneously, "dare to love God without mediator or veil . . . cast behind you all conformity, and acquaint men at first hand with Deity . . . live with the privilege of the immeasurable mind." He advised the young men to draw upon inner strength to safeguard against the societal criticism that inevitably fell upon those who took their own paths. He warned the graduates that it was too late to turn back; they could not revive a dead church, with its "smouldering, nigh-quenched fire on the altar." The time was at hand, he said, for these "newborn bard[s] of the Holy Ghost" to reinvent the church, each in his own manner and with a new faith that would be idiosyncratic, not uniform. And because new faith required a new view of Jesus, Emerson held up before the graduates and their appalled teachers the unachieved promise of a reconceptualized, idealized "new Teacher," whose message would be found only within separate hearts and independent minds.[24]

"I have written and read a kind of sermon to the Senior Class of our Cambridge Theological School a fortnight ago," Emerson wrote to Thomas Carlyle on August 6. "I hear [it] is very offensive." He vowed facetiously to "hold my tongue until next winter." For some time Emerson had been urging Carlyle to visit him and lecture in Boston. In the controversy following the address, Emerson became nervous and thought better of it, advising Carlyle to stay away, especially since his friend, "nowise guilty," had nonetheless been drawn by association into the tainted orbit. Carlyle, from a distance, praised Emerson for exercising "quiet tenacity" in the face of "the storm in our washbowl."

Another close friend, Emerson's uncle, Rev. Samuel Ripley, pleaded with him not to publish the controversial talk. "The world needs to be enlightened," Ripley conceded, "but I don't want to see you classed with Kneeland, Paine & co., bespattered and belied." Bostonian Abner Kneeland, an outspoken promoter of Thomas Paine's views, was convicted in 1835 of blasphemy and sentenced to sixty days in jail. Despite his conviction, two years later he published an edition of Paine's *The Age of Reason* in Boston. Uncle Samuel's warning was too late. "The Divinity School Address" was already on press and was published on August 21, 1838, by James Munroe and Company in an edition of one thousand copies.[25]

Six days later the furor began when Andrews Norton, a Harvard Divinity School professor and Emerson's former Sacred Literature teacher, aimed a blast at the address in the *Boston Daily Advertiser*, castigating it as "a great offence," an "insult to religion," and an "incoherent rhapsody." John Gorham Palfrey, dean of the Divinity School, concurred, observing that "the part of [the Address] which was not folly was downright atheism."[26]

Henry Ware Jr., whom Emerson had succeeded, and embarrassed, at the Second Church of Boston, had been in the audience as a Divinity School faculty member. He alerted Emerson that he was preparing a harsh sermon in response, in hopes Emerson might retract or soften some of what he had said. "I am not a stock or stone . . . and could not but feel pain in saying some things in that place and presence which I supposed might meet dissent," Emerson replied, mixing haughty resolve with indignant irony. "Yet . . . my conviction is perfect in the substantial truth of the doctrine of this discourse. . . . [I]n the present droll posture of my affairs, when I see myself suddenly raised to the importance of a heretic, I am very uneasy when I advert to the supposed duties of such a personage." In the last analysis Emerson flatly told Ware he would "go on, just as before." Even Aunt Mary Moody Emerson was offended, finding fault with her nephew, saying his talk "should be oblivion's, as under the influence of some malign demon."[27]

"Steady, steady," Emerson confided in his journal at the end of August, his appearance of equanimity and calm serving as a mask for anxiety. "The young people & the mature hint at odium, & aversion of faces to be presently encountered in society. . . . Society has no bribe for me, neither in politics, nor church, nor college, nor city." All he wanted to do now was absorb the Zeitgeist with extreme discrimination. He compared such quiet activity to a "net or frame" cast out from the shore of a river in order to snare and collect driftwood. He continued to pursue the road of the scholar and embraced the importance of unhurried, incremental composition, line by line, word by word, referring to working on "my book [Essays] which wants me" as the antidote to "these murmurers, these haters, these revilers" of his Divinity School talk. Fickle, "sour-faced" critics, disdained as "the cultivated classes," wasted Emerson's precious time by distracting him from the task at hand.

Emerson welcomed to the serenity of his home a faithful and sympathetic inner circle of friends led by his twenty-one-year-old Concord neighbor, "my brave Henry" Thoreau, with whom he escaped for moonlight rowboat rides and long woodland walks. After one such stroll, or, as Thoreau liked to call it, "sauntering," Emerson recorded in his diary an epigram drawn from the *Satires* of Persius by way of Michel de Montaigne's *Essays: Ne te quaesiveris extra*—"Look to no-one outside yourself"—which would become the motto for the "Self-Reliance" essay, a manifesto in defense of "one doctrine, namely, the infinitude of the private man." On Wednesday, December 5, he began a broad series of ten lectures, "Course on Human Life," at the Masonic Temple in Boston, beginning with "The Doctrine of the Soul" and ending in characteristic dialectical fashion with "Demonology." At Concord, on January 20, 1839, Emerson preached his last sermon.[28]

The Reverend Andrews Norton harbored residual anger with his recalcitrant former student, scorning the pollution of Emerson's transcendentalist thought by the subversive "intuitionists"—Spinoza, Schleiermacher, Strauss, Hegel, and their ilk. Still fuming, along with many of his colleagues, Norton took advantage of the occasion of the 1838 graduating class Commencement reunion as the first anniversary of the "Divinity School Address," to escalate the battle and to declare that "some of those opinions now prevalent . . . are at war with a belief in Christianity." Norton bluntly entitled the speech a "Discourse on the Latest Form of Infidelity." "The old tyrant [and] hard-headed Unitarian Pope," as Emerson described Norton, was at this time immersed in his monumental scholarly work, *Evidences of the Genuineness of the Gospels, 1837–1844*, a treatise based on research he had devoutly pursued for the past quarter century. Norton contended that the Bible was a definitive, historically viable text, its "miraculous character" beyond question. From that perspective, he would have to conclude, how could anyone be so blasphemous as to build a foundation for religious faith upon the unreliable, shifting contours of "undefined and unintelligible feelings, having reference perhaps to certain imaginations"?[29]

Norton's new volley was especially condescending since he took deliberate care not mention his adversary by name. The antagonism arrived when Emerson, at thirty-six, was devoting himself to writing and publishing more poetry, frequenting art galleries for imaginative inspiration, and hosting friends for intellectual soirees. He was picnicking on fair days, laboring in his garden, and extending "daily and nightly . . . medicinal" woodland strolls to "Walden Water [pond]" and beyond, into ambitious, remote field trips. In the winter of 1839, Thoreau's mother served as midwife to help Lidian welcome her second child into the world. The newborn girl was named Ellen in memory of Emerson's first wife. To adjust to additional commotion in the household, Emerson tried waking even earlier, to begin writing at six o'clock in the morning, but he remained just as enthralled with the children as ever, drawn often into the nursery to coddle and play with them.[30]

In the early fall of 1839, Emerson huddled with Theodore Parker, Frederic Henry Hedge, and Margaret Fuller to revive a project on his mind since their earliest Transcendental Club meetings, the establishment of a magazine that would serve as "an organ of a spiritual philosophy . . . one cheerful rational voice amidst the din of mourners and polemics." By so doing, Emerson heeded his own advice, "In hard times, cultivate yourself. And you cannot lose your labor." Emerson required "beautiful enemies" to drive him forward. His intellectual momentum was fueled by the antagonism of Norton and others. Emerson's utilitarian side exercised ecology of mind, recycling adversarial criticism and conservative resistance into greater strength: "I will call my enemy by my own name, for he is serving me with his might." His friend Carlyle knew and encouraged this necessity. "And if the Devil will be pleased to set all the Polarities against you and evermore against you," he wrote, "perhaps that is of all things the very kindest any Angel could do."[31]

Eldest daughter of a Newburyport lawyer, passionate scholar of the ancient classics, Shakespeare and Goethe, Margaret Fuller confessed when she reached twenty that "from a very early age I have felt that I was not born to the common womanly lot. . . . I should be a pilgrim and sojourner on earth . . . [with] the destiny of the poetic priestess." She agreed to edit the

Dial and planned for spring of 1840 publication of the inaugural number. The title of the magazine was suggested by Bronson Alcott with reference to the sundial. Fuller explained the metaphorical choice in a contentious lead editorial radically rewritten by Emerson to say that the kind of time-piece found in "the Garden itself . . . not the dead face of a clock," was most appropriate to alert "the sleeper . . . to what state of life and growth is now arrived and arriving." Somnolent members of the American culture at large were not cognizant of "the spirit of the time" within which "the progress of a revolution" was percolating; and—pertinent to the local scene—the especially "strong currents of thought and feeling . . . in New England."[32]

"When I behold a rich landscape," Emerson wrote, "it is to know why all thought of multitude is lost in a tranquil sense of unity." The blossoming height and heat of summer's end served to remind Emerson that his book of "Forest Essays," long in progress, should be organized before the pods of the slender gerardia flower filled with seeds. As Emerson picked his way among the riverside rocks one bright morning, he spotted the ubiquitous, purplish pink, four-petaled bloom, and jotted in a field notebook that the vivid "old acquaintance" seemed to talk to him, demonstrating by the pulsation of its yearly germination and renewal that Emerson likewise had work to do—and soon.[33]

During August and September, he drew up list after list for the table of contents of his new book. Among the dozen subject entries—"History, Compensation, Friendship, Prudence"—there was one piece "which had been longest in his mind" that he described as "new secrets of Selfreliance [sic]." It moved closer to the top of the roster in importance. "My chapter is not finished," Emerson restlessly admitted on October 23. "But selfreliance is precisely that secret—to make your supposed deficiency redundancy."[34]

O n New Year's Day 1841, Emerson sent the book manuscript off to his customary publisher, James Munroe. Within two weeks he received the first page proofs, and within three months his "little raft [was] afloat . . . no clipper, smack, nor skiff even, only boards and logs tied together." It was named, simply, *Essays*. The word "Forest" was dropped from the title, al-though like Rousseau, the "fine genius" he drew upon for inspiration, Emer-son had lived with nature and sought refuge many times in pristine wildernesses. He wanted to arrive at a place of divine ecstasy, a level of imaginative power capable of "strip[ping] man's nature naked," as Rousseau had hoped in the *Confessions,* one of Emerson's favorite books. The essay "Self-Reliance" was an inquiry into the nature of this "aboriginal self on which a universal reliance may be grounded."[35]

At first reading the essay seems tightly woven from dense fragments, as Emerson's writings frequently are. It begins to open up once we accept that the essential integrity of self-reliance is built upon cultivating one's spiritual aspects. "The secondary man" will be fated to remain rooted in mediocrity until he gives in to dependence upon God, "the divine fact." "Self-Reliance" begins as a hymn to isolation, advocating introspection, reverie, nonconformity, and proud inconsistency as the desired prerequisites to "the highest truth . . . the hour of vision . . . when a man lives with God, [and] his voice shall be as sweet as the murmur of the brook and the rustle of the corn."

Self-reliance does not mean that society should be ignored. Self-reliance must be cultivated in order for a man to emerge and transform society. If every man adheres to the regimen Emerson advocates, he will be remade as a result of that discipline, come to an educated understanding of his individual history, and thus democratic society will become the better for it. Calling for self-assertion hand in hand with self-surrender, Emerson poses huge demands. How many among you "parlor soldiers," he asks, have the confidence and resolve to "trust [to yourselves] for a taskmaster?" A great tidal wave of response will be required in order to "renovate . . . our social state."[36]

The last lesson of "Self-Reliance" is paramount. The conscientious reader, inspired to meet Emerson's standards, embarks upon an excited journey into himself, where he tests the faith in the God he discovers and deems it worthy. He then applies the energy of his newfound "Will" to the struggles and trials of the external world, leading to familiar results—"a political victory, a rise in rents, the recovery of your sick, or the return of your absent friend." From such conventional human accomplishments in the crucible of experience, a man's spirits are raised and he believes that he is vindicated. Would that social satisfaction were so simple. "Do not believe it," Emerson ends as he began, with another challenge, turning the thematic wheel around full circle, in modern American English this time instead of classical Latin, "Nothing can bring you peace but yourself. Nothing can bring you peace but the triumph of principles."[37]

The true believers of the persevering self-made man took Ralph Waldo Emerson as the patron saint of rags-to-riches America and read "Self-Reliance" as the manifesto of the strive-to-succeed ethos that became so central to our culture. After all, Horatio Alger Jr. (1832–99), the author of the *Ragged Dick* and *Luck and Pluck* dime novel series, was also a poet and a Massachusetts native, who attended Harvard Divinity School.

The ground for "Self-Reliance," the second piece in Emerson's book of *Essays*, is perfectly prepared by reading "History," the first essay in the collection, where he defines "the whole of history [as] one man, it is all to be explained from individual experience." Each personal mind, he writes, is connected to an overall "universal mind" by an invisible strand of consciousness. As with all of Emerson's work, beneath the abstraction and mysticism there is a practical foundation built from his lifelong habit of studying imported ideals as well as home-grown ones.

Emerson's precedents must be borne in mind. Thomas Paine's pamphlet sought to convince the disparate colonies they possessed a common cause. E Pluribus Unum, the succinct caption to the American picture, helps us understand Emerson's concept of the American individual's potential to stand as a representative for the entire society. And John Winthrop believed in a spiritual biblical contract that existed before it was made formally legal, implicitly connecting all of his people, whether they acknowledged it or not.[38]

Emerson was an intellectual and spiritual colossus, a giant bestriding the middle decades of the nineteenth century. His writing was like a powerful engine forcibly expanding the definition of the American personality, whose rapid growth required larger and larger geography for exercise. The insatiable push to stake out wider territory brought along unexpected consequences. We shall now discover that some—but not all of them—were beneficial.

John L. O'Sullivan

5

Manifest Destiny

There are some things this nation will never do. It will never be the forcible subjugator of other countries; it will never despoil surrounding territories; it will never march through the blood of their offending inhabitants; it will never admit within its own Union those who do not freely desire the boon.

—John L. O'Sullivan, *The New York Morning News*, November 1845

It is from the Democracy, with its manly heart and its lion strength spurning the ligatures wherewith drivellers would bind it—that we are to expect the great FUTURE of this Western World! a scope involving such unparalleled human happiness and rational freedom, to such unnumbered myriads, that the heart of a true *man* leaps with a mighty joy only to think of it!

—Walter Whitman, *The Brooklyn Daily Eagle*, January 1846

On page 426 of the November 1839 issue of the *United States Magazine and Democratic Review*, a popular liberal periodical coming out monthly from the District of Columbia, commenced an unsigned, vehement editorial, "The Great Nation of Futurity." The essay was noteworthy to the *Review*'s more than six thousand subscribers in many respects—for the passionate insistence that America was different from all other nations, disconnected from the outmoded, monarchical, and aristocratic European past; that American history bore no debt to antiquity, but rather operated from a clean slate with a collectively pure conscience; that America had been chosen by God to enact a sacred mission and bring democracy to the world, standing against the prejudices of privilege and "the tyranny of kings, hierarchs and oligarchs."

"The far-reaching, the boundless future will be the era of American greatness," the author rhapsodized, imagining an inevitable epoch when within a "magnificent domain of space and time, the nation of many nations is destined to manifest to mankind the excellence of divine principles. . . . Its floor shall be a hemisphere—its roof the firmament of the star-studded heavens, and its congregation an Union of many Republics. . . . Yes, we are the nation of progress, of individual freedom, of universal enfranchisement."[1]

The July 1845 edition of William G. Webster's *Elementary Spelling Book* defined *manifest* much as we would today as "apparent; plain; evident," and offered a more compelling definition of *destiny* as "Fate; invincible necessity." The author of the idealistic editorial was a twenty-six-year-old Columbia College graduate and "grand, world-embracing schemer" named John L. O'Sullivan. A man "eloquently infatuated" with the English language, he was responsible for placing these words in close proximity in print for the first of several significant times during a half-dozen years.

In a lead essay for the April 1859 issue, by which time O'Sullivan had long since left the magazine he had founded and brought to notoriety, the publisher proudly claimed that "from its birth until the present moment, [we have] advocated the **manifest destiny** of the American Republic."[2]

John Louis O'Sullivan was born on board a British man-of-war in Gibraltar harbor on November 15, 1813. He had an older brother, William; younger sisters, Mary and Adelaide, and two more boys, Thomas and Herbert, would follow. His father was John Thomas O'Sullivan of Dublin, a merchant mariner; his mother, "fine-grained and gently-bred," Mary Rowly of Bower End, in Staffordshire, England. O'Sullivan's father became the American consul to Mogador in Morocco and Tenerife in the Canary Islands and subsequently was "master, supercargo and owner in whole or part of sundry American ships." In 1824 he drowned in a shipwreck on a voyage off the west coast of South America while attempting to save the passengers. Mother and children were living in France at the time of the tragedy, awaiting Captain O'Sullivan's return so they could travel with him to the South Seas. Instead they moved to London, and then, in the fall of 1827, widow Mary departed with the family to New York City.[3]

John Louis O'Sullivan, well-schooled abroad, entered Columbia College at the age of fourteen, tutored freshmen in mathematics and classical languages, and graduated "with distinction" at the top of the class in the summer of 1831. He went on for an M.A. and read for a law degree as well, hanging his shingle at 63 Cedar Street downtown. Friends described the tall, dark-haired, thin young man as of "contemplative, intellectual appearance," with deep set blue eyes. He was by various accounts charming, gay, witty, talkative, gregarious, energetic, and gifted with a "light and pleasing" tenor singing voice.[4]

In 1835 the O'Sullivan family moved to Georgetown in the District of Columbia. His sister Mary married an Irish physician, Samuel Daly Langtree, and the couple set up household with the O'Sullivans. John Louis recalled with affection that in addition to being interested in medicine, Samuel was "decidedly literary," and through this shared passion, the brothers-in-law soon became friends. By the time he met Mary, Langtree had already started—and lost, in the space of one year—a magazine called the *Knickerbocker*. He was seeking another property through which to satisfy his lust for the printed word and convinced John Louis to come in with him to take over the *Metropolitan*, a semiweekly Georgetown newspaper. They ran book reviews and "Literary Intelligence" on the front page.[5]

In the fall of 1836, loyal vice president Martin Van Buren—known by virtue of his political adeptness as "The Little Magician"—succeeded Andrew Jackson after his two terms as president. Inspired by Van Buren's victory, O'Sullivan and Langtree boldly envisioned the revamped *Metropolitan* as "a new national literary journal of American democracy," devoted to "the sovereign nature of Democratic politics . . . striking the hitherto silent string of the democratic genius of the age . . . [with] a vast circulation throughout the Union. . . . Poetry and imaginative literature will be employed to relieve the graver discussions which constitute the main feature of the work." The president-elect and the rustic "Old Hickory" both signed as charter subscribers, publicly endorsing the mission of *The United States Magazine and Democratic Review* advertised by O'Sullivan in the October 15, 1837, inaugural editorial, which ran more than fifteen pages and advocated "at the present critical stage of our national progress . . . that high and holy DEMOCRATIC PRINCIPLE which was designed to be the fundamental element of the new social and political system created by the 'American experiment.'"[6]

After a token conciliatory gesture to "the Whigs," the new coalition party formed in 1834 by Jackson's political opponents, naming themselves after the seventeenth-century English Whigs who had defended civil liberties against the pro-Catholic Stuart kings, O'Sullivan moved quickly to address his true constituents, the rough-hewn public, "manly, intelligent millions of freemen . . . the sterling honesty and good sense of the great industrious mass of our people." They were the intended popular audience for the magazine's grand Jeffersonian masthead statement, "The best government is that which governs least." The sanctity of American individualism and faith in human nature was linked to "preservation of the present ascendancy of the democratic party as of great, if not vital, importance to the future destinies of this holy cause." The Democratic Party was established in 1832 as successor to the Democrat-Republican Party organized by Thomas Jefferson in 1792.[7]

O'Sullivan romantically imagined the uncharted territory of American literature and culture ripe for exploration stretching out far ahead of him. In his magazine he wanted to spotlight and advance native American genius and counter the widening inclination dangerously captivating editors of New England periodicals to import "high culture." "It is only by its literature that one nation can utter itself and make itself known to the rest of the world. . . . Our literature!" he wondered, ". . . when will *it* breathe the spirit of our republican institutions? When will *it* be imbued with the God-like aspiration of intellectual freedom—when will it assume *its* national independence? . . . Why cannot *our* literati comprehend the matchless sensibility of our position amongst all the nations of the world?"[8]

Aided by Langtree's connections and undeterred by a national bank crisis leading to the economic panic of 1837, O'Sullivan replied to these plaintive questions by launching a broad publishing program within the pages of the first number of *The United States Magazine and Democratic Review*. He acquired Ralph Waldo Emerson's Phi Beta Kappa Day oration, "The American Scholar," delivered six weeks previously at Harvard. The first issue also presented a new short story, "A Toll-Gatherer's Day," by that avowed Democrat, Nathaniel Hawthorne, loftily "affording [the author] a field for the exercise of his pen, and the acquisition of distinction." Following upon the acclaim and attention paid to the just-published *Twice-Told Tales*, O'Sullivan and Hawthorne became close friends, and "Uncle John," godfather to Hawthorne's daughter, Una, enjoyed many days of family conviviality at Concord. The author remained a consistent contributor even when the *Review* could only offer him a maximum of twenty dollars per article.

In succeeding issues O'Sullivan brought forth the poems of John Greenleaf Whittier, the magisterial historical essays of George Bancroft, the erudite literary criticism of Orestes A. Brownson, the exotic Mexico and Yucatan travel diaries of John Lloyd Stephens—as well as the fanciful stories of another radical Democrat, a twenty-two-year-old amiable, relaxed Brooklynite "with a ruddy pleasant face and a short beard" named Walter Whitman. The poet was still many years away from responding to the call issued in the *United States Magazine* for "the Homer of the Mass," *Leaves of Grass* would not be published until the fall of 1855.[9]

By the fall of 1840, the *United States Magazine* had come into its own as a force to be reckoned with in literary America, when the archives were destroyed in a fire, and Dr. Langtree, shocked and dispirited, lost interest in the daily labors of keeping the publication afloat. The satirical novelist and playwright Charles Frederick Briggs (writing under the pseudonym "Harry Franco") declared that "As Paris is France, and London, England, so is Broadway, New York; and New York is fast becoming, if she be not already, America." John L. O'Sullivan returned back home to the "bustling city" in the new year with renewed incentive to fight even harder for the Democratic cause. Transporting the magazine to a different center of gravity, he resolved to be a literary agent for change in the great metropolis, "seat and stronghold of this young power."[10]

It was the perfect moment for O'Sullivan's reentry. American society was conscious as never before of being in the prime of expansive youth and vigor. The tempo of the economy had recovered. Immigrant population from Europe bourgeoned. The Western territories were immense. Canals were dug, railroads "steaming up," and the telegraph was soon to be born. As the urban publishing marketplace grew, O'Sullivan included more industry reportage in the *United States Magazine,* initiating among other features in 1841 an exhaustive "Monthly Literary Record" of noteworthy new books and articles.

The *United States Magazine* gained stature, as well as support from the

Tammany Society and was universally regarded by Democrats as one of the liveliest journals of the day, a reputation further enhanced when, toward the middle of the decade, O'Sullivan hired away the ambitious editor Evert Augustus Duyckinck from the firm of Wiley and Putnam, and made him the publication's literary editor. Their alliance became the vital center of a full-fledged social movement called "Young America," emblematic of the "new spirit abroad in the land, restless, vigorous and omnipotent . . . plum[ing] its young wings for a higher and more glorious flight."[11]

Even before he met Duyckinck, O'Sullivan was attuned to the oracular voice of Ralph Waldo Emerson. O'Sullivan's familiarity with the Transcendental sentiments of "the Concord Sage" played an influential role in the ideological genesis of manifest destiny. Emerson and O'Sullivan had dinner in New York on Sunday evening, February 12, 1843, at the home of a mutual friend, the lawyer, free trade activist, and Stockbridge transplant David Dudley Field. In a letter to Margaret Fuller written later that night, Emerson assessed O'Sullivan as "politico-literary." His appraisal was succinct but not inaccurate. There were additional social evenings followed by further judgmental pronouncements from Emerson's side. From O'Sullivan's point of view came only respect and admiration.[12]

In a rousing speech before the Mercantile Library Association of Boston on February 7, 1844, published two months thereafter in the *Dial*, Emerson addressed himself directly to "The Young American," calling upon the current generation of movers and shakers to be inspired by the magnetic open continent, "boundless resources of their own soil . . . this great tract of land in the western hemisphere . . . the nervous, rocky West." He advised the youths to break away from the bondage of foreign cultures and heed only "a sublime and friendly Destiny by which the human race is guided. . . . Only what is inevitable interests us." Emerson sensed a grievous deficiency of spiritual and intellectual direction in the mind of the world at large. This was the moment for our young men to "advance out of all hearings of other's censures," and "give an aspect of greatness to the Future." They must do this neither for political expediency nor for materialistic gain but to build a "new and more excellent social state." That was the imperative for America as the current epoch's "leading Nation."[13]

At least one young American, John L. O'Sullivan, was listening. Emerson's *Essays: Second Series*, published in October 1844, was greeted by a dense and closely reasoned fourteen-page review in the *United States Maga-*

zine and Democratic Review. The anonymous author, writing with the by-line, "A Disciple," began with an epigraph from Coleridge attesting to "the discovery of essential unity," then anointed Emerson as "the great philosopher and poet . . . who understands the spirit of his age." The Disciple pointed out that the greatest legacy of all at this juncture of unprecedented potential in American heritage was Emerson's profound understanding that "in the very presence of the mighty past, men aspire to a future that shall confirm the great idea of unlimited Progress." Special note was taken of how the neo-Platonists of antiquity, as well as Schelling, Kant, and Carlyle flowed as tributaries into Emerson's accommodating intellect and of the "Berkeleyan idealism" in his essays, distinguished by their "unity of nature, where the whole reappears in all its parts."[14]

Alluding to a passage found toward the conclusion of *Essays: Second Series,* in the book's final entry, a lecture called "New England Reformers" dated March 3, 1844, the "Disciple" showed how thoroughly he had penetrated the book. Emerson wrote there with extensive praise of the "powerful and stimulating intellect . . . [and] the great heart and mind" of the idealist philosopher George Berkeley (1685–1753), the Thomastown-born, Irish bishop so enamored with America that he emigrated from London to live for four years in a farmhouse he called "Whitehall" about a mile from the shore at Newport, Rhode Island. Berkeley founded a scholarly society there in the late 1720s and wrote a book based upon his American sojourn. His poetic meditation on the promise of the new land, *Verses on the Prospect of Planting Arts and Learning in America* (1726) envisioning "the seat of innocence / Where nature guides and virtue rules" in stark contrast to "Europe breed[ing] in her decay," was a predictive anthem for manifest destiny. "Westward the course of empire takes its way," the bishop sang in the sixth and final stanza of the poem, confident that the great nascent country was fated to give rise to another "golden age / The rise of empire and of arts."

A visitor to the House of Representatives in Washington may view on the staircase wall of the Capitol Building the last great allegorical epic project of the painter Emanuel Gottlieb Leutze (1816–1868). The monumental twenty-by-thirty-foot 1861 fresco, named "Westward the Course of Empire Takes Its Way," in homage to Berkeley's poem, shows mountain men, immigrants, and a freed slave "surging across the picture from right to left," cresting a rocky cliff near sunset at the Continental Divide. Leading the group, a noble explorer waves his hat toward "God's tapestry," and in the reflected glow of the Golden Gate of the Pacific prepares to plant the Stars and Stripes, reminiscent of the image of Moses leading the Children of Israel behind a pillar of light, gazing from a distant desert summit upon the Promised Land.

To J. Hector St. John de Crèvecoeur in his third *Letter From An American Farmer* (1782), Americans were "the Western pilgrims, carrying along with them that great mass of arts, sciences, vigour, and industry." Half a century later, in *Democracy in America*, Alexis de Tocqueville exclaimed that "the gradual and continuous progress of the European race toward the Rocky Mountains . . . is like a deluge of men, rising unabatedly, and driven daily onward by the hand of God."[15]

O'Sullivan believed, like Emerson, in the gospel of American progress. From inception, the *United States Magazine* followed the path of manifest destiny into the literary realm while tapping into America's religious mission. Frederick Jackson Turner (1861–1932), historian of the "vast physiographic provinces" of the boundless American West, described O'Sullivan's generation as direct inheritors of Andrew Jackson's legacy—frontier Democracy. Turner wrote that O'Sullivan and his peers were, like General Jackson, men who valued "the unchecked development of the individual" and were also susceptible to "high religious voltage." Making that combination clear, O'Sullivan wrote in 1840 of Democracy as a consummation,"[I]n a true sense . . . the last best revelation of human thought. We speak, of course, of that true and genuine Democracy which breathes the air and lives in the light of Christianity—whose essence is justice, and whose object is human progress."[16]

Few young Americans in political life held greater faith in the Democratic creed than James Knox Polk (1795–1849). Named clerk of the Tennessee State Senate in Murfreesboro at age twenty-four, Polk had been a loyal son of the party ever since. He was a pioneer Jacksonian, voting to nominate "the Old Chief," Tennessee's favorite son, for president in 1823. Polk was speaker of the House of Representatives and in his seventh term in Congress when John L. O'Sullivan met and glowingly praised him in a lengthy profile interview in the May 1838 issue of the *United States Magazine*. Polk resigned from Congress in 1839 to run for governor of Tennessee.

He served one term—only to lose two "mortifying and incomprehensible" consecutive reelection races. His once-promising career was on the brink of dissolution when the savvy Polk opted to come in on the right side for Texas annexation.[17]

By the cusp of the federal election year 1844, the nation had doubled from thirteen to twenty-six states. The scales were evenly balanced—thirteen slave and thirteen free. How the fledgling independent Republic of Texas might enter this configuration was therefore pivotal. On April 27, five days after incumbent president John Tyler sent a Texas annexation treaty to the Senate for approval, Henry Clay, former secretary of state and Whig Party elder statesman, and former president Martin Van Buren, Democrat of New York, announced in two Washington newspapers their mutual opposition to annexation. The jury remains out among historians as to whether the adversarial presidential hopefuls came to a secret agreement against annexation as long as Mexico remained against it. The combined strategy of Clay and Van Buren was intended to defuse the issue and set aside any further public discussion about the ultimate disposition of the Texas Territory until after the fall elections.

In doing so, however, they misread the opinion of most Americans— Polk included—that the boundary separating Texas from the rest of the country was an artificial one that should be done away with as soon as possible. By the time of the Democratic Convention in May at Odd Fellows Hall in Baltimore, Andrew Jackson had abandoned Van Buren and turned to Polk, his new protégé, and darkest of the dark horses. Thanks to the last-minute strong-arm maneuvers of George Bancroft, the New York delegation put Polk over the top on the ninth ballot as the unexpected and triumphant nominee. Polk's selection added frenzy to the Texas issue, over which, observed the Alabama expansionist Dixon H. Lewis, public opinion "boiled and effervesced more like a volcano than a cider barrel."[18]

At this point John O'Sullivan again displayed astute political instincts. His finger on the pulse of the man in the street, O'Sullivan wrote that he had no doubt by peaceful means "sooner or later Texas would be part of the United States." Consistent with this altruistic point of view, O'Sullivan was already on record as being against capital punishment and similarly deplored nation building by bloodshed. In recent editorials he had gone so far as to espouse the creation of an international system of arbitration, like the

League of Nations, to put an end to "This War spirit . . . utterly antagonistic to the genius of American democracy."

Within three months of the Democratic Convention, O'Sullivan convinced candidate Polk and other party big-wigs of the necessity to provide an additional forum for their unified views. In concert with support from his friend, the prosperous railroad and real estate corporate lawyer Samuel J. Tilden, as business manager, O'Sullivan bolstered his publishing portfolio by establishing the *New York Morning News*. The new daily paper also put out a weekly national edition, like its predecessor, the *United States Magazine*, dedicated to government by the people—"The Democracy." Making certain that New York's electoral votes were delivered to Polk, now greeted as "Young Hickory," in the coming fall election, O'Sullivan looked beyond November to ensure his continuing influence in the White House corridors of power through the medium he knew best—the press.[19]

The Democratic leadership in the lame duck second session of the twenty-eighth Congress picked up where President Tyler left off the previous spring, and with Polk's blessing brought a joint resolution for Texas annexation before both Houses. It passed in January and February. Representative Stephen A. Douglass of Illinois captured the legislators' mood when he spoke of the necessity to "blot out the lines on the map which now marked our national boundaries on this continent . . . and make the area of liberty as broad as the continent itself . . . not suffer[ing] petty rival republics to grow up here, engendering jealousy with each other."

James K. Polk entered office on March 4, 1845, as the eleventh and youngest-ever American president. One of his first official actions that day was to endorse an annexation invitation conveyed by Andrew J. Donelson, the American chargé d'affaires in the Lone Star Republic. The *New York Morning News* heartily approved: "From the time that the Pilgrim Fathers landed on these shores to the present moment," O'Sullivan opined, "pioneer settlers have rolled forward in advance of civilization. . . . This is the natural, unchangeable effect of our position on this continent." Polk's action was the first step toward an exponential increase in America's "national domain." By the conclusion of Polk's self-imposed single term, the United States acquired more than 1.2 million square miles of territory, over one-third of the area it occupies today.[20]

All that remained was for Texas to grasp the welcoming hand offered by

Congress. The citizens of Texas voted approval at a referendum convention in June, but confusion still lingered in the summer months as Polk's spread-eagle diplomacy sent mixed signals to America's other southern neighbor. Secretary of State James Buchanan extended an olive branch to Mexico, insisting that continued good relations were of paramount importance, even though Capt. John Frémont was sent deep into Mexican country with an exploratory contingent of more than sixty men heading out from frontier Missouri toward the Great Basin.[21]

Accumulating tensions galvanized O'Sullivan—gripped by the enduring spirit of Andrew Jackson, who had died one month earlier in The Hermitage, his home near Nashville—to a double-barreled pronouncement. In the July 9, 1845, *Morning News*, O'Sullivan spoke of "our destiny to overspread this entire North America with the almost miraculous progress of our population and power." And the lead editorial for the July issue of the *United States Magazine*, an essay called "Annexation," was introduced as an exercise in "intelligent reflection." O'Sullivan sensed "a fever in the blood that steadily rose," reiterating an obsession that had threaded through his rhetoric for half a dozen years. "It is time now for the opposition to the annexation of Texas to cease," he declared indignantly. "It is time for common sense to acquiesce with decent grace in the inevitable."

O'Sullivan admitted that the slavery question was "a topic pregnant with embarassment and danger, intricate and double-sided," but it should not be the determining factor bearing upon the reception of Texas into the Union. As the country enlarged, the precarious balance was maintained by the admission of free and slave states alternatively, as Arkansas and Michigan had been on June 15, 1836, and January 26, 1837, respectively. Annexation, however, was part of the greater evolutionary flow of events, a trend pointing from the Mississippi valley to California and Oregon, and farther afield, to British Canada and the rest of Spanish America. For that matter, O'Sullivan carried on, "Away, then, with all the idle French talk of 'balances of power' on the American Continent." Texas was the entrée to "the fulfillment of our manifest destiny to overspread the continent allotted by Providence for the free development of our yearly multiplying millions." O'Sullivan warned that one hundred years in the future, in "the fast-hastening year of our Lord 1945 . . . three hundred millions—and American millions—[were] destined to gather beneath the flutter of the stripes and stars."[22]

The predicted century had nearly come to pass when the landmark study by Bernard De Voto, *The Year of Decision, 1846*, was published. In 1943 the historian and *Harper's Magazine* editor recalled the cultural fervor that had shaped O'Sullivan's language. De Voto considered "manifest destiny" to be "one of the most dynamic phrases ever minted." He saw the dual justifications of the expression, observing that to O'Sullivan manifest destiny allowed "occupying territory as well as practicing virtue. . . . In that phrase," he reflected, "Americans found both recognition and revelation."[23]

President Polk rewarded George Bancroft (1800–1891) for his loyalty to the Democratic Party by naming the distinguished historian to his cabinet as secretary of the navy. Worcester-born, Bancroft graduated from Harvard and spent four years abroad at the Universities of Gottingen and Berlin, where he studied with G. W. F. Hegel and came under the influence of the new German intellectualism and the belief in the providential, mission-driven nature of history. Within a decade of returning to America, Bancroft had become "an avowed apostate" from big banking and big government, shed his Brahmin trappings, and converted to Jacksonianism. He embarked upon a ten-volume *History of the United States of America from the Discovery of the Continent*. Leopold von Ranke praised Bancroft's long opus as the best history ever written from the democratic point of view, an appreciation that "annoyed as well as gratified" Bancroft. He moved up rapidly in the Democratic hierarchy. Appointed collector of the port of Boston by President Van Buren, from that power base he became the party "boss" for Massachusetts. Bancroft's political reputation was further burnished when he was chosen to deliver the official eulogy at Andrew Jackson's funeral.[24]

In Charles Grier Sellers's biography of James K. Polk, the author reports that within days of assuming office, the new president summoned Bancroft as the historian-in-residence to impart to him the four "great measures" of his term. In addition to lowering the tariff, re-creating an independent Treasury, and acquiring California from Mexico, Polk repeated to Bancroft a vow made at his inauguration to acquire "the whole of Oregon" beyond the Columbia River and all the way up to the Alaska line, wresting it away from the British. "Our title to the country of Oregon," Polk said, "is clear and unquestionable."[25]

Some modern scholars consider the report apocryphal because Bancroft did not set this incident down on paper until forty years later. Even if the conversation did not take place, Bancroft, the avowed Romantic, admired Polk's forceful expression of executive willpower. The president's conviction that the United States was the legitimate exemplar of "the law of growth" fit squarely into the succession of apprehensive American patriots, starting with John Adams in 1778 and extending through John Quincy Adams in 1846, suspicious of Britain's rivalry for any part of the continent. "So long as Great Britain shall have Canada, Nova Scotia, and the Floridas, or any of them," John Adams wrote, "so long will Great Britain be the enemy of the United States, let her disguise it as much as she will." America's open-ended right to domestic security expanded commensurate with the "emergencies" threatening her boundaries. In the *Farmer Refuted* (February 23, 1775), Alexander Hamilton expressed this right with poetic, moderated belligerence against "the pretensions of Parliament" as "written, as with a sunbeam, in the whole volume of human nature, by the hand of the divinity itself; and can never be erased or obscured by mortal power."

At the peak of congressional debate over the Oregon country, elder statesman John Quincy Adams also drew strength from the higher law in the holy writ. If America wished to claim the Northwest lands, he said, it was de facto the right thing to do. The Hudson's Bay Company of England was guardian of the area in name only and could no longer be permitted to stand in the way of thousands of American settlers moving by wagon train into the Willamette valley. Pausing in his peroration before the House of Representatives, Adams asked the clerk to read into the record a passage from the ancient Second Psalm of David: "Yet have I set my king upon my holy hill of Zion." The verses bore witness to the current American imperative. "Well, sir," Adams concluded, "our title to Oregon stands on the same foundation . . . to make the wilderness blossom as the rose."[26]

By the fall of 1845, most American newspapers had fallen into line on the chauvinistic "whole-of-Oregon" issue behind John L. O'Sullivan, who believed that the nation should put some spine into its internationalist posture. Acquisition of territory in the Americas could hardly be perceived as analogous to "invasions and conquests in the old world [Europe]. . . . We are above and beyond the influence of such views," he wrote with customary pride. "We take from no man; the reverse rather—we give to man. . . . [W]e can, therefore, afford to scorn the invective and imputations of rival nations."[27]

The president's disposition was not as philosophical. The ominous sound of a rattling sabre could be discerned in his first annual message to Congress on December 2. Polk asked for authority to set up a territorial government in Oregon—all of it, up to 54 degrees, 40 minutes latitude—and further, to notify Britain that the Anglo-American Convention of jointly shared occupation, in effect since 1818, was dissolved. Polk brushed aside fears expressed by Secretary of State James Buchanan and Sen. John C. Calhoun of South Carolina that such "rhetorical bravado" would lead to war, stubbornly disputing their plea that he respect a "balance of power" in the world. In the days after Christmas and before the New Year, the mood in the cabinet room was somber. On Saturday, December 27—the same day that Polk's cabinet members gathered to vote unanimously against arbitration with Britain—the New York Morning News published what has been called "the most famous editorial of the decade."[28]

John O'Sullivan began his column, "The True Title," with a tip of the cap to the president, referring to Polk's inaugural address almost word for word: "Our legal title to Oregon so far as law exists for such rights, is perfect . . . and the whole of Oregon, if a rood!" O'Sullivan may have feared that his piece five months earlier in the United States Magazine had not caught hold with a wide enough audience and so decided to repeat the message with vehemence. He may have moved to higher metaphorical ground to express his impatience with the equivocators in his party. America's claim to Oregon, O'Sullivan went on, "is by the right of our manifest destiny to overspread and possess the whole of the continent which Providence has given for the development of the great experiment of liberty and federative self-government entrusted to us. It is a right such as that of the tree to the space of air and earth suitable for the full expansion of its principle and destiny of growth—such as that of the stream to the channel required for the still accumulating volume of its flow. . . . [T]he American destiny . . . led and established here as we have been by the finger of God himself—that pervading tendency westward, westward, which marks the slope of our national movement, and bears us ever onwards toward the Pacific, like the attraction felt by the head waters of its own rivers that hear and in their flow obey the call of the great ocean of their destiny. . . ."

The Republic of Texas was admitted as a slave state, the twenty-eighth state of the Union at the end of December—Florida was the twenty-seventh and Iowa would soon become the twenty-ninth—and the Texas constitution was recognized in the first session of the twenty-ninth Congress on January 3, 1846. Riding the crest of an expansionist wave kept in motion by O'Sullivan's resourceful vocabulary, Rep. Robert C. Winthrop, Whig of Massachusetts, rose to address his colleagues in the House: "There is one element in our title [to Oregon] however, which I confess that I have not named," he said, "and to which I may not have done entire justice. I mean that new revelation of right which has been designated as the right of our manifest destiny to spread over this whole continent." Winthrop credited this illuminating usage to the *New York Morning News*, which he referred to as "a leading Administration journal," avowing "that this, after all, is our best and strongest title. . . . The right of our manifest destiny! There is a right for a new chapter in the law of nations; or rather, in the special laws of our own country." Although the sentiments had been simmering within American intentions since the seventeenth century, from that signal moment when Winthrop's speech was transcribed into page 99 of the appendix of the *Congressional Globe*, "manifest destiny" "passed into the permanent national vocabulary."[29]

The next morning, January 4, as the debate carried on in Congress, Rep. James Augustus Black, Democrat of South Carolina, called at the White House to express his trepidation. Writing in his *Diary* that night, the president remained steadfast, noting he had replied to Mr. Black "that the only way to treat John Bull [the popular cartoon personification of Great Britain] is to look him straight in the eye; that I considered a bold & firm course on our part [to be] the pacific one; that if Congress hesitated or faultered [sic] in their course, John Bull would immediately become arrogant and more grasping in his demands & that such had been the history of the British [sic] nation in all their contests with other Powers for the past two hundred years."

On the morning of January 5, a resolution to terminate the joint occupation of Oregon was introduced in the Senate, and John O'Sullivan stepped up to the bully pulpit once more, running a lengthy "Splendid New

Year's Compliment" letter on the *Morning News* editorial page addressed to his "political friends" in the Young Men's Democratic General Committee. Invoking the "aroused spirit" of Democracy at its best, O'Sullivan urged them to join in celebration of the "necessity of national destiny" resulting in the annexation of Texas. This action, he wrote, was a vivid illustration of "the growth of our national greatness . . . that great popular democratic movement towards territorial extension which so strikingly marks the present period." Now was the time to keep the momentum going, to move onward without delay to the Oregon Territory (which would eventually make up all of Washington and parts of Wyoming and Idaho). Then "the acquisition of California" would surely follow. And then, O'Sullivan said—onward to Mexico.[30]

During the winter and spring of 1846, the purpose and design of manifest destiny once gloriously conceived by John O'Sullivan began to take on an ominous tone, darkened by the resurgence of millennialist doctrine, that the course of American history under God's guidance must lead to a holy Utopia on earth. American millennialism drew its core of conviction from the prophetic book of the revelation of St. John, in which the "end," or goal, of man's universal history was to overcome the forces of evil. In order to defeat Satan and shrink his territory, a sanctified Anglo-Saxon nation had the right—the obligation—to unimpeded growth in its progressive desire for dominion.[31]

President Polk's acquisitive energies escalated. In mid-June the United States begrudgingly reached agreement with Her Majesty's government on the Oregon Territory "in regard to limits Westward of the Rocky Mountains." The boundary was extended along the forty-ninth parallel. While a two-thousand-mile journey from Missouri brought the Great American Migration pouring into the interior valleys of California, Polk arrogantly refused to reassure Britain and France that he had no intention of appropriating it by force. The Mexican situation degenerated as Gen. Zachary Taylor's four thousand troops moved further south, to disputed territory by the Rio Grande at Fort Brown, opposite Matamoros. Polk self-righteously insisted he was not scheming to extend American slavery by a war of conquest, hewing to a policy of transcontinental brinkmanship he euphemistically called "protective occupation."[32]

O'Sullivan's language, no longer altruistic and upbeat, turned cranky and patronizing. He lost his headstrong passion for preaching the attributes of "just, beneficent and peaceful continentalism." He no longer talked as he once did of adventurous American democracy transcending "the tyranny of kings, hierarchs and oligarchs," instead asserting that it was the fate of the unenlightened savages—Indians of Texas, Oregon, Louisiana, Georgia, and Florida—to be denied the new Eden. The Indians deserved the forced removal from their birthright lands perpetrated by Jackson and Van Buren. The indigenous population of "disadvantaged peoples" in "imbecile Mexico" also did not seem to understand the blessings that would arrive with the imprint of "the Anglo-Saxon foot." Mexicans were oppressed for so many centuries, O'Sullivan wrote, that they had become "unaccustomed to the duties of self-government." Trying to halt the inevitable American advance, they were bringing on hostilities and undermining their regeneration and future happiness. The mixed races of Mexico, for their own good, needed to be "schooled in the meaning and methods of freedom" under the light of the beacon of liberty.[33]

In a fit of disillusionment, O'Sullivan made a precipitous exit from the *United States Magazine and Democratic Review*, selling it to Thomas Prentice Kendall for the grand sum of five thousand dollars. His friend Samuel Tilden had long since left the masthead of the *Morning News*, and the paper was on the brink of insolvency. Financial mismanagement contributed to investor disenchantment. O'Sullivan was forced out, and the *Morning News* ceased publication in May.[34]

In the fall of 1846, at the age of thirty-three, O'Sullivan married Susan Kearny Rodgers, daughter of a New York City physician. They never had children. He was named a regent of the University of New York that year. In 1849 it appears that he was living in the South and active in the short-lived Free Soil Party as an abolitionist. He became involved in a scheme to overthrow Spanish authority in Cuba, then a failed attempt to purchase the island, and an abortive expedition to attack it. This fiasco led to O'Sullivan's indictment in New Orleans, but he was not convicted.

"How beautiful to think of lean tough Yankee settlers tough as gutta-percha, with [the] most occult unsubduable fire in their belly," Thomas Carlyle wrote to Ralph Waldo Emerson, "steering over the Western Mountains, to annihilate the jungle, and bring bacon and corn out of it for the Posterity of Adam." With the Mexican War won, the Southwest Territories became part of the Union, and President-elect General Zachary Taylor was inaugurated, succeeding James K. Polk. Gold was discovered in California. O'Sullivan's romantic ideal was perverted into rampant hunger for land at any cost. It was the end of the "heroic stage" of manifest destiny.

Designated by Pres. Franklin Pierce to be chargé d'affaires in Portugal, O'Sullivan was removed from this post in Lisbon in the summer of 1858 by Pres. James Buchanan. For two years O'Sullivan "lingered in Europe, living on borrowed money." After a brief return to New York, he sailed for London, where he resurfaced as the author of a series of pamphlets supporting the cause of the South during the Civil War, predicting the demise of the North, and urging the government of Great Britain to support the Confederacy. The war was terribly remote from the much-anticipated climax O'Sullivan joyously predicted when he first wrote of "The Great Nation of Futurity."[35]

There were unsubstantiated reports that O'Sullivan lived briefly in Paris in the early 1870s. By the end of the decade he was in New York again, a practicing Spiritualist, claiming with utter seriousness to James Russell Lowell that he had been in communication with Lowell's second wife, Frances, from beyond the grave. According to the National Cyclopedia of American Biography XII, O'Sullivan was chosen by the New York City administration to greet Ambassador W. A. LeFaivre and the French delegation at the unveiling of the Statue of Liberty on October 28, 1886, although contemporary newspaper accounts do not mention his presence at the ceremony. In 1889 he suffered a stroke. On March 24, 1895, at the age of eighty-one, following an attack of influenza, John L. O'Sullivan, his wife at his bedside, died destitute and without leaving a recorded will, in a single room at a "family hotel" on East Eleventh Street in Manhattan.[36]

In the end, the arc of O'Sullivan's dream of continental domination was surprisingly brief and narrow, barely a decade's worth of high-flown literary editorial rhetoric, and persistent lobbying where he roamed comfortably in the white marble corridors of his beloved "Democracy." Race consciousness and imperialism built up to become a volatile combination flaring in the election of 1892, by which time the Republican Party was in such an ebullient mood that the plank of outright "manifest destiny of the Republic in its broadest sense" was built into its official platform. The Hawaiian islands, Cuba, the Philippine ar-chipelago, and even Canada, all became expansionist targets through the turn of the century. The seed of manifest destiny was planted by John L. O'Sullivan with irrepressible, healthy confidence in the ongoing experiment of American possibilities. However, the maturing fruit tasted of a sour strain in the national character.

HENRY GEORGE

6

Progress and Poverty

This is the shore of the Pacific. This is the Golden Gate. The Westward march of our race is terminated by the ocean, which has the ancient East on its further shore. And yet here, in this new country, in this golden State, there are men ready to work, anxious to work, and yet who, for longer or shorter periods, cannot get the opportunity to work.

—Henry George, "Justice the Object—Taxation the Means," speech in Metropolitan Hall, San Francisco, February 4, 1890.

Henry George was born on September 2, 1839, in a two-story brick house on the east side of Tenth Street south of Pine, less than half a mile from the old State House in central Philadelphia where the Declaration of Independence was signed. He was the second child and oldest son of the ten children of Richard Samuel Henry George of New Brunswick, New Jersey, and Catherine Pratt Vallance of Philadelphia. Mr. George Sr., a pious vestryman at St. Paul's Episcopal Church, owned a publishing business specializing in Sunday School books. Mrs. George, the daughter of a Glasgow-born engraver, John Vallance, conducted a small private school for girls in association with her sister, Mary.[1]

When Henry was nine, his father sold the business and bookstore and became an "Ascertaining Clerk" in the Customs House at a government salary of thirteen hundred dollars a year. Henry entered the Episcopal Academy of Philadelphia but found formal classroom education to be constraining. The boy asked to be tutored privately as a transition to the new Philadelphia High School, where he lasted less than five months in the middle rankings of the seventh grade. At thirteen, anxious to be put to work, Henry left school for good, taking a job running errands for a china and glass importing house.

A faded daguerrotype from the period shows the distracted, pale, open face of a lad looking as if he had just rushed into the room moments before. He is wearing a hastily arranged white collar crimped unevenly over a wide bow tie, black jacket unbuttoned and flung open. Thick, wavy dark hair brushed back from a wide forehead curls down over and below protruberant ears. The mouth is set into a determined line, the brow slightly furrowed between keen eyes glancing off to the side. "Little Hen" or "Harry" George, even as an adult, tipped the scale at a delicate 113 pounds and never passed five feet, six inches.

At home in the evenings, Henry retreated from the crowded household sitting room to his back attic bedroom to read by gaslight—the family Bible as well as history and adventure stories picked up at second-hand shops or borrowed from the Quaker Apprentice's Library and the Franklin Institute. From his mother and her sister Mary, the beloved maiden aunt who helped raise him, Henry gained a lifelong love of poetry and tried his hand at it, interspersing labored and heavily edited verses among the pages of the pocket diaries he began at sixteen and kept daily for the rest of his life.

By this time the George family had moved to a larger house on Third Street, three blocks from the Delaware River, and Henry was a clerk in a nearby marine adjustor's office. On Sunday afternoons, following church services and Bible study, Henry and his father—who in his youth "could swim like a duck and handle a boat equal to anybody"—strolled along the wharves and admired the tall-masted schooners and steamships. One morning in mid-January 1855, Henry went out to the grocery shop and on the way home—as was his custom—stopped in at the library. There he read a notice in the *New York Herald* that the 586-ton merchant ship *Hindoo,* "an old East Indiaman," having just put in to New York harbor after a voyage from the Orient, would be heading out again in April, bound for Australia and India with a cargo of half a million feet of lumber. The captain was Samuel Miller, a friend of the George family. Henry seized the opportunity to try "the rough life of deck and forecastle," signing on as foremast boy to the crew of twenty men.

The ship rounded the Cape of Good Hope and entered the Indian Ocean, gales of hail and rain driving her toward Melbourne. Assigned to the midnight watch, Henry wrote in his journal. He reflected upon his first glimpse of hard times in the so-called "Land of Promise," when the crew went on strike at the Hobson's Bay docks in protest against low wages. In

Calcutta he described the "English palaces" along the banks of the Hooghly River branch of the Ganges, in stark contrast with the emaciated dead bodies of the starved poor floating in its waters, "covered by crows picking them to pieces."

After fourteen months at sea, the teenager returned to Philadelphia with a pet monkey, as well as the conviction, he wrote, that the voyage would "have a great influence in determining my position in life, perhaps more so than I can at present see." His father got him a job as a typesetter's apprentice in the firm of King & Baird. Henry quickly gained a reputation for being talkative, bright, and curious, with a tendency to engage the older men of the office in conversation in order to "stow away" facts and dates in his memory. After an argument with the job room foreman, Henry quit in a fury. Just before Christmas 1857, possessed with incurable wanderlust and daydreaming of a more exciting life in the West, he shipped out again, this time as ship's steward on the new lighthouse steamer *Shubrick* bound for San Francisco by way of Rio de Janeiro, Montevideo, and Cape Horn.

Seduced by the allure of Canadian gold deposits in the Fraser River in British Columbia, Henry spent a fruitless summer and fall prospecting in Victoria, retreating to San Francisco depleted, so broke he did not own a coat, confessing in a letter to his sister Jennie that since he left home he had become "even uglier and rougher looking."

Henry found lodging at a hotel for men, the What Cheer House, and was hired by the weekly *California Home Journal* as a compositor. He looked forward to his twenty-first birthday when he could qualify as a journeyman printer, join the union, and receive adult wages. Much to his parents' delight, he joined the neighborhood Bethel Methodist Church. He cast his first vote for Abraham Lincoln as president. He found a weekly reading circle where he began with enthusiasm to discuss the works of Emerson and Hawthorne, Scott and Dickens. And he met the one and only love of his life, a seventeen-year-old Australian-born orphan, Annie Corsina Fox, convent-educated and living under the guardianship of two uncles. They eloped on December 3, 1861, and there was no honeymoon. Henry was up as customary at 5:00 the next morning and off to work. The young couple moved to the state capital of Sacramento where Henry set type for the *Union*, rival to the *Bee*, then returned to San Francisco, as their family grew—two sons in four years.

In his mid-twenties, Henry George was still peripatetic, bedding down with his wife and babies in a fatiguing succession of shabby hotels, "house-keeping flats," and rented rooms. Barely above the poverty line, subject to the inconsistent vicissitudes of his trade, "unsettled and worried," he admitted to Jennie with embarassment that Annie had to take up needle-work, clean the landlady's apartment, and sell off some of her jewelry to help make ends meet. Henry was once so low on cash he bartered with the milkman, exchanging printed business cards for milk and eggs.

Henry George was proud to think of himself as a laboring man, a fellow who had always worked from morning till night, and then on again into the early morning hours of the next day if necessary. But he was ambitious, wanting to transcend the life of a substitute printer. The time had arrived to say as well as to do—"to have the dictionary at my fingers ends . . . to cultivate my mind and exert to a fuller extent my powers . . ." and, most fervently, "to endeavor to acquire facility and elegance in the expression of my thoughts by writing essays or other matters."[2]

H e began work on a novel. He wrote a reminiscence of his voyage on the *Shubrick*, a fanciful rumination upon the appeal of "the supernat-ural," and a retelling of a Northwest Indian legend. Over the signature of "H.G.," or significantly as "The Proletarian," he sent letters to the editors of various San Francisco newspapers, expressing opinions on issues of the day. One early effort encouraged workingmen not to shy away from ponder-ing "political and social questions." Soon enough George had a tragic op-portunity to practice what he preached. Distraught at the news of Lincoln's assassination on April 14, 1865, he left a plaintive eulogy called "Sic Sem-per Tyrannis!" in the mailbox of the surprised editor of the *Alta California*, the newspaper at which he worked setting type. Thus Henry George es-caped from compositor to composition. In the fall of 1866, the *San Fran-cisco Times* was founded. The diminutive fellow who had to stand on a wooden box to reach "the proper height to work on his type case" became a reporter, then an editorial writer, and finally managing editor.[3]

Bret Harte—friend of Mark Twain, Western tale spinner, printer-poet-bibliophile émigré from the East, and founding editor of the *Overland Monthly*—noticed Henry George's pertinent and lively journalism. Harte paid him forty dollars, a sum exceeding George's weekly pay at the *Times* by ten dollars, for a seven-thousand-word essay presented as the lead piece in the magazine's October 1868 issue, volume I, no. 4. "What the Railroad Will Bring Us"—a declarative statement, not a question—was the first signpost on Henry George's path as a social and economic critic who remained in the public eye for the next thirty years.

When he began the article in the late summer of 1868, Henry George was aware that the Central Pacific and Union Pacific railroads were racing across the Plains toward Promontory Point, Utah, their agreed-upon convergence point, tying together the Atlantic and the Pacific. He correctly predicted that by the middle of the coming spring, or summer at the latest, the "greatest work of the age" would be complete, more magnificent in its implications for the future of mankind than that other ambitious work in progress, the Suez Canal. On May 10, 1869, when the golden spike was driven, news of the hammer blows was transmitted instantly to a listening nation via the telegraph, another modern miracle.

George praised the marvelous, unprecedented feats of engineering, transforming wilderness into "populous empire," rich natural mineral resources revealed in profusion, regional economies linking into a glorious, national network of exchange. Thanks to the railroad companies selling land lots along the line, he noted a palpable, "keen sense of gain" in the "bracing" American air at the anticipation of material prosperity when primeval territory took on its true character by becoming occupied.

But who really was prospering? The railroad was tainted in a multitude of ways. Chinese workers in the Sierras went on strike. Lawless outposts commonly derided as "Hell on Wheels" towns sprouted up. Sioux in Powder River valley and Cheyenne in Nebraska vandalized tracks and killed crews. George wondered what would ultimately happen when the California metropolises in general, and San Francisco in particular, were "penetrated by the locomotive." Feeling his way toward the ominous downside, he envisioned, again presciently, the overreaching Southern Pacific Railroad assuming a monopoly and dictating the level of transportation costs for freight coming into and out of the Oakland Bay area.

He feared the inevitable consequences of growth at the mercy of "the great laws of compensation which extract some loss for every gain." Would the high tide raise all boats, or, more likely, would the completion of the Transcontinental Railroad and the concomitant increase in corporate business "be of benefit to all of us, [or] only to a portion?" With rhetorical confidence, Henry George built his case, posing probing questions at a measured pace. Answering them suddenly, like a striking snake, he transfixed the stark and paradoxical issue that would become central to the immense corpus of his work. He said it was "the tendency of the time" that benefit came most rapidly to those who were wealthy. During the boom those who did not have the luxurious financial resources of the "new elite" class would be left behind. Those who already possessed lands and mines would become richer for it, while "those who have only their own labor will become poorer, and find it harder to get ahead."

His hopeful conclusion took on a humanist cast, leavened with a warning. "The future of our state, our nation, of our race, looks fair and bright," George said, adding with a sense of history that "perhaps the future looked so to the philosophers who once sat in the porches of Athens. . . . Our modern civilization strikes broad and deep and looks high," he wrote, however, "so did the [Babel] tower which men once built almost unto heaven." He managed to depict the economic quandary of American society and he needed to find a way to articulate the solution.[4]

By the end of the year, Henry George left the *Times* for a brief stint at the *Chronicle*, then signed on with the *San Francisco Herald*. Bankrupt and silent during the Civil War years, the paper was revived with an infusion of new capital under the entrepreneurial guidance of veteran publisher John Nugent, who understood that a wire service connection was crucial to success in the telegraphic age. Someone needed to make an important journey back East to New York City and make arrangements for the *Herald* to affiliate with the Associated Press. Chosen by Nugent for the mission, George sent Annie and the three children, including a year old daughter, Jennie Theresa, ahead to stay with his parents in Philadelphia.

For the next six months, George traveled between his hometown and New York, meeting with Western Union as well as the Associated Press. Received unenthusiastically in both offices, he compared their impersonal atmospheres to "big manufactories." The wire services, already represented at other dailies on the west coast, were reluctant to contract with a newspaper perceived as having a checkered past. George became belligerent and impatient as the weeks wore on. For a while, he attempted to run an im-

promptu telegraphy press shop out of his father's rented coal shed on Third
Street.

One benefit derived from the grueling commuter life. Always a believer
in the healthy value of constitutional walks to clear one's brain, George
spent time before catching the return train exploring the neighborhood
streets of New York City. These perambulations served to reinforce his "appalled" perception of the severe gap "between monstrous luxury and debasing want" in the so-called land of opportunity, a phenomenon that would
not have registered the last time he had been in the city as a seventeen-
year-old.

Henry George described these revelatory field trips in a confessional letter to a friend, the Reverend Thomas Dawson of Glencree, Ireland. "Once
in daylight, and in a city street," George recalled the epiphany, "there came
to me a thought, a vision, a call . . . every nerve quivered. And there and
then I made a vow. Through evil and through good, whatever I have done,
and whatever I have left undone, to that have I been true."

"There are worlds and worlds—even within the bounds of the same
horizon," he continued. "The man who comes into New York with plenty
of money sees one New York. The man who comes with a dollar and a half,
and goes to a twenty-five-cent lodging house, sees another. There are also
fifteen-cent lodging houses, and people too poor to go even to *them*. . . .
That 'one-half of the world does not know how the other half live' is much
more true of the upper than of the lower half," he declared. "Social suffering is for the most part mute. The well-dressed take the main street, but the
ragged slink into the by-ways."[5]

N ot one to waste time between appointments and on the alert for free-
lance writing assignments, George called in lower Manhattan upon
the city's first Whig daily, the *New York Tribune*. Since 1841 it had been under the management of legendary founder Horace Greeley. Yet another
American with printer's ink in his bloodstream whose sporadic formal
schooling ended before he reached the age of fourteen, in the truest tradition of Horatio Alger, Greeley had served as a typesetter's apprentice, and
more than once in his storied career hovered on the fringes of bankruptcy.
"We cannot afford," Greeley said in an early statement of editorial position,

"to reject unexamined any idea which proposes to improve the moral, intellectual or social position of mankind." A worthy editor "must have an ear open to the plaints of the wronged and suffering, though they can never repay advocacy." Greeley's "literary newspaper" was a popular success, boasting a circulation in excess of a quarter of a million readers. Greeley published his *Overland Journey*, an account of a trip to San Francisco in the summer of 1859, and recently had produced a two-volume history of the Civil War and his memoirs, *Recollections of a Busy Life*.[6]

The *Tribune*'s managing editor was John Russell Young, one year George's junior. Young's journalistic career began with the *Philadelphia Press* in 1862. He went on to become minister to China in the early 1880s, and in 1897 Pres. William McKinley appointed him the eighth librarian of Congress. The two contemporaries struck up an immediate friendship. Young found George to be an excellent listener, "a serious man . . . wanting to know a thing exactly." His "direct and urgent way" and "fine intelligence" were appealing. Nights when George decided to forego the last train out of Pennsylvania Station, the comrades "prowled about Printing House Square," at the convergence of Park Row and Nassau Street, "and chummed with printers and newspaper men doomed to late hours."[7]

During one of their nocturnal conversations, George brought up a matter much on his mind, the chronic dilution of California workingmen's pay so much at odds with the capital growth spurred by corporate monopolies. George implied that he was going to lay the blame for this imbalance upon the unrestricted availability of Chinese immigrant labor. Young challenged his friend to write an article on the subject for the *Tribune*, and commissioned it for the princely sum of sixty-five dollars. Before George set to the task, however, he realized he needed to do some research and find out "what political economy had to say about the causes of wages."[8]

George went straight to the wellspring, consulting the classic text of the "dismal science," *Principles of Political Economy with Some of Their Applications to Social Philosophy*, by John Stuart Mill (1806–73), "the dominant figure in English intellectual life in the latter half of the nineteenth century." George had no difficulty finding Mill's "rapidly-executed" book in the Philadelphia Library. The first American edition was published by Little,

Brown and Company of Boston in 1848, the same time as the first English edition. The second, two-volume American edition was brought out to critical acclaim in early 1864 by D. Appleton & Company of New York City, followed the next year by an inexpensive "People's Edition" subsidized by Mill so as to place it "within the reach of the labouring class."[9]

Mill's challenge to think organically and "study all the determining agencies equally" inspired Henry George. Mill's appeal to George resided in his "intellectual catholicity"—the way he scrounged for diverse, "scattered particles of important truth" among all social theorists, always testing himself against those with whom he disagreed. Mill's eclectic, brilliant, well reasoned, and humane themes first informed—and when his style matured, reinforced—George's ideology.[10]

One of Mill's first papers was published in the *Parliamentary History and Review* when the young philosopher and logician was nineteen and had already been working for three years as a clerk in the East India Company. The paper put forward a correlation between the aggregate capital of a country and the growth of its population as the basis for the rate of wages. Mill's forte was to insist upon context, cause and effect, when analyzing economic forces, understanding that such interdependent factors characteristic of all societies as environment, laws, race, class structure, and people's "habits or propensities" must be taken into consideration. Since society was naturally a physical construct, political and economic knowledge should represent actual conditions and not be abstract or "intellectualist." Mill saw economic process without blinders. The "present wretched education" and "wretched social arrangements," he said, were "the only real hindrances" to human happiness. In a progressive, fluid society, government must not be permitted to hinder the urge for self-betterment or the right of women's suffrage, which Mill championed thanks to the strong "promptings" of his wife and stepdaughter.[11]

"I am not charmed," Mill declared, "with an ideal of life held out by those who think that the normal state of human beings is that of struggling to get on." All who participate in the chain of events of labor—all workers whose "productive power" leads to the presence in the marketplace of desired and valued commodities—deserve to reap commensurate benefits from that labor.[12]

Under the headline, "The Chinese in California," Henry George's *New-York Daily Tribune* essay was displayed on the front page of the Saturday,

May 1, 1869, "triple sheet" edition with the subheads, "Character of the Asiatic Immigration—The Problem of the Pacific Coast." George's spring-board was his interpretation of Mill's "wage-fund theory." He latched onto Books II and IV of Mill's *Principles* dealing with "Labour, Capital and Land" and "The Influence of Progress." He wrote in the *Tribune* that the indiscriminate importation of a willing, obliging workforce for mining, railroad construction, road building, "chamber-work," cooking, gardening, fruit harvesting, stock tending—in this case, "the race which started from the plains of Central Asia"—was exercising an injurious effect upon the economy of the western American states. George was so proud of the essay that he sent a clipping to the Master himself.

Mill sent an equivocating reply in October. On a theoretical level, Mill wrote, it might be possible to agree with George's "difficult and embarassing" assertion that Chinese labor was overcrowding the American labor market, thereby driving wages downward. "But there is much also to be said on the other side," Mill continued, pointedly asking George if, on a practical level, in the greatest competitive democratic society in the world, it was "justifiable to assume" that the condition, "character and habits of the Chinese are insusceptible of improvement." Rather than the government "put[ting] a stop . . . by force" to immigration, Mill advocated increased efforts to include Chinese children within the American system of education. Twenty-five years after the *Tribune* article, George looked back upon the piece and criticized it as "crude," symptomatic of an early time when his well-intentioned assimilation of Mill's economic philosophy was as yet unformed. George's close reading of John Stuart Mill's work eventually came to be the liberal, utilitarian core for his forays into the literature of political economy and universal history.[13]

By the summer of 1869, Henry George had returned to the west coast and was making plans to start his own newspaper in order to reduce his dependence upon the whims of other editors and control a regular outlet for his irrepressible assortment of social theories. With job printers William M. Hinton and Frank Mahan on board as partners, one double flat-bed press, and a grand total of eighteen hundred dollars among them, Henry George launched the *San Francisco Daily Evening Post* toward the end of 1871. The four-page, eleven-by-fourteen-inch paper sold for a penny a copy. It was "Democratic in the higher, wider sense," the editor declared, "that is, it will

oppose centralisation and monopoly of all kinds." This it did with a
vengeance for the next four years.

The *Evening Post* was the perfect forum in which to serialize George's
important new essay, "Our Land and Land Policy, National and State." In
December 1900, Henry George Jr. introduced a posthumous edition of his
father's explorative pamphlet as "bearing the relation of acorn to oak"
when read as the test run for the great opus to come, *Progress and Poverty*.
The metaphor is an apt one as George comes to more intelligent terms with
John Stuart Mill, moving beyond wage issues to a wider, more significant
subject—a man's proper rights in his use of property as these rights flowed
naturally out of his inalienable "right to self."[14]

In the lexicon of classical economics, "land" referred to all naturally oc-
curring resources. Land was one of the three factors of production, the
other two being capital and labor. Since land was not "produced," its market value needed to be understood differently from labor or produced goods.
In the throes of composing the "Land" essay, George may well have recalled a corollary expressed in his youthful readings, Ralph Waldo Emerson's hymn to the sanctity of "any relation to land, the habit of tilling it, or
mining it, or even hunting on it," as "generating the feeling of patriotism."
Sam Houston said it just as truly if less eloquently: "There is not an American on earth but what loves land." In Henry George's David and Goliath
vision of what ailed his beloved country, the first thing that needed to be
done was to wake up to the fact that government was engaged far too
deeply with renegade speculators, "Grain King" middlemen, and rapacious
railroad promoters granted unregulated title to millions of acres of unim-
proved public domain. "Since the day when Esau sold his birthright for a
mess of pottage," George exclaimed indignantly, "we may search history in
vain for any parallel to such concessions . . . and reckless prodigality!"[15]

As Mill stated repeatedly in Book II of the *Principles*, the point was not
to rue the existence of private property, but to consider whether it existed
in its best form. Henry George agreed that property, in and of itself a veritable "condition of civilization," was not the problem. "Monopolisation—
standing between the man who is willing to work and the field which
nature offers for his labor"—that, George wrote, was the "national crime."
The time had arrived, he insisted, to make a wholesale, leveling revision in
the American tax structure, to strip away all existing tax burdens from the

realms of production and exchange, and instead concentrate upon one tax source, based upon the value of land ownership. In George's view, the state should *"give*, not sell" all remaining open territory *"in limited quantities"* solely to *"actual settlers"* for the use of their individual enterprises.

A thousand copies of *Our Land and Land Policy* were sold. Despite the appearance of lively excerpts from time to time in the *Daily Evening Post*, Henry George's views on the benefits of the new "land tax" and its potential to correct once and for all the rampant economic inequities of the most prosperous civilization in the world received little sympathy.[16]

Henry George, the early riser, left his sleeping wife and three children at dawn (a fourth, christened Anna Angela, because she was born on the Feast of Angels, arrived October 2, 1877) in the two-story house covered with white climbing roses on Valencia Street in the Mission District. He walked over to the stable nearby and by first light mounted his bony, tan-colored mustang—"a small, shaggy, wiry native animal"—for the solitary "thinking ride," loping easily down to the *Evening Post* on Montgomery Street. His office, more like a cell, contained a massive table piled high with papers flecked with cigar ashes, the surrounding floor obscured by back issues. He engaged in a "nervous . . . unsystematic method of work," scribbling a paragraph here and a paragraph there. George's foolscap pages were replete with "inserts," brief passages interleaved and sequenced alphabetically through the main text, as if he were expanding from within when subsidiary thoughts occurred. On occasion he leapt from his chair in midsentence and flung himself down upon a ragged, old sofa in the corner or walked over to the balcony and gazed out upon the street below, so lost in thought he did not hear visitors entering through the always-open door.[17]

In November 1875 George parted ways with the *Evening Post*. The paper had added a seven-day morning edition and stumbled financially, unable to repay extended credit. Along the way George also made some ill-advised investments in a mining company that went under. He wrote a desperate appeal to the Democratic governor-elect of California, former state senator William S. Irwin, hoping to obtain a political appointment that would allow him to devote more time to his "long-cherished plan," a big book percolating in his mind. Irwin thought highly of George and was grateful for his steadfast editorial support during the election campaign. He came through with the exceptionally undemanding post of state inspector of gas meters.[18]

To supplement his income and to rehearse before varied audiences the arguments of *Progress and Poverty*, Henry George hired himself out as a lecturer. Despite his diminutive stature, he possessed a ringing voice that carried well. He delivered two major public speeches within four months. The first, on March 9, 1877, was by invitation to the students and faculty at the new Berkeley campus of the University of California, where Henry George was under consideration for the academic chair in political economy. Introduced by John Le Conte, president of the university, George spoke for forty-five minutes. At a time in higher education when economics was becoming recognized as a bona fide profession, George's presentation rivaled the shocking effect produced by Ralph Waldo Emerson before the students at Harvard Divinity School. "The Study of Political Economy" was an opportunity for George to invoke "the dark side of our boasted progress, the Nemesis that seems to follow with untiring tread." He challenged the professors to marshall their brain power and help alleviate the struggle of the laboring man, instead of hiding in their ivory tower. This endeavor, he warned, might prove difficult, because economic science had not evolved in the one hundred years since Adam Smith's *Wealth of Nations*. He accused the academy of being at fault for failing to discern the moral identity in economics. They must change their laggardly approach and unleash the knowledge they had gained for "practical utility" and the betterment of the common man. In developing "intellectual self-reliance" the professors must find a reason for being in the society that needed their leadership or become fated to obsolescence.[19]

George's suspicion of the academy eventually proved fatal to the perpetuation of his economic theories. He had worked up several additional lectures as a proposed series, but was never asked to return to the campus. He was chosen by the San Francisco city administration to be "Orator for the Day" at the annual Fourth of July ceremonies in the crowded California Theatre downtown. Stepping to the podium following a dramatic reading of the Declaration of Independence, George shifted to his Christian side from the self-appointed gadfly role shown at Berkeley for a speech he called "The American Republic: Its Dangers and Possibilities." His message was framed in stark contrasts. America exemplified "the apotheosis of Liberty," but only "in broken gleams and partial light," because "Justice" was still cruelly denied to so many of her citizens by the transgressions of the wealthy few who "misappropriated the gifts of the Creator with impunity." America, engendered as a nation under God, had—in the guise of modern progress, concealed by steam and energized by electricity—strayed perilously from her initial charter. The result was an insufferable aura of hypocrisy, "prating the inalienable rights of man and then denying the inalienable right to the bounty of the Creator."

On the 101st anniversary of the founding of the Republic, Henry George stood before the good people of San Francisco, announced that there still existed the possibility of "a glorious vision" of the future, and said that he felt a kinship with St. John, whose book of Revelation was conceived on the "remote Aegean island of Patmos." Henry George came before his townspeople this day to preach about a future America, an America that should accomplish her mission and become "the City of God on Earth, with its walls of jasper and its gates of pearl!"[20]

The journal entry read, simply, "Tuesday, September 18, 1877. Commenced Progress & Poverty." This date was the documented beginning. The eventual subtitle—"An Inquiry into the Cause of Industrial Depressions and of Increase of Want with Increase of Wealth"—had been an obsession for many years by the time the book was written in concentrated fashion over eighteen months. George paid scant attention to his municipal patronage job. Rarely leaving his house except for a brisk walk by the docks or a half hour horseback ride, George preferred to remain in his yellow dressing gown, unshaven, ensconced in a second-floor workroom with three windows overlooking San Francisco Bay, contentedly surrounded by the eight hundred volumes in his personal collection. He did not have a fixed writing routine. When the spirit moved him, any time of day or night, he set down a few lines, always equidistant, left-hand margin plumbline straight, copperplate penmanship uniformly slanted, "t"s crossed with a flourish—followed by hasty, scribbled pencil afterthoughts.

The stop-and-go, methodical then feverish rhythm reflected the peak years of the "Discontented Seventies" in California, the uncertain maelstrom against which *Progress and Poverty* came into being. While Denis Kearney incited the Workingmen's Party to new heights of xenophobia, federal troops were brought in to break up strikes. While quintessential Gilded Age mansions reared up on Nob Hill, the Bank of California collapsed. While the state legislature formed a new constitution, the holdings of the Central Southern Pacific Railroad increased in excess of eleven million acres.[21]

When Henry George fixated upon "progress" in the six hundred closely textured pages of the book, he did not restrict himself to the most proximate definition of positive growth. The final chapter, "The Problem of Individual Life," was an open-ended speculation about the capacities of humankind. Drawing aside the monetary veil, he wrote: "It is first necessary to live, before one can aspire to live well." In that respect, abiding by the American doctrine of "each for all," the individual was the prototype for an entire common "race" or society, the many reflected within the one. It was in the personal, ethical arena that the struggle against greed commenced and the antidote to industrial "paroxysms" was defined.

Henry George came full circle to the crux of economic determinism as defined in his failed pamphlet of 1871: the primal component of the natural order, he wrote, was land. To the "arch-idealist" philosopher of *Progress and Poverty*—"the ardent knight-errant from out [of] the newest West"—this claim could no longer be the sole province of the robber barons and owning classes. Opportunity for advancement must be shared with the exploited blue-collar men on the "treadmill of toil," whose wages were incommensurate with their "exertions." Leave the labor-earned income of the workingman alone, George said. Bank interest was just another meaningless example of debilitating "false capital." Instead, levy one mode of tax, to be incurred by property owners and measured relative to the market value of their land. In the throes of the Gilded Age, "Harry" George had the audacity to lay out "facts of common observation and common knowledge." He believed his corrective tax would reconcile—literally "justify"—the flawed, discordant system through which wealth was disproportionately gained and distributed in America: "Society has no just claim," he said, "upon what society has not produced."[22]

Setting aside the tardiness of his essentially agrarian panacea at a time when America was moving so quickly toward industrialization, there can be no doubt that when he sat down to write *Progress and Poverty*, Henry George thought of himself as a well-versed, confident, and self-made economist. He improvised upon and challenged the dicta of his favorite theorists, starting with the "classical school" of Britain and the so-called "father" of modern economics and exponent of freedom in the social order, the Scotsman Adam Smith; David Ricardo, early authority on taxation, best friend and colleague of James Mill, father of John Stuart Mill; and Thomas Robert Malthus, author of the influential book, *Essay on the Principle of Population*. Further into the historical tradition was the Physiocratic ("Rule by Nature") philosophical school of the French Enlightenment, *les économistes* surrounding founder François Quesnay—the court physician to Louis XV—and their espousal of the *impôt foncière unique* ("single tax"). George admitted to the "second-hand" influence of the Physiocrats only later on in his career because he said he could not read French.[23]

"Henry George was a self-taught economist, but he *was* an economist," was the assessment of Austrian-born Harvard economist Joseph A. Schumpeter (1883–1950), inventor of the concept of the "business cycle," and arbiter of the modern field. Along with a detailed history lesson on the lineage of political economy, Henry George wove into the fabric of *Progress and Poverty* many evidences of well-thumbed, popular Victorian texts taken from the shelves of his home library. Frequently cited was the laissez-faire, evolutionary sociology of Herbert Spencer (1820–1903), and his faith in the influence of individual character upon the collective personality of the competitive state, exemplified in his great work, *Social Statics, or, the Conditions Essential to Human Happiness Specified and the First of Them Developed*; the two-volume opus of Henry Thomas Buckle (1821–62), whose mammoth exegesis, *History of Civilization in England*, attempted to summarize the natural, scientific laws governing the destiny of all nations, and made frequent appearances in George's midnight reading; and William Winwood Reade's (1838–75) cult saga, *The Martyrdom of Man*, rooted in the author's voyages to "Negroland" (Inner Africa) in search of support of his belief in universal history—that "our own prosperity . . . is founded upon the agonies of the past," and must not be taken for granted.

In testimony to the huge imaginative appetite of "the Prophet of San Francisco," dozens of tidbits from other intellectual and moral voices were fed to the readers of *Progress and Poverty*, from Charles Darwin and Louis Agassiz to Edmund Burke and Samuel Taylor Coleridge; from Thomas Carlyle and Alexis de Tocqueville to Moses and Plutarch; from Benjamin Franklin and William Wordsworth to the Koran, the Bible, and the Ramayana. Conspicuous by their absence, however, from Henry George's entire oeuvre were two intellectual giants. The first was Jean-Jacques Rousseau. It is difficult to accept that in all his reading, George—a tried-and-true Jeffersonian his entire life—never came across Rousseau's claim in the *Discourse on the Arts and Sciences* (1750) that "the first man who, having enclosed a piece of ground, bethought himself of saying 'This is mine,' and found people simple enough to believe him, was the real founder of civil society."[24]

It is not as difficult to determine why Karl Marx receives such short shrift in Henry George's work as a whole, and no mention at all in *Progress and Poverty*. "We differ from the socialists in our diagnosis of the evil [of economic imbalance] and we differ from them as to remedies," George wrote a dozen years later in one of his last books, *The Condition of Labour*. "We have no fear of capital . . . [and] we see no evil in competition, but deem unrestricted competition to be as necessary to the health of the industrial and social organism as the free circulation of blood is to the health of the bodily organism." Marx could not have disagreed more. In a letter to Friedrich Sorge, a German émigré radical in the vanguard of the labor anarchist movement in America, Marx disdained Henry George as "a self-advertising Yankee . . . utterly backward . . . wandering about in speculations which follow the English model." He ridiculed George's "sentimental" veneration of private property as if it were "a primordial human condition," and criticized his sovereign, "fundamental dogma [,] that everything would be all right if ground rent were paid to the state in order that it may serve as a substitute for taxes. This is a frank expression of the hatred which the industrial capitalist dedicates to the landed proprietor." Marx's ideal communist economy would follow upon capitalism's inevitable death throes and flourish in an emancipated society ruled by the no-longer-alienated working class. Nothing short of wholesale change would suffice. George's ideal society, on the other hand, did not require an all-out class war because it was wedded to systemic reform through the redistribution of economic benefits. While Marx, the intellectual snob, conceded that *Progress and Poverty* was a "sensation," he insisted that the book remained an "unsuccessful attempt at emancipation from orthodox political economy."[25]

Early in March 1879 Henry George completed *Progress and Poverty* "in the dead of night, when he was entirely alone." He fell down upon his knees and wept. His old friend, John Russell Young, visiting San Francisco at the time, said George was completely bereft of his familiar "breezy . . . sea manner" and looked exhausted, as if "he had given the book his very soul." On March 22 George sent the manuscript to D. Appleton & Company in New York, publishers of Mill and Spencer. The editors thought the book was "written with great clearness and forthrightness," but was "very aggressive." Harper's and Scribner's likewise declined.

Henry George decided to print the book himself. He personally "set the first two stickfulls" of lead type. An author's proof edition of five hundred copies, temporarily entitled *Political Economy of the Social Problem*, was run off. George sent an unbound galley to Appleton, and they replied they would take a chance on the book if George provided the original plates. In January 1880 the regular market edition of *Progress and Poverty* went on sale at a cover price of two dollars. Within the year three subsequent printings came from Appleton, and Kegan Paul of London published the first European edition. Lovell's Library of New York serialized the book in its magazine, and then produced an inexpensive edition for twenty cents. Kegan Paul's paperback went for sixpence.

Progress and Poverty landed on the leading cusp of the era of big business in America, but Henry George preferred to situate the source of power in the realm of the workingman. "Labor is the active and initial force," he wrote, in a deliberate reversal of the assumed causality, "and labor is therefore the employer of capital." This timely, passionate rhetoric seized the attention and sympathy of workingmen when their quality of life was under threat. The book was tinged with nostalgia for a simpler marketplace whose attributes were shared by craftsmen, small shopkeepers, and local tradesmen, and permeated with warnings about the dire consequences of inordinately concentrated wealth—specifically, cash.

Within five years, there were German, French, Swedish, Danish, Norwegian, and Dutch translations; Spanish, Italian, Hungarian, Russian, Bulgarian, Chinese, and Yiddish followed, making the book a worldwide sensation. By the turn of the century, there were more than two million copies in print. Sales of *Progress and Poverty* before 1900 in America were second only to the Bible.[26]

As the book gained momentum, George was in demand as a public speaker. He relocated with his family to upper Manhattan, published a book on *The Irish Land Question* in 1881, and embarked upon a speaking tour of the United Kingdom financed by American partisans of the Irish

Land League. In 1883 he joined the Knights of Labor. A series of essays called *Social Problems*, originally published in *Frank Leslie's Illustrated Weekly*, was presented as an expansion of the themes set forth in *Progress and Poverty*, in order to show more relevance to "industrial questions and to public utility problems that beset large cities." This book was followed by *Protection or Free Trade?* In 1886 the United Labor Party, at the instigation of Samuel Gompers, gathered thirty-six thousand signatures on a petition to put Henry George up as their New York mayoralty candidate against the Tammany Hall bosses. During the course of a month of campaigning, George spoke more than a dozen times a day. "Look over our vast city, and what do we see? On one side a very few men richer by far than it is good for men to be, and on the other side a great mass of men and women struggling and worrying and wearying to get a most pitiful living," he told applauding, cheering crowds at Cooper Union on October 5, 1886. "The aim of this movement," George said—above spontaneous cries from the audience of "Bully for you!' and "Hear, hear!"—"is the assertion of the equal rights of man. . . . It is our duty as citizens to address ourselves to the adjustment of social wrongs." Although he lost the race to Abram Hewitt, George did come in ahead of a "young politico" named Theodore Roosevelt.[27]

An international network of "Single Tax" clubs sprang up under the leadership of New York corporate attorney Thomas G. Shearman, author of *Natural Taxation* (1888). Although those two catchwords were never used by Henry George in *Progress and Poverty*, the grassroots organization gave impetus to his social philosophy, and to the sales of the book. George toured England again in 1888 and 1889 and went on for three months of speaking engagements in Australia and New Zealand with his wife and daughters, pushing himself to such an extreme that he suffered a stroke.[28]

Returning from a round-the-world trip, George produced *The Condition of Labour* in 1891, taking issue with what he perceived as contradictions in Pope Leo XIII's encyclical on land ownership. "You give the gospel to the labourers and the earth to the landlords," George upbraided the pope, "you give us equal rights in heaven, but deny us equal rights on earth!" This tract was followed in 1892 by *A Perplexed Philosopher*, a critique of Herbert Spencer. That same year Henry George also commenced work on his final study, *The Science of Political Economy*, intended as a "textbook" pedagogical response to his critics and a wider "propagation of the truths . . . making clear to the world" what had been first set down in *Progress and Poverty*. The author feared, despite popular acclaim, that his gospel was marginalized by the academic community, and that his legacy might not stand the test of time.

In declining health and against medical advice, George was pulled again into the race for mayor of New York as an independent Democrat against the liberal Republican Seth Low. Five days before the election, on October 28, 1897, George delivered four speeches. The final one was at the Metro-politan Opera House and lasted past eleven o'clock. He did not return to his room at the Union Square Hotel until midnight. Early the next morn-ing he suffered a stroke and died in his wife's arms. He was fifty-eight years old.

All day Sunday, October 31, his body lay in state in the Grand Central Palace, a vast exhibition hall at Lexington Avenue and Forty-third Street. More than one hundred thousand people filed by the bier as countless thousands more who never made it inside milled about in the street.[29]

The epitaph in metal letters set into the headstone of Henry George's grave on a hill crest in Brooklyn's Greenwood Cemetery begins, "The truth that I have tried to make clear will not find easy acceptance." That rueful prediction was all too true. While he was in the thick of writing *Progress and Poverty*, Henry George genuinely hoped it would survive to be "a book for the twentieth century." He believed that a fluid and fair Amer-ican economy was not only possible but imperative. As a writer with one foot in the privacy of his study and the other in the artisan's workshop set-ting his own words into lead type, George held on to a venerated labor sys-tem and honored its vanishing practitioners. The single-tax movement was the final—and utopian—manifestation of a simple domestic economic agenda reacting to the stirrings of an increasingly complex international one. A disciple of John Stuart Mill to the end, George instigated the single-tax movement to protest against the inordinate weight of government and the infringement of special interests upon the lives of regular citizens. But the movement peaked too quickly to provide momentum for the genera-tion of "Georgists" still struggling in the name of their patron saint into the second decade of the twentieth century.

With Progressivism front and center on the national electoral scene in 1912, the attributes of George's political philosophy were handily co-opted and subsumed by both reformers, Theodore Roosevelt and Woodrow Wilson, neither of whom so much as acknowledged the influence of the home-grown radical who had blazed the trail ahead of them. "Not as a political leader shall those who honor Henry George hold him in remembrance," wrote John Russell Young, eulogizing his old friend. "To them he was no gladiator, but a thinker, a philosopher who lived only to benefit his fellow man." Henry George's "remedy" for American society now seems naive, cumbersome, and even impracticable. But his contribution to the script of the American drama must be reappraised. The sustained urgency of his desire to reconcile what he saw as "The House of Have and the House of Want" was supremely noble, and in this ideal, Henry George had enlightened predecessors. When Thomas Jefferson modified the third imperative for the Declaration of Independence into the encompassing right of the "pursuit of happiness," he was well aware of John Locke's original insistence upon "life, liberty and *property*."[30]

JANE ADDAMS

7

The Sphere of Action

I have just been reading your *Democracy and Social Ethics*, and with such deep satisfaction that I must send you my tribute of thanks. It seems to me one of the great books of our time. The religion of democracy needs nothing so much as sympathetic interpretation to one another of the different classes of which society consists; and you have made your contribution in a masterly manner.

—William James to Jane Addams, September 17, 1902[1]

This heady praise for Jane Addams's first book came from America's first psychologist, self-styled "genuine philosopher," and distinguished exponent of pragmatism to a social worker who had been residing in Chicago's worst slum for seventeen years, devoting every waking moment to ameliorating the problems of the immigrant poor. When *Democracy and Social Ethics* arrived on the doorstep of William James's mountain summertime retreat in Chocorua, New Hampshire, from Macmillan publishers in New York, James took it up immediately and did not wait until he had finished reading to send a note. "Religion of democracy" was the right turn of phrase. The necessity that "the real backbone of the world's religious life" should exist in support of "the material of the blessed life" of the "single private man" (and woman) was James's great preoccupation. He believed there was something reverent and faithful about Addams's egalitarian commitment to the mission of Hull-House, the community center she founded.

The doors of the settlement were open from the very first hour of the very first day to thousands of desperate people a week who came through in search of food, clothing, and shelter as well as nutrition for their minds from an array of activities, including reading groups, language classes, and studio art. The thriving institution exemplified Jane Addams's concept of democracy as a way of living. Her book, *Democracy and Social Ethics* was, among other things, an outspoken tract on behalf of modern women. Jane Addams's path to that self-confident definition of democracy in action was long and arduous.[2]

Laura Jane ("Jennie") Addams was born seven months before the start of the Civil War, on September 6, 1860, in Cedarville, Illinois, a rural village north of Freeport in Stephenson County. She was the youngest child of John Huy Addams, a prosperous and respected Lincoln Republican, grist mill owner, railroad builder, banker, and Illinois state senator. A Hicksite Quaker, Mr. Addams believed "the light within" was more powerful than Scripture. Sarah Weber, her mother, died from childbirth complications when Jane was two years old. In 1864, Mr. Addams married a handsome widow, Anna Hostetter Haldeman. Along with a glamorous, sociable stepmother, whom Jane viewed as a rival for her beloved father's attentions, she inherited two stepbrothers, Harry and George Haldeman. As a teenager, Jane was slightly built, pigeon-toed and painfully self-conscious about her stooped posture, the result of spinal tuberculosis. She wore her light brown hair pulled back into a tight bun and was blessed with wide, luminous brown eyes and a calm, low voice. In the fall of 1877, she left home to board at the Rockford Female Seminary, thirty miles from Cedarville. Her father, proponent of the virtues of "mental integrity," was on the board of the school, established to instill Christian values of "duty, responsibility, and helpfulness to others." Each student was expected to build her own fire, keep her linen clean and her room in immaculate order.

Distinguished as a top-notch scholar in all her courses, Jane resolved in an early English class essay that the properly educated and mature young woman of the nineteenth century should "develop her intellectual force and her capabilities for direct labor . . . not to *be* a man, nor *like* a man, but she claims that same right to independent thought and action." She quickly found herself at the nucleus of a group of headstrong and energetic young ladies, first among them Ellen Gates Starr, with whom she would enjoy a long colleagueship.[3]

The girls steeped themselves in history, the Gospels, Greek and Roman classics, the inspirational writings of the great Victorians, Dickens, Arnold, Tennyson, Browning, Carlyle, and most favorably of all to Jane, John Ruskin, whose "abstruse parts" she "liked the best." Ruskin appealed to her because his works helped Jane to think profoundly about "doing one's duty," her personal brand of "religion in the practical sense." His well-wrought essays, especially "Unto This Last" (1862) and "Lilies: Of Queens' Gardens" (1864) extolled the importance in an industrial society of man's right to unfettered enjoyment of his craft and correct payment for his professional "labour," whatever it might be, and likewise, woman's equal right to reap the benefits of her "noble teachings" and make use of that awareness to determine her proper place in society, exercising her "power . . . office and dignity" to the fullest extent in order to find autonomy.[4]

Jane was elected president of the class of seventeen girls, wrote extensively for the school magazine, and graduated as valedictorian. In a brief and refreshingly forward-looking commencement speech, she declared, "We stand united today in a belief in beauty, genius and courage, and that these expressed through truest womanhood can yet transform the world."[5]

Six weeks later, just before her twenty-first birthday, Jane's beloved "Pa" died suddenly and prematurely at fifty-nine. "The greatest sorrow that has ever come to me has passed," Jane wrote to her friend, Ellen Gates Starr. The venerated "father-god" removed from her life, Jane drifted into a netherworld of nervous tension. She moved to Philadelphia where she had planned to attend the Women's Medical College, but lasted only half a year before retreating to Cedarville. A corrective spinal operation rendered her bedridden for the better part of another year, after which she set forth for Europe, in the customary manner of many middle-class young American women of the time. The extended cultural-enrichment and shopping tour to the British Isles, Holland, Germany, Austria, Italy, Greece, Switzerland, Berlin, and Paris with a group of friends was conducted under the close supervision of her stepmother. Jane returned to Cedarville "always blundering . . . spiritually more confused than when [I] left . . . absolutely at sea as far as any moral purpose [is] concerned."

Without the essential anchor of her husband, gregarious Anna was desperate to escape small-town confines and broaden her social life. At her stepmother's insistence, spinster Jane relocated to Baltimore to help her keep house. "I am filled with shame," she confided to friend Ellen, "that with all my apparent leisure I do nothing at all."[6]

Between uninspiring art history and zoology lectures at Johns Hopkins,

drawing and French lessons, concert going, whist parties, tea time, and vac-
uous parlor conversations, Jane Addams's "sense of maladjustment" was
thankfully relieved in books. At about this time she discovered the works
of Leo Nikolayavich Tolstoy (1828–1910). *My Religion* was published in
English in 1885, and Addams read it in Baltimore in the fall of the following year. Isabel Hapgood's translation of *What to Do?* (1887), subsequently
published with the more accurately rendered and pertinent title, *What
Then Must We Do?* changed Addams's life profoundly. It was, she said, a
transformative, "vital experience . . . a trenchant challenge, written with
overwhelming sincerity and simplicity."[7]

The "challenge" came to Addams through Tolstoy's choice for the opening epigraph for the book, the citation from Luke 3:10–11. These were the
words of a human Jesus: "And the multitudes came to Him, saying, What
then must we do? And He answered and said unto them, He that hath two
coats, let him impart to him that hath none; and he that hath food, let him
do likewise." Casting about fitfully during these years for a purpose to push
her forward, Addams was aware of the needful "other half" from her occasional, fleeting charity visits in Baltimore to an orphan asylum and to a small
shelter for elderly indigent black women. The "deep furrows" she said were
driven into the "smooth surface of nineteenth-century satisfaction with the
belief that progress was inevitable" might equally have been the worry lines
in her maidenly brow.

Addams admired Tolstoy for addressing widespread problems of poverty.
Here was an intellectual born into a wealthy, noble family, and married
into wealth, yet profoundly dissatisfied, actually "horrified at the delusion"
of his dissolute lifestyle, "living on the backs of the working folk." After
War and Peace, after *Anna Karenina*, Tolstoy experienced a conversion of
moral conscience in middle age: "I, a very prolific writer who for forty years
have done nothing but write" suddenly realized that the possession of talent and privilege were not birthrights. They were "a call to serve" the less
fortunate. He turned away from the domestic routine of a "mental worker"
constructing epic novels, abandoned worldly goods, and took solace in the
"new simplicity" of social action and hard manual labor. He set up an open
soup kitchen in aid of famine relief for overworked peasants on the grounds
of his estate at Yasnaya Polyana, outside Tula, and embarked upon philanthropic forays into destitute city neighborhoods in the dead of winter. A
major thrust in Tolstoy's writing for the last thirty years of his life was di-

dactic pamphleteering on the virtues of religion and education, the skewed economics of Russia, and imperatives for the State to improve itself through the good works of its better-off citizens.

With her health reasonably restored, and an inheritance from her father's estate that provided her with an income of three thousand dollars a year, Jane Addams decided to make a return trip to Europe, ostensibly to collect art reproductions to donate to her alma mater, recently accredited as Rockford College. She was of an age to travel unchaperoned. With Ellen Gates Starr and a Rockford teacher, Sarah Anderson, Addams arrived in Southampton just before Christmas 1877: "Everywhere it was 'Madame' with the utmost respect," she wrote, "and I felt perfectly at my ease and dignified all the time."[8]

The traveling party made their way during winter and spring through Paris, Stuttgart, Munich, Florence, and Rome. A tour through Spain included a stop in Madrid where Addams witnessed an especially gruesome bullfight. The companions returned to Paris, after which they parted ways. Addams wanted to head for London in order to be there in time for the World Centennial Congress of Foreign Missions in early June. Starr returned to Italy for more museum hopping, accompanied by her art history students from Miss Kirkland's School for Girls in Chicago.

On the way up to London, Addams and Anderson visited Canterbury and toured the magnificent Gothic cathedral. They encountered the wife of the bishop of Dover, who invited the two American women to tea. They met the "liberal Christian" Canon William Fremantle, former rector of St. Mary's Church in London. He urged Addams and Anderson to pay a visit to the Toynbee Hall Settlement on Commercial Street in the Whitechapel District of London's impoverished East End. The place was thriving under the able joint wardenship of the canon's protégé, the Reverend Samuel Augustus Barnett, vicar of St. Jude's Church, and his wife, Henrietta.[9]

Toynbee Hall was a lay mission founded in 1884 by friends of the idealist social reformer and political economist Arnold Toynbee as a memorial to his life and work one year after his "nervous collapse" and death at thirty. Born in London and educated at Pembroke and Balliol colleges, Oxford, Toynbee's great book, *Lectures on the Industrial Revolution of the Eighteenth Century in England* was published posthumously. "It would be well," he wrote, "if, in studying the past, we could always bear in mind the problems of the present." To that end Toynbee advised his elite students that the only way to derive applicable significance from the dogma of untested scholarly learning and infuse their lives with meaning was to take a step across the insular boundary between social classes, go back to the people, and become truly useful citizens by "settling" in economically disadvantaged areas. "We—the middle classes, I mean, not merely the rich—we have neglected you," Toynbee declared in what would be his final lecture in January 1883, directed to the urban poor of England. "Instead of justice, we have offered you charity, and instead of sympathy, we have offered you hard and unreal advice. . . . We work for you in the hope and trust that if you get material civilisation, if you get a better life, you will really lead a better life."[10]

Canon Barnett took the two women on a tour of the Tudor-style mansion to show them the library, the gymnasium, the lecture hall, and the dining hall. He spoke of education in evangelical terms. It must transcend the academic setting, "cultivating personality through contact with what is excellent in human achievement." The Victorian charity organizers of Toynbee Hall adhered to a special dynamic that made the education offered by the institution function properly: "One by one, face to face contact between helper and helped," Barnett told Addams and Anderson, was the "best system . . . 'to raise the buried life.'" The fifteen Oxford and Cambridge graduates in residence at Toynbee Hall paid their own room and board and held jobs in the city of London during the day, performed relief work on evenings and weekends when they visited the poor, provided free legal aid, ran workingmen's activity clubs, sponsored "fresh air" field trips to the countryside for the neighborhood children, and conducted a full curriculum of university extension lectures.

Addams was responsive to the structure of the Toynbee Hall program. "It is a community for University men who live there, have their recreation and clubs and society all among the poor people," she observed in an enthusiastic letter to her sister, Alice, "yet in the same style they would like in their own circle." She noted with approval that the stance of the residents was clearly "free from 'professional doing good,' so unaffectedly sincere and so productive of good results in its classes and libraries so that it seems perfectly ideal. . . . The mission side of London is the most interesting side it has," Addams decided. She "put very much to the front & in no account [would] give up" the point that the men of Toynbee Hall chose to live there with the primary motivation of bettering themselves. Charitable benefits received by the "neighbors" followed as a matter of course.[11]

Addams returned to Cedarville in June 1888. Deeply impressed by the "element of permanency" in the London settlement style, for the first time she saw the glimmer of a solution to her troubled wanderings. "I had confidence," she wrote, looking back upon that pivotal moment, "that though life itself might contain many difficulties, the period of mere passive receptivity had come to an end, and I had at last finished with the everlasting 'preparation for life,' however ill-prepared I might be." Surely there must be other educated women like herself who needed "to learn of life from life itself." There had to be a building in a neglected neighborhood where the Chicago counterpart to the male-dominated Toynbee Hall in London could be established. Putting her substantial inheritance to its most effective use, Addams figured she could afford to spend one hundred dollars a month in additional maintenance expenses after furnishing such a place, where she and her colleagues would grapple with the issues of the crowded slums, "share the life of the downtrodden," and "drink at the great wells of human experience."[12]

Jane Addams and Ellen Gates Starr reunited on home ground and discussed the settlement plan percolating in their minds. Starr knew her dear friend's psyche best of all. After a drawn-out social evening, having to "see people" and be "up to things," Addams would come home exhausted. However, after a morning spent with indigent neighbors or taking care of children, she emerged in fine form. "Nervous people do not crave rest," Ellen observed, "but activity of a certain kind."

The women were not able to take immediate action on "the scheme," as they had privately taken to calling their plans for a settlement house. Domestic obligations, the pressures of the "family claim," took hold. Addams dutifully moved to live for six months with her older sister, Mary Linn, in rural Geneseo—northwestern Henry County about twenty miles east of the Iowa border—to help care for her sickly youngest son. Finally, at the beginning of January 1889, Addams took the train to Chicago and rented a room with Starr in a boardinghouse at 4 Washington Place near Lake Michigan so they could begin to look for additional funding and for the right real estate in the right location.[13]

Starr's connections to prominent families in Chicago society through her aunt, Eliza Ellen Starr, and through Miss Kirkland, the headmistress of the school at which she taught, were of help from the outset. Meetings with the exclusive Chicago Women's Club led to enthusiastic "at-home" receptions for smaller groups of "certain young ladies" sponsored by well-intentioned "Wellesley girls and Smith graduates," intrigued by the possibility of joining the effort in the coming winter, as if it were a kind of therapeutic retreat. "Nobody ever shows them a place & says, 'Here *do this,*'" Starr wrote to her sister. "I *know* that girls want to *do.* I have talked with enough of them, poor little things! They are sick and tired of society, simply because 'It's a man's recreation, but it's a woman's business.'"

Addams sought out the influential religious leaders of the city, among them David Swing, head of the Central Church of Chicago, Frank Gunsaulus, pastor of Plymouth Church, and C. F. Goss, minister of Moody's Church, and the directors of such social service organizations as the Society for Ethical Culture and the Charity Organization Society. These were the men who knew in which "disreputable" communities the people's needs were greatest.[14]

By the time spring arrived, Addams and Starr, with the advice and authority of the mayor, secured the building that would become their settlement—a two-story house in a sea of ramshackle wooden tenements and sweatshops between a saloon and a mortuary, "with a hooded top story of fanciful brick . . . long windows and a wide doorway," set back from the unpaved, garbage-strewn street, surrounded on three sides by a broad piazza. Real estate magnate Charles J. Hull had built the place in 1856. It was on the corner where Polk Street met Halsted Street, a thirty-two-mile-long north-south road running through the fourteenth precinct of the nineteenth ward, a few blocks west of the Chicago River. Once a pleasant pastoral suburb, the area had been gradually abandoned by the moneyed class moving south and east toward Lakeshore Drive and ceded predominantly to Italian, German, and Eastern European immigrant families. The neighborhood was a rundown slum, "a seething, savory stewpot of humanity . . . the human spectrum presenting some of its darkest shades."

Addams and Starr negotiated with the owner, Helen Culver, Mr. Hull's cousin and heir, to rent part of the first floor and the entire second floor at sixty dollars a month. They spent the summer remodeling and feverishly recruiting women to "come into residence." Within the year, Miss Culver, won over to the cause, offered to lease the building rent free for the next four years. In gratitude, Jane and Ellen formally named 335 South Halsted Street as "Hull-House . . . a rock of permanence, about which the tide of population flows and shifts and changes."[15]

The two women, joined by a housekeeper, Mary Keyser, began a series of Saturday community receptions so that wives and mothers of the neighborhood could come to know them in a friendly fashion. Carriages were sent to bring the elderly who could not walk far enough. In harmony with their intention to gain "Neighboring" trust through the women, the first official program launched within a month after the settlement opened its doors on September 18, 1889, was a "serious kindergarten, alleviated by a sand-pile [on the outside porch] and a monstrous doll's house." The kindergarten immediately enrolled "twenty-four little people," with a waiting list of seventy-five children. The classes began at nine o'clock every morning and were conducted by twenty-two-year-old Jennie Dow, a "society girl" who donated her time, laid out her own pocket money for supplies and streetcar fare to commute to and from work, and sang songs to the children, accompanying herself on a donated piano.

The second Hull-House communal activity was a popular, once-a-week, after-dinner "reading party" especially for the many neighbors of Italian descent, invited into the dining room decorated with Renaissance art reproductions and photographs to hear Ellen read aloud from George Eliot's novel, *Romola* (1863; Chicago, 1885). In the densely populated swirl of late-fifteenth-century Florence, Romola is the religiously devout, beautiful and gifted daughter of a blind scholar who has dedicated herself to live in service among the poor and plague stricken. She enters into an ill-starred marriage to a handsome and ultimately unfaithful Greek. With her increasing worldliness, she learns that the true inspiration to love others can only come from helping them. Romola abandons the church and the seductions of "patriarchal politics" to find spiritual—but lonely—fulfillment in the harshness of "the common life," resolving to "go through the heart of the city; it was the most direct road."[16]

From one daily kindergarten class for "the ragamuffins" and one reading circle, Hull-House grew steadily during the first year of its institutional life. Following the kindergarten, a nursery creche room was established where working mothers could drop off babies to be "minded" for the day. For a fee of five cents, the little ones were guaranteed "the neatness of a bath and the sweetness of a nap in a little white bed all to oneself." The four hundred-volume Home Library Association allowed children to borrow books overnight. A group of high school boys started a Shakespeare class, which grew into a club. A drawing class for children began under the tutelage of a teacher from the Art Institute of Chicago. Cooking classes were conducted three times a week in the kitchen. There was a German *klatch* and a sewing club for women on Mondays, a Thursday evening "physiology and hygiene" discussion, and a social science club for men on Saturdays. Two additional bathrooms were built with funding from Miss Culver, "and kindergartners, much to their dismay, were subject to frequent 'tubbings.'" On New Year's Day, the neighborhood elders—Addams called them "pioneers"—were invited to attend for a reminiscing session, to recall for each other, and for succeeding generations who sat and listened, the hardships they had encountered upon first arriving in America.[17]

Within two years, the weekly schedule of "Lectures, Clubs, Classes, Etc." included a Debating Club, Athletic Class, English Composition, a club for "discussion of subjects supposed to be of interest to young citizens," classes in singing, women's gymnastics, electricity—"With Experiments," clay modeling, a Plato Club "with a small membership who meet every Saturday afternoon to read philosophic essays," and a "Jolly Boys' Club." The Reading Party, guided by "Miss Jane Addams (B.A., Rockford Seminary)" moved on to *Felix Holt: The Radical,* another favorite George Eliot novel. There were college extension courses presenting "speakers of every opinion and circumstance," a public reading room, a Diet Kitchen for delivery of soup and hot meals to the homebound, an employment bureau for women's labor, and a summer school at Rockford Seminary.[18]

Aside from expansion within the main building made possible when the final renting tenant vacated opening up the entire first floor, an art gallery, a wooden-timbered coffeehouse "with rows of blue china mugs," and a gymnasium "mildly noisy with its afternoon classes of girls," were established on adjacent property. More "tributaries" would flow outward up and down Halsted Street toward the end of the decade, including a public playground with shady area and benches for mothers to sit, a Children's Building, the "Jane Club," a cooperative boarding for factory girls, and a new gymnasium, as the entire block, as well as houses across the street, were taken over.[19]

To many in the neighborhood, regardless of how much Hull-House grew, it was always referred to as "the place where Miss Addams lives." She was the constant presence. When the fifteen residents gathered every night for dinner and debriefing, she sat in a leather-upholstered chair at the head of the sixteen-foot-long polished oak table and orchestrated "the meeting-ground of the day," urging the free exchange of conversation with slight inclinations of her head, smiles, and gentle commentary.

Addams resisted the title of "president" urged upon her when Hull-House was formally incorporated by the Board of Trustees. Preferring to be called simply "Jane Addams of Hull-House," she never took a salary and was the first to remind visitors that she was anything but alone in this constant work. "Of course we are undertaking more than we ourselves can do, that is part of the idea," Addams wrote to her sister during the early months. Hull-House attracted many strong, independent-minded women with financial means. The most active of these women who helped Jane Addams build an unequaled sisterhood included Mary Rozet Smith, who usurped Ellen Gates Starr's primary place in Addams's affections and became her confidante, traveling companion, and faithful patron. Smith was frail in health, good-natured to a fault, and ethereally beautiful. The daughter of a wealthy paper manufacturer, she often donated money anonymously and wholeheartedly gave her time to the children of Hull-House, who adored her. Another outstanding colleague was Julia Lathrop, a Vassar graduate, businesswoman, activist for childrens' rights, and member of the Illinois Board of Charities. Florence Kelley, "the finest rough-and-tumble fighter for the good life for others," a Socialist *divorcée* with three children who moved to Chicago after working at the College Settlement in New York City, was a member of the inner circle. There was "hard-boiled" Mary Kenny O'Sullivan of Hannibal, Missouri, a bookbinder by trade and a labor movement organizer; and Alzina Stevens, an advocate for working women "quick to join the picket line," who went on to become active in the Juvenile Protective Association.[20]

As Hull-House became a magnet for philanthropic attention, Addams received requests for speaking engagements in Chicago and farther afield. These proselytising talks provided vivid insight into how she deliberately formulated a platform for explaining her social theory predicated upon daily practice. By way of introducing Miss Addams at the February 4, 1892, meeting of the Chicago Sunset Club "Ladies' Night" to speak on the provocative subject of 'How Would You Uplift the Masses?' the chairman, Miss Willard, noted with emphasis that "while others have been talking about what might be done for the masses, one brave-hearted woman has set about doing something." The life of the large, industrialized American cities had become chaotic and bifurcated, Addams began. The poor—"Bohemians, Italians and Poles, and Russians, and Greeks and Arabs of Chicago"—had no access to major institutions of art, culture, and health. Their main gathering locale was more likely than not the saloon. Their potential for broad social contact was as "cramped" as their dwelling places. "Cultivated people," the very ones who could bring richness of all kinds into the lives of the poor, not only monetary, were staying away: "The Settlement is a protest against such division . . . a center and impetus to keep intellectual and social activity alive." It was up to "the fast-growing number of so-called 'favored' young people" in the middle class to "add the social function to Democracy."[21]

This local speech was a rehearsal for employing much the same language on a wider stage. Addams's advocacy "gained national notice" the following summer when she delivered two lectures on consecutive days during a conference at the School of Applied Ethics in Plymouth, Massachusetts. The first, and most impressive, "A New Impulse to an Old Gospel," was titled and published in 1893 as "The Subjective Necessity for Social Settlements" in a collection called *Philanthropy and Social Progress*. Addams laid out three "reasons-for-being" for social settlements. In the process she set in motion her vision of a wholesale expansion of the ingredients of Democracy. The first reason for establishing the settlements, she said, was "to make the entire social organism democratic . . . to make social intercourse express the growing sense of the economic unity of society." Second was the pressure for dissemination, to employ the "primordial . . . impulse to share the [human] race life . . . to bring the accumulation of civilization to those portions of the race which have little." And third, she reiterated Tolstoy's theme that there was a need to move beyond an acceptance of Christianity as only "a set of ideas" and, by means of hands-on association, to "express the spirit of Christ . . . [through a] movement toward its early, humanitarian aspects."[22]

With Hull-House a focal gathering place, Florence Kelley worked to make the settlement a "launching point" for investigations into the social problems of Chicago. Addams wanted to exploit the prominence of her institution to find as many ways as possible to publicize the plight of the immigrant poor in order to stimulate municipal government to enact humanitarian reform. An opportunity came in early 1892, when Congress commissioned the Department of Labor to conduct a nationwide survey, *A Special Investigation of the Slums of the Great Cities*. Since she was politically well connected as the daughter of a Pennsylvania congressman and had a law degree, Florence Kelley was chosen to direct the effort in Chicago. During that spring and summer and into the following year, while the sprawling, gaudy cacaphonous World's Fair "White City" a few miles away frenetically advertised a different face of America, Kelley, Julia Lathrop, and Alzina Stevens conducted an exhaustive, block-to-block, door-to-door canvass of every tenement and dwelling in the Hull-House district, "determined," said Kelley, "to turn the searchlight of inquiry" upon the fifty thousand people from eighteen nationalities living within the one-third of a square mile confines of the Nineteenth Ward. Kelley's aversion to sentimentality in talking about the lives of the poor is evident in the graphic narrative of *Hull-House Maps and Papers*, published on January 1, 1895, by Thomas Y. Crowell Company in New York City. This was the first of twenty-three analytical investigations conducted by Hull-House residents during the next thirty-eight years.[23]

In the "Prefatory Note," Addams acknowledged the genesis of the landmark study, citing the mission of Canon Barnett in London as a natural precedent, as well as her admiration for another important member of the Toynbee Hall circle, British social investigator Charles Booth, (1840–1916) and his monumental, seventeen-volume *Life and Labour of the People of London*. The Liverpool-born Booth was a wealthy Victorian with a social conscience and profound sympathy for the working class. Beatrice Webb, the social reformer and Booth's cousin by marriage, praised him as a man who exemplified the "Time-Spirit" of her generation. Booth made an immense fortune in the steam-powered shipping business, demonstrating such an aptitude for facts and figures that he took issue with the lord mayor over the findings of London census returns with regard to the supposed percentage of people living below the "poverty line," a term Booth invented. He decided to fund a team of investigators under his own supervision to undertake a new survey to supply "a true description of the social landscape." His methodology involved living for several weeks at a time with working-class families. Booth's purposes coincided with those of Canon Barnett and, by extension, with the women of Hull-House.[24]

Hull-House Maps and Papers were fashioned after Charles Booth's study in two ways. They included detailed patchwork-quilt maps of each street in the district, meticulously color coded by hand to represent the demographics of every household, including income graded "from $5 a week to over $20;" and the Hull-House maps, like *Life and Labour*, were supported by a series of powerful essays recording picturesque, "insistently-probing" observations of neighborhood life, including Kelley's unsparing critique of fetid sweatshops squeezed into windowless, inner rooms without ventilation or running water, Alzina Stevens's clear-eyed assessment of the uncontrolled epidemic of emaciated children in the work force, and Agnes Holbrook's disconcerting commentary on the ubiquitous wooden "garbage boxes" filled to their brims with refuse and debris, lining backstreets out of sight behind the houses and presenting unconscionable health hazards for the neighborhood children, who played in and around them at all hours of the day and night for lack of anywhere else to go. The negative publicity surrounding the wretched garbage boxes attracted such a furor of attention after *Hull-House Maps and Papers* was published that Addams was appointed garbage inspector for the Nineteenth Ward, the only salaried job she ever held.[25]

Among the earliest settlement institutions were Andover House in Boston, the Neighborhood Guild and the College Settlement in New York, Welcome Hall in Buffalo, and the Eighth Ward Settlement House in Philadelphia. The "settlers," as the urban pioneers familiarly called themselves, had reached critical mass as a full-fledged movement, and in 1893 the members held their inaugural professional conference in Chicago during the throes of a national economic depression. While women always remained the dominant force, a "healthy minority" of the settlers were men. By 1895 there were more than twenty settlements in America; by 1910 more than four hundred would be established. On May 15–17, 1899, the annual Conference of American Settlements convened at Hull-House was so crowded that almost every session held in the lecture room was standing room only. "Heart-searching and self-examination were the keynotes of the Conference," wrote a magazine reporter. "What is our work and our purpose? Are we honestly doing what we purport to do? Is our elaboration of method and detail really in the service of the neighborhoods into which we have come?"

The participants covered a wide spectrum of issues, for example, the increasing influence of settlements upon local politics, the effectiveness of the "cooperative" way of operating, the best methods for bringing intellectual culture into the neighborhood, and how to balance group identity with the personal needs of the individual resident. In summary remarks presented at the closing reception sponsored by the Chicago Federation of Settlements on the evening of the last day of the conference, host Jane Addams spoke about the "simplicity, purity and warmth" that should always exist in daily relationships with visitors, and the stringent requirements of fairness and accuracy to be maintained as more community-based statistical studies were published.[26]

Addams's singular ability to honor "relationships of affinity" in community advocacy, as well as her insistence upon "scientific objectivity" in neighborhood investigations, made her attractive to the collegial circle of distinguished professors in the country's first Department of Sociology, founded in 1892 at the new University of Chicago. Chief among Addams's partisans in the department was the first chairman, Albion Small. The son of a minister, he attended Newton Theological Institution in Maine before receiving a Ph.D. from Johns Hopkins in 1889. He came to the university at the request of Pres. William Rainey Harper, a fellow Baptist. "Sociology," Small wrote, "is the holiest sacrament open to men . . . because it is the wholest career within the terms of human life . . . assuming the same prophetic role in social science which tradition credits to Moses in the training of his nation." Small founded the *American Journal of Sociology* and published an essay by Jane Addams in the inaugural issue of March 1896, as well as four more articles in subsequent numbers. Five of Addams's books were reviewed in the *Journal*. Small was a frequent and enthusiastic visitor to Hull-House and used *Maps and Papers* as an integral text in his classes. At least twice Small offered Addams staff positions in his burgeoning department, including a half-time stint on the graduate faculty. She turned these down and declined President Harper's plea that she annex Hull-House to the University, determined to remain as independent as possible.

Addams did consent to Small's request that she teach in the university's Extension Division. In the summer of 1899 she presented twelve lectures under the overall rubric of "Democracy and Social Ethics," dealing, she said in the introductory prospectus, "with those situations in which the new conception of life has not yet expressed itself in social changes or legal enactment, but rather in a mental attitude of maladjustment, and a sense of divergence between conscience and conduct." The lectures brought into convergence for the first time the multiple intellectual influences Jane Addams had absorbed in her active life and served as the bridge to "her first and still freshest book . . . laying down the general lines of thought she would continue to develop for the next forty years."[27]

A ddams's hurried, angular, longhand penmanship was almost indecipherable. Using a typewriter for the first time, she labored over the lectures for several hours every day, cutting the pages into strips, then using straight pins to arrange and rearrange the sequence of her thoughts. Addams admitted to Mary Rozet Smith, summering abroad with her mother toward the end of July, that she was not sure how well the introductory "General" talk went. But soon she began "to feel the swing." Forthright with her students on the first day of class, Addams reminded them that all persons in society are interdependent. "Our social morality demand[s] that we devote ourselves to the good of the whole, [therefore] we must have some idea of the experiences of the whole." And what exactly did she mean by social ethics? "We can only discover truth by a rational and democratic interest in life," Addams the pragmatist explained, "and to give truth complete social expression is the foundation of social ethics."

The subject matter of her talk was taken from the exhortatory *Essay on the Duties of Man Addressed to Workingmen* (1898) by Giuseppe Mazzini, the exiled Italian nationalist and patriot, founder of the Young Italy Society, and champion of the oppressed working poor. "Country is not a mere zone of territory," Mazzini wrote. "The true Country is the Idea to which it gives birth." Six years later, on June 22, 1905, the one hundredth anniversary of his birth, the Chicago branch of the Young Italy Society presented Hull-House with an heroic bust of Mazzini for display in the main foyer. His portrait also hung on the wall of Addams's Hull-House office to remind her that when she was a girl growing up in Cedarville, her father had idolized Mazzini.[28]

The second lecture, "City Politics," extended the imperative of social engagement, asserting that "corrupt men" in government subverted "moral progress" by bending ethical standards to suit their needs. For lecture three Addams relied upon the writings of her friend, Mary Ellen Richmond, pioneer in professional social work and author of the influential new book, *Friendly Visiting Among the Poor* (1898). "There is no relation in life which our democracy is changing more rapidly," Addams said, "than the charitable relation." She went on to say that in order to come to terms with the essential nature of charity, we must suspend all "traditional assumptions" about the superiority of rich over poor.[29]

The fourth lecture, "Educational Methods," placed pragmatic emphasis upon "the learner, the child himself, and the social value of his daily experience." Addams endorsed the foundational role of the school to help the child understand his place in the world and accept his relationship to the rest of society. Stressing the importance of formative personal experiences in shaping the way problems are faced and solved, Addams paid tribute to one of her most important mentors, John Dewey, chairman of the University of Chicago Department of Philosophy, Psychology, and Pedagogy. First visiting Hull-House in 1892, Dewey became an instant convert, describing the settlement house a decade later as the quintessential democratic community. Dewey joined the Hull-House Board of Directors and invited Addams to speak to his classes at the university. He admired her subtle charisma, the magical way her sheer "presence" informed the "spirit and method" of the settlement. "Every day I stayed there only added to my conviction that you have taken the right way," he wrote to her. Dewey's essay, "My Pedagogic Creed," first appeared in the *School Journal* (January 16, 1897), and was the central background text for Addams's fourth lecture.[30]

At this point in the course the influence of Prof. William James of Harvard became evident. The previous August, in a lecture called "Philosophical Conceptions and Practical Results," delivered at the University of California at Berkeley, James used the term "pragmatism" in public for the first time. He made a statement that seized Addams's attention: "Beliefs, in short, are really rules of action. . . . The ultimate test of what a truth means is indeed the conduct it dictates or inspires." James's pragmatism held that

an idea could only be evaluated by testing its consequences in the "laboratory of life." This thought became embodied in Addams's most recent essay, published in May 1899, "A Function of the Social Settlement." For his
part James remained one of Addams's most devout admirers, writing in response to her 1909 book, *The Spirit of Youth and the City Streets*, "I do not
know why you should always be right, but you always are. . . . The fact is,
Madam, that you are not like the rest of us, who *seek* the truth and try to
express it. You *inhabit* reality."[31]

In her fifth lecture, "Industrial Relations," Addams returned to favorite
works of Arnold Toynbee and John Ruskin and what these men had taught
her about the "clash between individual or aristocratic management, and
corporate or democratic management." Lecture six elaborated on the consequences of this conflict. Addams used a discussion of "Trades Unions" to
promote the ongoing advocacy of her Hull-House colleagues on behalf of
"the little children . . . to protect [them] from premature labor by the enactment of child labor laws."[32]

In her seventh and eighth lectures, "Filial Relations" and "Domestic
Service," Addams sympathized with the quandary of the contemporary
woman. She showed how problematic it became for the traditional family
when "the grown-up daughter attempts to respond to the newer democratic
ideal" and decides to transcend her "historic position as that of a family
possession." The family, Addams said, must accept their daughter's affinity
with "the social claim," allowing her to go forth and meet her "larger conception of duty." Within the household the unseemly traditional devalua-
tion of the female "domestic employee" must come to an end. Now, as
always, Addams kept current with the popular literature on these emerging
issues, recommending such protofeminist texts as *Woman's Share in Primitive
Culture* (1894) by Smithsonian Institution cultural historian and ethnolo-
gist Otis Tufton Mason; *Women and Economics: A Study of the Economic Relation Between Men and Women as a Factor in Social Evolution* (1898), by her
lifelong friend Charlotte Perkins Gilman (Stetson), who had been in residence at Hull-House for a year and whose work was praised by the *Nation* as
"the most significant utterance on the subject since John Stuart Mills's *The
Subjection of Women*"; and *Domestic Service* (1897), by Lucy Maynard
Salmon, a pioneer in the field of statistical compilation and Vassar College's first history teacher.[33]

In Lectures nine and ten, Addams led her students into the world of Leo

Tolstoy as an exemplar of "the supreme personal effort—one might almost say the frantic personal effort—to adjust his activities to the mass of the working people." She selected *What Is Art?* and, of course, *What Then Must We Do?* to illustrate the difference between naturalistic and historic views of life.

Addams concluded the course with two linked lectures. Number eleven provided a history of the settlement effort by examining *English Social Movements* (1891) a testament of the American profession's debt to the idealistic ferment of Toynbee Hall, by Robert A. Woods, head of the South End-Andover House in Boston; *The Ways of Settlements and Missions* (1897), by Canon Samuel Barnett; and her own seminal essays in the collection *Philanthropy and Social Progress* (1893). Lecture twelve, "Social Control," provided, Addams said, "of necessity merely an outline" of the consequences of the influence of "the modern state" upon the ethical climate of the settlement house. She made background use of Thomas Kirkup's *A History of Socialism*, and Bertrand Russell's first book, *German Social Democracy* (1896). Florence Kelley, a proudly "outspoken Socialist," translated Friedrich Engels's writings and engaged in spirited correspondence with him in the early 1890s. But Addams disapproved of Karl Marx's doctrine because of what she perceived as his aversion to compromise and his rigid ideological adherence to "cataclysmic" change rather than to the orderly societal movement she preferred.[34]

During the half dozen years between 1893 and 1899, Jane Addams published thirty-five articles. Roughly one-third of these, material from selected speeches and the notes and references for her University of Chicago Extension course were distilled into the seven sections that composed the manuscript for her first book, *Democracy and Social Ethics*. On February 26, 1902, she signed with Macmillan to bring it out in April as part of a new series called "The Citizens' Library," edited by Richard Theodore Ely, progressive thinker, historian of the American labor movement, cofounder of the American Economic Association, and professor of political economy at the University of Wisconsin. Ely first came to know Addams through Florence Kelley when he acquired *Hull-House Maps and Papers* "in the vanguard of the Social Gospel" for the Crowell Library of Economics and Politics. Although he was only six years her senior, Addams affectionately called the evangelistic Ely her "sociological grandfather." His letters during the eighteen months leading up to the publication of her book are filled with praise, bolstering her confidence, encouraging Addams to stay on message, and admonishing her to stop saying how "ashamed" she was for taking so long to get the book done. During a difficult stretch in the summer of 1901, Ely moved into Hull-House to work on the manuscript with Addams daily for three weeks.[35]

The book successfully enjoyed three big printings within the first five months, and was adapted by reading circles and women's clubs across the country. Her publishers at Macmillan pleaded for a second book as soon as possible. *Democracy and Social Ethics* "struck some of her contemporaries with the force of revelation. . . . She made it clear that the working class represented not merely a class but a culture." Presenting inherent lessons about American democracy, where it had come from and where Addams hoped it was going, the book stressed the need for purposeful understanding between people at different levels of the American social structure. Democracy in the progressive sense, she said, must be built upon reciprocity—authentic relationships between individuals—because "the individual struggle for life may widen into a struggle for the lives of all."

The book was equally about the inevitable momentum of women's changing status in a modernizing democratic society. Coming at a time when the middle-class "women's sphere" was supposed to be located primarily in the home, Addams believed that a talented single woman was perfectly capable of maintaining her "maternal" instincts while enacting her "sense of responsibility" through "civic housekeeping," daring to enter a public arena controlled by and considered exclusive to men. Addams and her friends were emboldened by the possibilities of that reforming enterprise.[36]

Jane Addams saved the crescendo of *Democracy and Social Ethics* until she reached the last half-dozen pages at the end of the final chapter. "We continually forget," she declared, "that the sphere of morals is the sphere of action, that speculation with regard to morality is but observation and must remain in the sphere of intellectual comment, that a situation does not really become moral until we are confronted with the question of what shall be done in a concrete case, and we are obliged to act upon our theory."[37]

A dangerous consequence of prosperity is that it distracts attention from the hard work of preserving social balance. Jane Addams stood at a different point on the immense spectrum of reform from Henry George, an original inhabitant of the working class, who theorized his way higher and higher through articles and books of increasing density until he thought he had reached a global panacea that was finally appreciated more for its intent than its enactment. Addams, emerging from the shelter of the middle class, rolled up her voluminous silk sleeves to practice her helping philosophy within the crowded community of the less fortunate. Both progressives struggled to define the role of government when faced with the persistent quandary of the poor in ways that have not changed since the waning of the nineteenth century. George wanted government's cumbersome and intrusive presence pulled back from daily life. Addams wanted government to enact corporate regulations that would assist disenfranchised individuals—especially mothers, child laborers, slaughterhouse and factory workers—immediately and directly. Jane Addams went on after the publication of *Democracy and Social Ethics* to serve as a member of the Chicago Board of Education, help found the National Association for the Advancement of Colored People (NAACP), become vice-president of the National American Woman Suffrage Association, organize the Woman's Peace Party, and help create the American Civil Liberties Union. During the Depression years, the journalist and literary critic Edmund Wilson visited the gray landscape of Chicago, "the darkest of great cities," and found Jane Addams still to be a dominant force, even in her seventies defiant against doctors' orders to spend no more than four hours a day at Hull-House.

On December 10, 1931, in Oslo, Sweden, Halvdan Koht of the Nobel Committee read aloud Jane Addams's citation. She was the first woman to receive the Peace Prize. "America has fostered some of the most spirited idealism on earth," Koht declared in her praise. "American social idealism expresses itself as a burning desire to devote work and life to the construction of a more equitable society." Suffering from a weak heart and unable to travel to the ceremony, Jane Addams lay in a Baltimore hospital. She donated her entire award to the Women's International League of Peace and Freedom.[38]

ISRAEL ZANGWILL

8

The Melting-Pot

The United States are the greatest idealistic experiment in government by the people that the world has ever tried. If it fails it will be the last great experiment of humanity. America is thus carrying mankind.

—Israel Zangwill, 1908

I sought in my play *The Melting-Pot* to bring home to America her manifest mission that she carried humanity and its fortunes. The twentieth century, I wrote, will be America's critical century. Will she develop on the clear lines laid down by her great founders? . . . If America breaks away from her ideals, humanity's last chance will be gone. O if America were less conscious of her greatness and more conscious of the greatness of her opportunity!

—Israel Zangwill, 1909[1]

He was an angular, slightly stooped, and familiar figure in London at the turn of the century, dashing from his rooms in the Temple along the Strand to an afternoon rehearsal at a West End theater. Long, black frock coat and flannel trousers hanging loosely from his tall and gangly frame, he was in a hurry in soft, incoherent speech as well as motion. He was pale in complexion, a pince-nez balanced on the tip of a smooth, prominent nose, a massive head adorned with abundant curls of brown hair beneath a soft, shapeless cap or fedora. "Scorning an umbrella in any weather," Israel Zangwill reminded one gossip columnist of the White Rabbit. His first novel, *Children of the Ghetto*, was successfully published before he reached the age of thirty. Zangwill was hailed by literary critics on both sides of the Atlantic as "the most striking Anglo-Jewish genius since Disraeli," and "the Jewish Dickens . . . of that aristocracy to which the greatest of writers belong . . . one of the mightiest intellects of modern times." This son of impoverished East End immigrants went on to write a play that gave emotional expression to his lifelong dream of America.[2]

He was born a Cockney, "within the sound of the Bow Bells" at Ebenezer Square in the Whitechapel District on January 21, 1864, the second of five children of a Polish mother, Ellen Hannah Marks, and a Latvian father, Moses Zangwill, a traveling peddler and old-clothes trader, who never earned more than a pound a week. The family was pious and poor. For lack of a coal fire, the house was often cold, and the children had "a slice of bread each and the wish-wash of a thrice-brewed pennyworth of tea as their morning meal, and there was no prospect of dinner." Israel was a serious youth with little interest in games and play. At the Jews' Free School, he showed early literary promise. He went on to a triple-honors degree in French, English, and Mental and Moral Science from the University of London, studying by night and teaching by day. He resigned or was dismissed from his teaching post and began earning a scant living selling poetry, opinion columns, and short stories to Jewish periodicals and humor magazines, publishing under the pseudonym of "Robin Goodfellow." Zangwill also tried his hand at a detective mystery, some playlets, and a whimsical novella called *Motso Kleis* ("Matzoh Balls"), which—to his surprise and delight—sold four hundred copies.[3]

All this productivity drew Zangwell into the center of an "intellectual force"—"*not* the celebrities," he pointed out, "but the men of *brains*," an affinity group meeting at the home of the Romanian-born, Talmudic scholar Solomon Schechter. Lucien Wolf, chief editorial writer and later editor of the *Jewish World*; historian Joseph Jacobs; artist Solomon J. Solomon; Asher Myers, editor of the influential *Jewish Chronicle*; medievalist and founder of the *Jewish Quarterly Review* Israel Abrahams; Zangwill's brother, Louis, a fledgling novelist; and others gathered fortnightly, sharing a passion to understand the shifting nature of Jewish identity in their emancipated society. The debates focused upon ways to reconcile the traditional demands of the faith with the pressures of assimilation in modern Britain. Calling themselves informally "the Mosaics" or "the Nomads," the men often strayed from the predetermined discussion of the evening. Mrs. Schechter once walked into the parlor and remarked that they were "wandering from the subject, like a lot of wandering Jews." Zangwill exclaimed,

"What an excellent name! Let's call ourselves that." "The Wanderers of Kilburn" evolved by 1891 into an elite club called The Order of Ancient Maccabeans, in turn leading to the formation of the Jewish Historical Society, which laid the foundation for the culture of Anglo-Jewry.[4]

Although Zangwill's recollection of Mrs. Schechter's comment might seem frivolous, the Wandering Jew—referring to the dispersion of the Jewish people condemned to roam the earth in alienation until Judgment Day as punishment for the "unpardonable sin" of scorning Christ—was an emotionally charged, ambivalent theme in his work. In an essay called "The Position of Judaism," published in the April 1895 issue of the *North American Review* three years before his first visit to New York City, Zangwill wrote: "The fall of the Ghettos has left Israel dazed in the sunlight of the wider world without, his *gaberdine* half off and half on. If he throws it off, will he throw off his distinctiveness and fade into the common run of men? If he keeps it on, can he keep his place in the new human brotherhood?" The *gaberdine* was a long, coarse cloak, frock, or "mean dress" traditionally worn by Jews during the Middle Ages at a time when they were forbidden to engage in handicrafts or manual labor. Its name derived from the Old French *galvardine* to the Middle High German *wallevart*, meaning "pilgrimage." Emancipation—the end of professional restrictions, Ghetto seclusion, and high walls—supposedly brought with it integration of the Jew into the mainstream of European "civic Christendom," and offered the historical moment to shed his garment. Yet if the Jew were to take the path toward assimilation or, as Zangwill called it, the "process of interfusion" in his parent country, would he continue safely protected or open himself up "Quixotically" to the "biting blast" of anti-Semitism? "For the Jew belongs to a race as well as to a religion," Zangwill went on, "and may wish to remain in either, or both, or neither." From the time he was a teacher-in-training at the Jews' Free School, Zangwill always carried a mezuzah with him. The commandment in Deuteronomy 6:4–9 requires that this small case containing a tiny roll of parchment with the words of the Shema prayer inscribed by hand be placed on "the doorposts of thy house and upon thy gate." Even to his beloved wife, Edith, Zangwill never explained the reason why he kept the mezuza on his person. Perhaps it was meant as a reminder that the Jew never enjoyed a permanent "home" except within himself.[5]

Israel Zangwill's struggle with the quandary of Jewish placelessness led him to maintain an affectionate and yearning eye on America. By the time the Ancient Maccabeans Club was founded, Zangwill had reached an echelon of literary prominence. From this position, he felt compelled to continue to write and talk about "the Jewish problem." He often did so using the American background and that nation's coexistence with Jews as far back, he reminded readers on several occasions, as the merchants who financed Columbus's voyage and the five Jews who accompanied the great explorer to the new land. "It is perhaps worth while remarking," he told an early lecture audience, "that the first place in [civilized] North America to which Jews came was New York."

Zangwill took delight in publicly reciting melancholy lines from a classic American favorite, Henry Wadsworth Longfellow's "The Jewish Cemetery at Newport," composed on the evening of July 9, 1852, after the poet had spent the morning on a solitary visit to the secluded and "shady nook at the corner of two dusty, frequented streets, with an iron fence and a granite gateway." Longfellow's walk among the low marble "sepulchral stones, so old and brown," spurred a meditation on the long-ago voyage "o'er the sea—that desert desolate—[of] These Ishmaels and Hagars of mankind," in hopes, Zangwill interpolated, of finding hospitable refuge in "the New Jerusalem . . . which created the prosperous New York of to-day." Zangwill took equal pleasure in the ringing verses of "the eminent American poetess, Emma Lazarus . . . appealing to [him] by name." He regaled fellow Maccabeans at an evening dinner celebration, reciting her resounding Chanukah lyric, "The Feast of Light," "Clash, *Israel*, the cymbal, touch the lyre, / Blow the brass trumpet and the harsh-tongued horn; / Chant hymns of victory till the heart take fire."[6]

On a visit to London in September 1890, Judge Mayer Sulzberger of Philadelphia asked Lucien Wolf to arrange a visit with Israel Zangwill in order to make the noted author a proposition. Sulzberger was an antiquarian book and manuscript collector, a scholar, and magazine editor who had collaborated on a translation of Maimonides, served as a member of the governing board of the Young Men's Hebrew Association, and was chairman of the publication committee of the new Jewish Publication Society

of America (JPS). The society, disturbed by the paucity of substantive por-
trayals of Jews in contemporary American fiction, was enamored of Zangwill's work. Sulzberger was prepared to offer Zangwill an advance of two
hundred pounds as a commission to create "a reputable Jewish-oriented
novel" to be published by the JPS in America. After some initial disputes
over artistic freedom, the society assured Zangwill he would enjoy carte
blanche to write exactly what he wanted.[7]

Within two years the result was *Children of the Ghetto*, a brilliant inter-
generational panorama of Jewish life in nineteenth-century London,
chronicling the exhausting trade of the "old clo's man" plying his wares,
peering inside the cramped workrooms of the "sweaters," capturing the reassuring domestic rituals of the Sabbath, the match-making machinations
of a closely knit family aspiring to a better life for their daughter, and the
rabbi's droll ruminations at home, at bar mitzvahs and weddings, and at
Shul. In lyrical language and dialogue so natural it read as if overheard,
Zangwill guided the uninitiated reader with abiding compassion for his
characters, as young and old tried to find common ground within their heritage, conveyed by the clear mirror the author held up to his past with un-
embarassed nostalgia.

Children of the Ghetto was the first Anglo-Jewish best seller. Its triumphant publication was the stimulus for a three-decade correspondence
between Mayer Sulzberger and Israel Zangwill that chronicled their contentious friendship—the only kind of friendship the writer could sustain.
Zangwill reveled in Sulzberger's "causticity" as "merely criticism." He wrote
to the judge: "I hate to differ with you, because I know I am probably wrong.
My only consolation is that if I agreed with you about everything, one of us
would be superfluous in this world." In the fall of 1892, as the novel gained
ascendancy, Sulzberger turned to Zangwill for advice on recommending a
qualified Jewish scholar in London suitable for a rabbinical position at the
prestigious Temple Rodeph Shalom in Philadelphia. The judge exploited
the discussion of the merits and liabilities of Zangwill's colleague Israel
Abrahams to hint, somewhat in jest, that Zangwill himself might be well-
disposed to make the crossing. Sulzberger hoped that at some point "America may be attractive enough to withdraw some of the good fellows from
England. . . . We have a superfluity of eloquence on this side," he admitted,
"but very little of much talent, knowledge, and character. . . ." On more

than one occasion after he became the first president of the American Jewish Committee in 1906, Sulzberger extended a hand across the sea to his friend, saying he would "hail with pleasure your coming hither."[8]

On the foggy afternoon of November 21, 1895, Theodore Herzl, newly arrived from Paris and feeling chilled and "a bit low in spirits," finally located Israel Zangwill's home after a ride through the narrow streets of Kilburn in northwest London. "Like one dropped from the skies," he knocked on the door of Zangwill's book-lined study, where he found the writer sitting at a huge, disordered writing table with his back to a roaring fire. Herzl carried a letter of introduction from their mutual friend, Hungarian-born writer and psychiatrist Max Nordau, who had chosen Zangwill as the most effective access point to the London Jewish intelligentsia. Herzl came across the Channel for one reason: to define and promote the mission of the nascent Zionist movement, gaining adherents from among the ranks of "those Jews who are strong and free of spirit" for the "universal idea" to resettle in the ancestral Promised Land, "securing for the Jewish people a publicly-recognized home in Palestine . . . and bring an end to Exile."[9]

"I am Theodore Herzl. Help me to build the Jewish State," he said simply, to open the conversation. As the Paris correspondent for the *Neue Freie Presse* of Vienna, Herzl encountered anti-Semitism in its most overt form while covering the military trial of Alfred Dreyfus, a Jewish captain in the French army accused of spying for Germany. Herzl witnessed Dreyfus's public degradation, saw him stripped of his epaulettes on the parade ground, and heard the feverish cries of the crowd calling for "Death to the Jews." He resolved from that transformative moment to devote the rest of his life—Herzl died at age forty-four in 1904—to "find a soil of our own . . . a secure haven, under public law."[10]

Three days after the meeting, Zangwill introduced Herzl with propriety and pride at a Maccabean dinner, giving him the platform he sought to "present to the world the first exposition of his scheme" for "The Jewish State." The pivotal speech was acquired and published by Zangwill's friend Asher Myers in the *Jewish Chronicle* on January 17, and again one month later by M. Breitenstein and Company in Vienna as the booklet "Der Judenstaat," Herzl's introductory manifesto. "The Jewish question is a national question," he wrote, "and to solve it we must first of all establish it as an international political problem to be discussed and settled by the civilized nations of the world in council." Toward that end Herzl called together the First Zionist Congress at Basel in the summer of 1897. More than two hundred delegates and three hundred guests and news correspondents gathered in the city's concert hall. Zangwill was among those in the audience seated in cane chairs facing the green baize dais eager to hear the proposal of the "Jewish dreamer . . . the very modern Moses . . . a tall, impressive, black-bearded figure with a head like an old Assyrian king's."[11]

Theodore Herzl was a timely catalyst. Zangwill had been hungering for a more active and engaged role in the public arena, a constructive medium "beyond [his] pen-point" toward which to direct his surplus energy. Taken in by Herzl's evangelizing personality, Zangwill readily draped the mantle of politics across his own narrow shoulders. Even more than Herzl's statesmanlike sensibility in counterpoint to the "impassioned rhetoricians" of the Zionist Congress—Zangwill realized as he listened to the president conclude his speech on August 29, 1897, "amid the thunder of hands and feet and the flutter of handkerchiefs"—he identified with Herzl's "unbending dignity." Here, Zangwill understood with relief, was a Jew, very much like himself, "who did not crawl."[12]

Speaking that day of "a cause too great for the ambition and wilfulness of a single person," Herzl convinced Zangwill of the romantic inevitability of Zionism. At the same time Zangwill, the inveterate, introspective contrarian, was not as certain that the only road to Zion led explicitly to Palestine as the unifying place for Jews. His compass did not automatically point eastward. Zangwill made a crucial early distinction regarding the object of Zionism as "not . . . to ingather Israel." This qualification resonated with the emphatic declaration by Columbia University professor and director of the Oriental Division at the New York Public Library, Richard James Horatio Gottheil, who served as the first president of the American Zionist Federation. Speaking at its inaugural convention in New York City in July 1898, Gottheil also insisted that Zionism "does not mean that all Jews must return to Palestine. . . . What does Zionism offer the not ingathered?" he asked rhetorically. ". . . It wishes to give back to the Jew that confidence in himself, that belief in his own powers which only perfect freedom can give."[13]

Amerika, du hast es besser
Als unser Kontinent, das alte.

[America, you are better off
Than our continent, the old one.]

The glowing promise of Johann Wolfgang von Goethe's 1827 poem "Amerika" held great allure for the earliest wave of German Jews who came westward in the 1830s and 1840s, and just as much appeal for the Eastern European Jews who flooded these shores from the early 1880s and onward for four decades.

Israel Zangwill was overjoyed by his maiden voyage to America. Crossing the Atlantic in the summer of 1898 for the first time he "came face to face with [his] own century." He thrilled at the sight of *Liberty Enlightening the World* when she loomed into view in Upper New York Bay. He granted many interviews, expounding willingly on subjects ranging from his affinity with Tolstoy, whose seventieth birthday was being celebrated on September 8—"The true man of letters must always be a lay priest," to the Chosen People—"The God Abraham chose was the God of Justice," to impressions of American women in Baltimore—"They are not stay-at-homes." In Philadelphia, the City of Brotherly Love, Zangwill chatted with Judge Sulzberger—whom he called "the Nathan the Wise of American Judaism"—in his magnificent private library and visited the legendary Wanamaker's, unlike any department store he had ever seen. The popular writer of homespun memoirs, William Dean Howells's protégé Hamlin Garland, who hosted Zangwill in Chicago and later visited him in London, said that "no recent visitor so stirred our literary circles." Zangwill's American lecture tour, Garland later recalled, took over the daily headlines and "made the Spanish war a stale drama for the time."[14]

The most important public appearance on Zangwill's calendar was a meeting of the prestigious Judaeans Club in New York on October 24, 1898, to which he was invited as the guest of honor. Zangwill began his warmly received talk, "The New Jew," with a humorous disclaimer. "There are those who hold that it is always a mistake for a literary man to show himself in the flesh," he said. "The flesh is generally disappointing. An author should be a disembodied spirit." This was Zangwill's moment to voice his hopes for "American Progress," and for the new American Jew who would open up "the isolated diffusion" of his religion in "a land, raw and new, whose cultured spirits pant for historic associations." American Jews were being given the chance—even more, the responsibility—to return the ideal of Israel to its rightful location at "the centre of the world-stage." If they accepted the reality that there was "a nobler era to come," American Jews were positioned to commence a cultural "Renaissance . . . to set the jewel upon the forehead of the future." Within the coming year, Zangwill's inspiration would take him so far as to endorse a powerful force for religious regeneration, "Washington is our Zion."[15]

Among the American poets Israel Zangwill enjoyed reading, another lifelong favorite was Walt Whitman, a writer who, like Zangwill, was "very large" and "contained multitudes." The epigraph "Do I contradict myself? Very well then I contradict myself," taken from "Song of Myself," appeared slightly misquoted as "Do I really contradict myself?" on the fly-leaf of one of Zangwill's last books, published in 1925, the year before his death. In 1903 his only volume of poetry, Blind Children, was published, an idiosyncratic compendium of juvenilia, spiritual hymns, romantic lyrics, and translations of prayers giving voice to his love of paradox. In "the swing and rush of verse" Zangwill found the right genre to come to terms with his affinity for both sides of an argument the deeper he delved into his political and artistic selves. "Hear O Israel, Jehovah, the Lord our God is one," he wrote in the poem "Israel," confessing to the fissures in his attitude toward Zionism, "But we, Jehovah His people, are dual and so undone." In another poem, bluntly titled "A Working Philosophy," he encouraged him-self in Shakespearian echoes to "Speak out the word that to thy soul seems right, / Strike out thy path by individual light," concluding that " 'tis con-tradictory rays that give the white."

There were also love poems sprinkled throughout Blind Children, some melancholy laments, but more often celebratory, along the lines of "life re-born at radiant dawn," or "For thee, my darling, I will spread / Within my court a golden bed." These were inspired by Zangwill's fiancée of three years, the twenty-eight-year-old, brown-haired, brown-eyed "gentle, gra-cious, lovely, ethereal-looking"—and non-Jewish—Edith Ayrton. An ac-complished fiction writer and graduate of Bedford College, she was the daughter of Prof. W. E. Ayrton, an electrical engineer and physicist, and Matilda Chaplin, a medical doctor, who died when Edith was eight years old. The professor's second wife, Phoebe (Hertha) Marks, was Jewish and a great admirer of Zangwill's short stories. The couple were married in a civil ceremony in a London registry office on November 26, 1903. The bride did not wear white, preferring a terra-cotta–tinted embroidered dress with matching broad-brimmed hat. Most of Zangwill's Jewish colleagues, silently disapproving of his intermarriage, were absent from the Ayrton family reception following the brief service.[16]

Edith eventually became involved, along with her stepmother, in Jewish philanthropy, and after her marriage she was active in the pacifist movement and campaigned ardently for womens' suffrage. She was indefatigable in support of her husband's career, worried about Israel's tendency to overwork to the point of exhaustion, and constantly concerned about his uneven health and disposition. Edith kept meticulous records of box-office receipts of his plays and answered the door when would-be dramatists and out-of-work actors appeared at the threshold of their country home at Far End, by the sea in Sussex. She was an attentive and doting mother to the three Zangwill children—Ayrton, Margaret, and Oliver—hiring and then dismissing nannies on a moment's notice when the little ones showed the slightest complaint, and she kept a humorous journal of their endearing turns of phrase as they grew up.[17]

Israel Zangwill was dismissive of the implicit and explicit criticism he received for marrying outside the faith. The rabbis were "too rigid and sectarian. It remains with them to broaden out their principles. . . . My wife has the same Jewish ideals as those which you credit me," he told an interviewer in later years, noting acerbically that "Judaism is spiritual and you appear to make it racial." Edith Zangwill remarked to a family friend after her husband's death that Israel often assured her "my religious outlook was nearer to his own than any Jewess he had ever met. . . . I am a Jewess by conviction."[18]

Triggered by the assassination of Czar Alexander II on March 1, 1881, reckless and violent attacks on Jews in Russia, called pogroms, extended through the subsequent accessions of Alexander III and his son, Nicholas II, both vowing to maintain complete autocracy. Agents of the Minister of the Interior Vlacheslav Plehve encouraged anti-Semitic agitation among the officials of the Bessarabian provincial administration led by Piotr Krushevan, who circulated a libel-laden newspaper leading to the Easter murder of forty-nine Jews and the looting of hundreds of houses and businesses at Kishinev on April 6–7, 1903. With the complicity of the town police chief, Vladimir Levendal, whose garrison of officers stood by and did not intervene, the mob ran rampant through the Jewish quarter. Immortalized the following year by the Odessa author Hayyim Nahman Bialik in his poem, "City of Slaughter," the Kishinev pogrom became a symbol of Jewish oppression in Russia.

Two years later, on October 19–20, 1905, an even worse orgy of monarchist violence broke out again at Kishinev and in waves throughout czarist Russia. By the end of the first decade of the twentieth century, more than one-third of the Jews of Eastern Europe were uprooted by this incessant, terrifying persecution. The remaining two-thirds would be baptized or starve to death. By 1920 two million wanderers from the Russian Pale of Settlement as well as from Austria, Romania, and Galicia, comprising half of the entire world's Jewish population, would gather in the cities of *di goldene medine*—the Golden Land, America.

"Kishinev will make Zionists of everybody," Zangwill told Mayer Sulzberger before heading to Basel for the Sixth Zionist Congress in the summer of 1903. The pogroms added a sense of dire urgency to the proceedings. The chief question of the moment was *Wohin?* ("Whither?") Where, Zangwill asked, would the Jews "illuminate their beacon of fire upon Zion's hill?" What could be done to find a refuge to accommodate the Russian Jews in perennial danger? English colonial secretary Joseph Chamberlain met with Theodore Herzl and offered a large section of Kenya to serve as a temporary self-governing Jewish settlement. Zangwill joined forces with Herzl to bring the "Uganda Plan" before the Congress delegates. "All my weight would be thrown on the State," Zangwill said, imagining that this broader vision beyond "classical" Zionism might reach fruition. "I would allow religion to have a great place, but not the controlling place. . . . Unless it be a modern state with the highest play for individuality, it seems silly to recreate it." After a fractious debate—"Uganda is not Palestine and it will never be Palestine"—a commission was authorized to examine the semitropical eastern African territory, at five thousand square miles nearly the size of Wales, thirty hours by train from the seaport of Mombasa.[19]

Herzl died suddenly of exhaustion the following year in Vienna. Zangwill viewed the passing of his friend as a signal to start "the second stage" of Zionism. He was convinced that neither the Turkish government, to which

Palestine belonged, nor the Arabs, would cede their ancient homeland or any area in that neighborhood of the world. Plucking up the baton of his fallen comrade, Zangwill built a head of steam propelling him into the 1905 Seventh Zionist Congress, resolving that "Palestine at one jump is too great an effort for us. I should be inclined to turn elsewhere. . . . Any territory which was Jewish, under a Jewish flag, would save the Jew's body and the Jew's soul." Despite his ardent appeal, the delegates rejected the Uganda Plan. In an impulsive burst on a hot and stormy August day, Zangwill told the assembly it was consequently incumbent upon him to "create a second organization *ad hoc*" to explore non-Palestinian alternatives for mass Jewish settlement. "The Jewish Territorial Organization takes as a body no position towards Zionism," he said. "No land whatever is excluded from our operations." He walked out of the meeting and returned to London. His first announcement as president from the organization's headquarters was that "all existing machinery for dealing with the great stream of Jewish emigration is obsolete and inadequate."[20]

As part of fund-raising efforts for the new organization, Zangwill engaged in a prolonged correspondence with Jacob H. Schiff, the aristocratic German-Jewish banker and philanthropist. Since 1885 Schiff had been chairman of the investment firm Kuhn, Loeb & Company in New York, second in size to the House of Morgan at the turn of the century. The men had met at the Judaeans Club during Zangwill's American visit and had begun a dialogue based upon mutual, if occasionally grudging, respect. Schiff shared Zangwill's skepticism about the practicality of a homeland in Palestine as well as his concern for the fate of the oppressed "co-religionist" *yidden* in Russia, and he was monitoring the immigration crisis in America. From recent meetings with immigration authorities, Schiff knew there was an imminent threat of legislative imposition of quotas because eastern ports were becoming overcrowded. Perhaps, Schiff suggested to Zangwill in the fall of 1906, the Russian Jews should be steered away from the swamped North Atlantic seaports and "toward the Gulf ports, whence they can be readily distributed over the interior of the country . . . the American hinterland. . . . Surely the carrying out of this project will furnish the relief which is imperatively needed." The shift exemplified Schiff's "effective compassion" and his desire to integrate Jewry into America as a whole, to bring "the great Jewish problem to a nearer solution." He told Zangwill he was willing to put down a half million dollars toward "The Galveston Plan" if matching amounts were raised by the Jewish Territorial Organization in England, France, and Germany. In such case Schiff, who demanded anonymity in his generosity, would give the organization "all the glory of initiating this immigration in Europe." Zangwill thought that if the plan took hold in Galveston, it could be replicated in self-governing enclaves—"colonizations" in the southern states, Nevada, or Southern California.

It was a noble dream, but resistance within the executive council of the Jewish Territorial Organization, logistical complexities of marshaling Russian émigrés and convincing them to separate from other *landsmen*, the inability of contentious European relief committees and the unwillingness of competing steamship companies to direct the flow of masses away from New York City, sporadic deportations by uninformed government inspectors, and an economic depression in the States—all conspired toward failure. Between 1907 and 1913, fewer than ten thousand Jewish immigrants made Galveston, Texas, their home, while Iowa and Missouri took in perhaps one thousand Jews.[21]

Israel Zangwill's hopeful gaze toward America intensified even when the Galveston Plan dissipated. He would not concede that the plan never lived up to its promise. He was proud of the ten thousand Jews who resettled: "*The Melting-Pot* sprang directly from the author's concrete experience as president of the Emigration Regulation Department of the Jewish Territorial Organization . . . founded shortly after the great massacres of the Jews in Russia," Zangwill recalled in January 1914 in a bout of revisionist history. In fact the seeds for the play were sown well before the creation of the Jewish Territorial Organization. When fellow Kilborn Wanderer Solomon Schechter was lured away by Mayer Sulzberger in April 1902 to lead the Jewish Theological Seminary in New York, Zangwill sent him off with a valedictory blessing to America, "a country which—*en attendant* the Seminary of Jerusalem—is probably destined, through the fusion of Western and Russian Jewry, to set the standard of Judaism for the modern diaspora." As the pace of immigration reached an historic high during the first six months of 1907, a period when six hundred thousand more people passed through the gates of America than went out, Zangwill's rhetoric swelled in tandem: "America is far and away the best land for the Jewish emigrant" drawn by the light of "a lamp cheering all humanity with the radiance of a nobler world."[22]

In early spring 1908, Zangwill told his American producer, George Crouse Tyler, cofounder with Theodore Liebler Jr. of Liebler and Company in New York, that he was working on the "germ" of an idea for a play dominated by "a Jewish hero" that would be "tremendous in significance." The company were great Zangwill fans, having already mounted several of his shows on Broadway, including a dramatization of *Children of the Ghetto* at the Herald Square Theatre in the fall of 1899, followed by *Merely Mary Ann* at the Garden (1903) and *The Jinny* at the Criterion (1905).[23]

On April 18 Zangwill wrote an agitated letter to Tyler, who was in Marseilles about to head northward on his annual European foray to call upon playwrights and gather promising new scripts to bring home. "I think of calling the play simply 'America,'" Zangwill said, "and making it symbolic of the great part America is called on to play in the history of mankind, if she will remain true to her root principles of liberty, equality and fraternity. . . . 'America,'" Zangwill continued, "as seen by all those yearning eyes of the oppressed of all races. . . . 'America,' as the promised land in which the best human ideals shall ultimately find solution." By the time Tyler reached Zangwill's home at Far End in July, three months later, the title of the play had been changed to *The Crucible*, whereupon the wary producer reacted by telling the playwright that he "[had] a little doubt as to whether the public would understand this word." In August, within half an hour after his ship docked in New York, Tyler handed the fresh, "precious manuscript" to his friend, the actor Walker Whiteside, who had driven down at top speed from his home in Hastings-on-Hudson and was waiting at the pier. The script was titled *The Melting-Pot*.[24]

Twenty years had passed since the dashing, nineteen-year-old hailing from Logansport, Indiana, took Broadway by storm with a sensational debut as "a youthful phenomenon . . . the boy Hamlet." From that time Walker Whiteside had worked and traveled steadily as an actor, producer, and director, founding his own repertory company in the Midwest and "establishing a route stretching from Western Pennsylvania into Kansas, and extending north from Michigan into Wisconsin." From his taproots in Shakespeare, Whiteside always favored the substantial roles he found in classical literature. He read *The Melting-Pot* overnight, astonished by the emotional power of the lead character, David Quixano, a young, Jewish, immigrant violinist living in a New York City tenement and trying to exorcise the memories of his turbulent past. Whiteside insisted upon meeting the author without delay. Tyler underwrote Whiteside's spontaneous steamer trip and pilgrimage to England. Zangwill greeted him with the words, "You Americans rush everything so tremendously." Playwright and actor spent a week huddled over the script, honing some finer points in the third act, then presented an impromptu reading in a "dingy" rented hall in Littlehampton, charging one shilling admission. The audience was small but appreciative.

Casting in New York soon followed, and rehearsals began there in early September under Zangwill's close supervision in anticipation of the gala American premiere to be hosted by Pres. Theodore Roosevelt on the night of October 5 at the Columbia Theatre in Washington, D.C.[25]

The Melting-Pot begins in the shabby living room of the immigrant Quixano household, a small home "in the Richmond or non-Jewish borough of New York." The "Stars and Stripes" are pinned over the street door, the bookshelves sag with "large mouldering Hebrew" texts, Nietzsche next to the Bible. David Quixano enters on a wintry afternoon singing, "My Country, 'Tis of Thee." He makes a living teaching music at a settlement house by day, returning by evening to compose his magnum opus, a "New World" symphony in tribute to his adopted land. David hopes it will be performed by a full orchestra under the direction of the avuncular German conductor Herr Pappelmeister. David's beloved Uncle Mendel gives piano lessons at home and tries to maintain a semblance of equilibrium, while lonely Grandmother Quixano sits in a shabby armchair by the fireplace and reminisces in Yiddish about the Old World. The sharp-tongued maid, Kathleen, bustling about in preparation for the Sabbath, provides comic relief, in comments under her breath in a broad Irish brogue, about "the haythen Jews" and the "ould lady's" mystifying kosher rules and regulations.

Into this insular setting glides the beautiful Vera, a different sort of Russian immigrant. She is Christian and "exotic," and performs social work at the settlement, where she has met David and become attracted to him. Vera's father and stepmother, Baron and Baroness Revendal, arrive on a surprise visit from Russia, escorted by the pretentious Quincy Davenport, a superficial country-club type in pursuit of Vera's hand. In a visceral confrontation with David over Vera's affections, the baron—rudely expostulating on "the Jewish problem" during an ugly, anti-Semitic rant—reveals a terrible secret. He had been in command of the police in Kishinev, or "Kishineff," as it is spelled in the play, during the bloody Easter pogrom.

Can David overcome the heartrending shock that Vera's father was responsible for the gruesome butchering of his entire family in the Russian Pale? Can the romance between David and Vera be consummated under these agonizing circumstances? The star-crossed couple rendezvous on the roof garden of the settlement house at sunset during the July fourth premiere of David's symphony. At the crescendo, David and Vera, Jew and Gentile, embrace, while the torch of the Statue of Liberty glows in the distance like a guiding star over the darkening water. They agree that "only in America" would a paradox such as their love find resolution. Coming full circle, the curtain comes down to the strains of "My Country, 'Tis of Thee," as David cries, "Yes, East and West, and North and South, the palm and the pine, the pole and the equator, the crescent and the cross, how the great Alchemist melts and fuses them with his purging flame! Here shall they all unite to build the Republic of Man and the Kingdom of God. . . . Peace, peace to all ye unborn millions, fated to fill this giant continent."[26]

The events of The Melting-Pot, melodramatic verging upon operatic, are transparent representations of the issues that had been swirling in Zangwill's imagination for a decade and more. Zangwill underscored the propelling metaphor of the play—its "concrete symbolism"—while continuing to make textual adjustments in New York during the weeks before the Washington opening. David's outburst comes in Act 1 when he accuses Vera of not understanding the cause of his transcendent artistic inspiration: "Not understand!" he rages, "You, the Spirit of the Settlement! Not understand that America is God's Crucible, the great Melting-Pot where all the races of Europe are melting and re-forming! Here you stand, good folk, think I, when I see them at Ellis Island, here you stand." In the script, Zangwill firmly inserted the capitalized words "The Great Melting-Pot" in deep black ink, and also strengthened the second incidence of the word "melting," changing it to "fusing" in black ink, then revising it back again while reviewing page proofs for the published version in 1909. To Zangwill, the beauty of American assimilation was that people of diverse origins shared an attachment to the values of a free society, no matter what those origins might have been. Jews did not cease to be Jews when they became "citizens of a secular Republic. . . . America does not attempt to fuse by force the various peoples that seek her shores," he said several years later. The wise Reb Shmuel had long ago maintained in *Children of the Ghetto* that "the Jew cannot put off his Judaism. His unborn soul undertook the yoke of the Torah at Sinai." The "New Jew" David Quixano perpetuates this conviction. He can respect the old ways while looking to the amalgam of the future. Zangwill believed that American society was sympathetically "founded in the Mosaic tradition by the Pilgrim Fathers . . . and Puritans are practically Jews. The social life in New England was of the Hebraic pattern." Modern America, he said, was "diversified beyond all historic experience" to the point where "all race-differences and vendettas [would] melt." Anyone—not only the Jew, but of course the Jew was Zangwill's starting point—could preserve his identity in America at the same time as he became integral to the culture as a whole, unashamed to live singularly—one among many.[27]

Every seat in the house was filled on opening night. President and Mrs. Roosevelt, and his secretary and close adviser William Loeb and his family, invited Edith Zangwill to share their box. The first two acts passed in respectful silence. At the conclusion of the third act, with the turbulent, "powerful climax" of the dispute between David and the baron, the entire audience, cheering, leapt to their feet—which pleased Walker Whiteside, since he had prevailed upon Zangwill during readings and rehearsals in the summer and fall to build up David's recollections of the harrowing Kishinev tragedy. During the ovation the president leaned over, whispered into Edith's ear, and "positively raved . . . 'I'm not a Bernard Shaw or Ibsen man, Mrs. Zangwill. No—*this* is the stuff.'" Cries for "Zangwill!" rang out until the author was brought out on stage in front of the curtain for a final bow with the cast. Roosevelt shouted to him, "That's a *great* play, Mr. Zangwill, a great play!" Zangwill asked the president if he would allow the first published edition to be dedicated to him, and Roosevelt consented. "To Theodore Roosevelt," read the dedication page, "in respectful recognition of his strenuous struggle against the forces that threaten to shipwreck the great republic which carries mankind and its fortunes."[28]

The *Melting-Pot* was at capacity for the rest of the week then moved on to Baltimore, where its run at the Academy Theater was also sold out. An open-ended stay followed at the Chicago Grand Opera House, where, according to George Tyler's reports to Mrs. Zangwill, the "'pot' simmered nicely, [bringing in] from six to nearly eleven thousand dollars a week." Throughout the spring of 1909, *The Melting-Pot* toured the Midwest before opening at Broadway's Comedy Theatre on September 6, where it ran for 136 performances into the following spring—and then was off to Providence, Boston, Buffalo, and other venues until the middle of 1911. Walker Whiteside kept his role of David the entire time. After a hiatus of three years, the play opened in London, once again starring Whiteside. On May 30, 1915, the movie was released at New York's Hippodrome, as the first silent feature of the Cort Film Corporation, with Whiteside making his screen debut.[29]

The play was an unqualified success at the box office, but the immediate response was divided. Jewish religious leaders and reviewers were uneasy about what they saw as the danger of Zangwill's "assimilationist" message. Dr. Judah Magnes, associate rabbi at Temple Emanu-El in New York, preached that "the symphony of America" required that the various nationalities "keep their individual and characteristic note." Baltimore journalist and social worker Louis Levin cautioned that Zangwill's "new type of man" did not have to "throw upon the scrap heap" everything he stood for in the past.[30]

The mainstream American critical establishment was enraptured. To Burns Mantle, drama critic of the *Chicago Tribune*, the play was "something of a master work." Percy Hammond of the *New York Tribune* said it was "sincere, from the heart, and thrills with conviction." Augustus Thomas, the respected dramatist who became president of the National Institute of Arts and Letters, wrote that "Mr. Zangwill [possessed] wide human sympathy, charity and compassion." Holbrook Jackson, editor of *New Age* magazine, suggested that "not since Walt Whitman's *Leaves of Grass* have we had so inspiring a picture of America."[31]

The English critics lambasted *The Melting-Pot* as "Nonsense . . . Romantic claptrap" in 1914. Zangwill returned fire by calling them "sluggish and sensual" in the "Afterword" to the London edition. He reserved the last sentences of gratitude for the patriots enlightened enough to welcome his play as "a revelation of Americanism" to Washington, New York City, and points north and west "throughout the length and breadth of the States."[32]

By the time *The Melting-Pot* was written, America was already in tremendous multicultural flux. Had Zangwill published the play thirty-six years later, he would no doubt still have agreed with the evaluation of another foreign observer, Gunnar Myrdal (1898–1987), the Swedish sociologist, economist, and member of Parliament who discussed "the American creed" in his 1944 study, *An American Dilemma*. Myrdal saw this nation as the repository for five key values: liberty, egalitarianism, individualism, populism, and laissez-faire—a country that could look back for its resolutely individualistic culture to seventeenth-century Anglo-Protestants. Modern Americans, according to Myrdal, were a people remaking themselves in a country "continuously struggling for its soul," possessed with the self-consciousness that they could always do better. No matter how diverse their origins, he wrote, this ameliorative drive was one quality they had in common.[33]

Conversely, Myrdal would have agreed with Zangwill that "assimilation" did not require complete self-sacrifice. While becoming immersed in the American way of life, it was possible, even preferable, to maintain aspects of one's original culture. The melting-pot was a symbolic antidote to the nativist epidemic bridging the nineteenth and twentieth centuries, demonstrating that transformation worked in two directions. By choosing America and acknowledging that the journey and the adjustment would not be without hardship, the immigrant changed the country for the better; by taking in the immigrant, America reciprocally could change him for the better.[34]

The Carnegie Corporation had originally commissioned Myrdal to study the issue of *The Negro Problem and Modern Democracy*. This subtitle to his book revealed the negative side of the American dynamic, a polarizing aspect that Zangwill did not talk about. Even though the American creed placed egalitarianism at the top of the system, and even though every citizen was theoretically permitted the same starting point on the path, in fact, for 250 years, blacks were slaves, and, for the ensuing century, they lived and labored in the shadow of Jim Crow. Myrdal identified racism as the debilitating "split in the American moral personality." We now turn to an idealist who decided to try to mend this massive flaw.[35]

Carter G. Woodson

9

The Negro in Our History

Year in and year out, Carter Woodson worked diligently to promote a new American history that would reject the notion that the Negro had no history or that he should be treated in some special way. No one was a more vigorous protagonist of the idea that the history of the United States should be completely integrated. No single person did more to promote a New American History—a democratic, egalitarian American history—as far as racial and ethnic groups are concerned.

—John Hope Franklin, "The New American History,"
Negro Digest (February 1967).

Carter Godwin Woodson was born in rural New Canton, Buckingham County, Virginia on December 19, 1875, twelve years after the signing of the Emancipation Proclamation. He was the seventh of nine children of former slaves. When his mother, Anne Eliza Riddle, was eleven years old, she witnessed the sale of her mother and her two younger brothers. James Henry Woodson, Carter's father, escaped from his master in Fluvanna County, Virginia, sixty-five miles north of Richmond, after a brutal beating, and served in the Union army under George Armstrong Custer. After the war, James dug ditches, made furniture, built fish traps, worked on the railroad, and finally scraped together enough cash to buy a ten-acre tobacco farm on the banks of the James River.

Enlisted from an early age to help with chores, the Woodson brothers had little time to attend the five-month term of the one-room district school taught by their uncles, John Morton and James Buchanan Riddle. Carter's "fundamental" geography, spelling, arithmetic, and American history lessons were sporadic and brief. His early experience with reading was encouraged by his educated uncles. He picked out letters of the alphabet from the family Bible, then sounded out words. His father gave the boy copies of discarded newspapers, and in the evenings, Carter read aloud to his illiterate parents. Big for his age, he loved the outdoors, amusing himself on barefoot walks by catching insects and fishing. The family was poor and wanting for food. In late winter and early spring, the children often left the table hungry and wandered into the woods to scavenge persimmons from the trees and sour grass from the meadows. To be properly clean and neat for Sunday school, Carter went to bed early on Saturday night so that his mother could wash and iron his one set of clothes.[1]

When the C & O Railroad embarked upon a branch line extension from Thurmond to Dunloop Creek in Fayette County, southern West Virginia in the early 1890s, his older brother Robert convinced Carter to follow him across the state border for better paying work. After a short time laying track, they found jobs in the thriving coal mine at Nuttallburg. Buckingham County, Virginia, had no secondary schools for Negroes, and so the rest of the Woodson family moved to Huntington, West Virginia, in 1893, where the two youngest children, Susie and Bessie, entered the new Frederick Douglass High School.[2]

Resting between bouts of subterranean labor, Carter continued his reading, bravely taking on the works of Cicero and Virgil. After the day's shift was done, he headed to informal gatherings at the commissary cabin of Richmond-born fellow miner Oliver Jones. In payment for reading aloud to eager coworkers, the daily Negro newspapers, the *Mountaineer* and the *Pioneer,* as well as journals from farther afield, including the *Pittsburgh Telegraph, Toledo Blade,* and *Cincinnati Commercial Gazette,* Jones provided Carter with all the ice cream, fresh fruits, and watermelon he could eat. News of the day soon escalated to excerpts from "interesting books . . . giving the important achievements of the Negro." Joseph T. Wilson's *The Black Phalanx* (1888) "gave light" to the "manly and noble deeds" of Negro soldiers in the Revolutionary War, the War of 1812, and the Civil War. *Men of Mark: Eminent, Progressive and Rising* (1887), by William J. Simmons, the son of an escaped slave, was a biographical dictionary of 177 entries in which the author, a Baptist minister and president of the Normal and Theological Institute of Louisville, Kentucky, "hoped to demonstrate to intelligent, aspiring young men and women everywhere that the Negro race is still alive, and must possess more intellectual vigor than any other section of the human family." The Negro miners' reading circle was a turning point for teenage Carter Woodson, a welcome setting in which "the history of the race was discussed frequently," he remembered five decades later, "and my interest in penetrating the past of my people was deepened and intensified."[3]

At twenty Carter left the mines to enter the Frederick Douglass High School with advanced standing. He completed the work in a year and a half, then went to the coeducational and interracial Berea College in Kentucky, where he stayed for little more than a semester before transferring with the aid of a scholarship to Lincoln University in Pennsylvania. Founded in 1854 as the Ashmun Institute, the school was dedicated to providing an education for "promising young men of African descent." From 1898 to 1900, Carter taught high school at Winona in West Virginia, before returning home in triumph to Huntington to become principal of his alma mater high school, where he served ably for three years while taking correspondence courses from the University of Chicago in order to apply credit toward a Bachelor of Literature degree from Berea College, conferred in June 1903. Later that summer his application was accepted to teach English for the Bureau of Education in the U.S.–occupied Philippine Islands at an annual Civil Service salary of twelve hundred dollars. On November 20 he boarded the SS *Korea* out of San Francisco. After a fifty-six-hour steamship voyage from Hong Kong, Carter Woodson arrived in Manila on his twenty-eighth birthday "with twenty-six missionaries who were going to take the Orient by storm."[4]

Woodson was assigned to take up residence and teach primary grades in the remote town of San Isidro in the province of Nueva Ecija, thatched houses surrounded by lush cotton and tobacco fields. Promoted to supervisor of schools in the towns of Agno and Bani in the neighboring province of Pangasinan, he worked to indoctrinate and train new teachers. He was astonished that for lack of suitable curriculum materials, the children were compelled to use a popular American textbook, *The Baldwin Primer*. The book opened with illustrations of a red apple and polar bears cavorting in the snow, and simple, patriotic verse about George Washington. These alien cultural references were to Woodson "a striking example of how people . . . should *not* be taught." Surely it was better to have the children sing "Come Shake the Lomboy Tree"—the ubiquitous *jambolan*, a fragrant, hardy evergreen with juicy, clustered plumlike fruit—than "Come Shake the Apple Tree." And surely it was better for the children to study the life of José Rizal—martyred Philippine revolutionary hero, physician, poet, and apostle of nationalism, executed at thirty-five before a firing squad at Bagumbayan in 1896—than the father of a faraway country, George Washington. "Hold on to the real facts of history as they are," Woodson cautioned, "but complete such knowledge by studying also the history of races and nations which have been purposely ignored."[5]

Chronic stomach problems forced Woodson to leave the Philippines in early 1907. He took half a year to meander home westward—with characteristic purpose—stopping at Singapore in the Crown colony of the Straits Settlements (on and adjacent to the Malay Peninsula) and at villages in India to examine the local school systems, then proceeding to Egypt, Palestine, Greece, and Italy. He remained for several months in Paris to study at the Sorbonne and became fluent in French, adding to his already self-taught Spanish. Rematriculating at the University of Chicago, this time in residence there, Woodson completed his bachelor's as well as his master's degrees by the end of the summer of 1908. In September he entered Harvard as one of thirty-six students in the History Ph.D. program.[6]

W oodson's major instructor at Harvard was the McLean Professor of Ancient and Modern History, the formidable Edward Channing, son of the liberal Unitarian minister and erstwhile abolitionist William Ellery Channing. Prominent at Harvard from 1883 until his retirement in 1929, Edward Channing was a "scientific historian," who espoused the necessity of ploughing through primary source material in support of the virtue of objectivity. His magnum opus, A History of the United States was published in six volumes over a twenty-year period from 1905 to 1925. The final installment, on the Civil War, would win the Pulitzer Prize in 1926. Revered at Harvard, Channing expressed a myopic view pervasive in mainstream American academia. During a seminar on the American Revolution, Channing facetiously alluded to Crispus Attucks—the mulatto seaman "who shed the first blood" of the war at the Boston Massacre—by scoffing that "the Negro had no history." In one parenthetical phrase, he dismissed such landmark works as William Wells Brown's The Black Man: His Antecedents, His Genius, and His Achievements (1863) and the two-volume classic by George Washington Williams, History of the Negro Race in America from 1619 to 1880 (1882), written, the author had said, "not as a blind panegyrist nor as a partisan apologist, but for a love for 'the truth of history.'" Professor Channing also seemed to have forgotten about "The Conservation of Races," a speech by the first black man to receive a Ph.D. from Harvard, W. E. B. Du Bois, delivered at the Lincoln Memorial Church in Washington at the inaugural meeting of The American Negro Academy on Friday morning, March 5, 1897—127 years to the day after Attucks was gunned down in front of the Customs House on King Street. "He who ignores or seeks to override the race idea in human history," Du Bois said, "ignores and overrides the central thought of all history."[7]

Woodson was quick to retort to Professor Channing that "*no people lacked a history.*" Negro historic tradition, Woodson would come to believe, possessed intrinsic value, the "arsenal of facts" to be unearthed there serving as more than merely a "defensive bulwark against the . . . distortions of scholars." Completing a year of required course work at Harvard, Woodson set forth to prove this case. He took a teaching job at a Negro school in Washington, D.C., so that he could be close to the Library of Congress and begin research on his dissertation, "The Disruption of Virginia."[8]

Dressed in "hayseed clothes" and with barely "enough money to pay for a haircut," Woodson moved into a rooming house at 1924 Eleventh Street in northwest Washington. The adjoining room was occupied by another ambitious, self-taught young man, twenty-seven-year-old Louis R. Mehlinger, a native of Donaldsonville, Louisiana, by way of Bolivar County, Mississippi, where his father ran a plantation store. Mehlinger attended business school part time and worked as a $660-a-year stenographer-typist in the Department of the Treasury. Of an evening Mehlinger took dictation from Woodson as he labored on his dissertation. The two became lifelong friends.[9]

After a stint at Thaddeus Stevens School, Woodson settled in for almost a decade to teach French—the social realist novels of Balzac were his favorites—Spanish, English, and History at the M Street School for "Washington's black bourgeoisie," later renamed Paul Lawrence Dunbar High School. During period changes, Woodson stood impassively outside the door of his classroom to supervise the passing students. He was not tall—about five feet eight—but robust and erect in stature, with a powerful torso from many years of hard manual labor. His expression was stern, almost dour, his manner formidable. In the classroom Woodson was inclined to lecture in complete sentences without referring to notes. He was tough on the students, expecting them to give their best. When he was in charge of study hall, he used the time to work on his own research projects, sitting ramrod straight at his desk at the front of the room. But in private conversation with the young people he loved and encouraged, Woodson's serious demeanor gave way to soft-spoken compassion, quips with a twinkle in his eye, and even, at times, boisterous laughter.[10]

Oh! For a Negro pen to record the lives of our great men and women! I would not circumscribe the fields of learning nor rob the white children of their pride of lineage; but I would teach Negro children the glorious deeds of Negro men and women *FIRST!*" pleaded Charles Victor Roman, M.D., in 1911, first black graduate of Hamilton Collegiate Institute in Ontario and one of the founders of the National Medical Association.

Carter Woodson heard and heeded these words. He anthologized Dr. Roman's speech in his collection of *Negro Orators and Their Orations* (1925). In 1912 Woodson received a Ph.D. from Harvard. Following in the footsteps of Du Bois, he was invited to join the exclusive American Negro Academy in 1914, presenting a paper on "Educating the Negro Before 1860" at the annual meeting in December of that year. The talk was a preview of Woodson's first book, *The Education of the Negro Prior to 1861*, published the following April by G.P. Putnam's Sons, "with the hope," the author declared in the Preface, "of vitally interesting some young master mind in this large task."[11]

Woodson traveled to Chicago in the early fall of 1915 for research at the university. He took a room at the new YMCA at Thirty-eighth Street and Wabash Avenue on the city's South Side. On the evening of September 9 he met in the office of the executive secretary of the "Y," Alexander L. Jackson, an old friend from Washington; along with surgeon George Cleveland Hall, chairman of the Board of Management of the "Y" and chief of staff at Chicago's Provident Hospital; insurance executive James E. Stamps, future founder of the National Alumni Council of the United Negro College Fund; and scholar and teacher W. B. Hartgrove. The group of five assembled "for the purpose of considering definite plans for the organization of a society devoted to the study of the Negro . . . to treat the race scientifically, and to publish the findings to the world." The *Association for the Study of Negro Life and History (ASNLH)* was born. Carter Woodson told his friends "how in time the inspiration given in these releases and publication could not only play an important part in changing the image of the Negro, but would awaken and arouse our youth to study for achievement. We do not wish to duplicate controversial material," Woodson wrote early on, in a spirit of moderation, to the Reverend Jesse E. Moorland, first secretary-treasurer of the association. "We must consider the race situation dispassionately."[12]

The Executive Board authorized "the thrifty and frugile [sic] bachelor" Woodson to rent an office in Washington at a cost of $13.50 a month and to employ Miss A. H. Smith, a part-time office worker, at a starting salary of $10 a week. Without consulting the board, and much to their chagrin, Woodson proceeded to take $400 out of the savings from his M Street School teaching job, using the money to fund the publication of the first issue of *The Journal of Negro History* on January 1, 1916. The theme of the inaugural magazine was "the mind of the Negro . . . what the Negro was thinking . . . the attitude of the free Negro." W. E. B. Du Bois was suitably impressed. By the time the *Journal* was in press, Du Bois had brought forth two master works, *The Souls of Black Folk* (1903), a collection of essays identifying "the color line" as the paramount problem of the twentieth century, and *The Negro* (1915), "a sociological examination of the African diaspora." He had helped to found the Niagara Movement and the National Organization for the Advancement of Colored People (NAACP), and was editing *The Crisis: A Record of the Darker Races*, the association magazine. From this vantage point, Du Bois praised Woodson's new periodical and predicted the multiplication of its "subscription list by at least ten in the next twelvemonth."[13]

After some grumbling about fiscal responsibility, Woodson's colleagues came around to accepting that the *Journal* was going to be a platform for the philosophy of the headstrong "lone wolf" editor, and they had no choice but to give him latitude. Woodson used a review of *The Negro in Literature and Art,* a new book by Benjamin Brawley, poet, minister, and dean of Morehouse College in Atlanta, to comment upon the "lofty" importance of recognizing "Negro genius. . . . There is among Negroes," Woodson reminded readers at every opportunity, "a growing scholarship which must be reckoned with in the thought of this country." Grudging acceptance emerged from unexpected quarters. Professor Channing of Harvard weighed in on the verge of the fifth volume of his *History*, dealing with the first abolitionist movement up to 1850. "If you have any suggestions as to the mode of treatment or as to facts," Channing respectfully queried his former student, "I should be very grateful for them."[14]

In 1910, nearly a half century after the Civil War, 90 percent of all blacks in America still lived in the South. Starting in the middle years of the century's second decade, they fled the cotton crop failures, meager tenant farming, dismantled civil liberties, punitive Jim Crow color line laws, and racial violence of the rural South in search of industrial jobs and (perhaps) a better life. Epitomizing the situation in many burgeoning northern cities, the black population of Chicago doubled by 1920. Seizing an historical moment at the end of World War I "when black migration was at its peak," Woodson brought forth his next important book, *A Century of Negro Migration* (1918), tracking the roots for the phenomenon earlier than the postbellum "refugee" years of Reconstruction. Writing of the "blighted hopes for freedom" in the South, Woodson meditated upon the core of the "Negro problem"—a constant necessity to relocate, even from the countryside to towns within the South. Despite urban rioting over jobs and housing, "out of this [Great Migration] came some very *useful* Negroes," he said, a further example of Woodson's intent to develop positive implications for the Negro future drawn from the harsh, oppressive lessons of his past.[15]

In 1919 Woodson left M Street School to take the job of principal at Armstrong Manual Training School. The immense structure in the Renaissance Revival style, situated at First and "P" Streets in northwest Washington, was dedicated in a celebratory speech by Booker T. Washington on opening day, 1902, as the city's first secondary school for blacks. The following fall Woodson was appointed dean of the School of Liberal Arts and head of the Graduate Faculty at Howard University. For several years preceding his arrival, distinguished professors Alain Locke in philosophy, Kelly Miller in sociology, and Charles H. Wesley in history, as well as Howard trustee and Association for the Study of Negro Life and History board member Jesse E. Moorland, had been pushing for the formal development of a syllabus in Negro studies. The first course on this subject in the Howard College of Arts and Sciences to be sanctioned by the Board of Trustees was offered by Carter Woodson when he taught a two-semester

M.A. sequence in Negro history for five students preparing to become teachers.[16]

"Why study Negro history?" he asked the class rhetorically on the first day after issuing the blunt warning that anyone not able to carry a "B" average would be summarily dropped. Woodson began by tracing the evolution of the Greek word, *historia*, meaning "searching to find out." He told the students they needed to broaden their conception of history beyond political and military records to encompass "social conditions of the periods under study," to look for "the continuous threads binding" events, places and dates, because "if a race had no recorded history, it would thus become a neglible factor in the thought of the world." During one memorable lecture at the conclusion of the final quarter, Woodson demonstrated the breadth, "romance and spice" of his knowledge by reading excerpts from the work of Frederika Bremer, a Swedish novelist and social activist who had traveled throughout the United States in the mid-nineteenth century. Documenting her visit in a book called *The Homes of the New World: Impressions of America* (1853), she noted that "the romance of American history is the fate of the Negro."[17]

Woodson's year at Howard ended unceremoniously in a dispute with Pres. J. Stanley Durkee. He moved on yet again, this time to become dean of West Virginia Collegiate Institute outside Charleston. Woodson successfully restructured the curriculum at the institute while continuing to develop the programs of the ASNLH. He created a related business entity called the Associated Publishers, a private corporation in which he held 90 percent of the stock. The new imprint gave him the opportunity to publish more books by Negro scholars beyond "what others permit them to bring out." Such offerings included his study on *The History of the Negro Church*, the "pioneer" scholarly, "psychological and geographical" effort to "trace the rise and spread of institutionalized Christianity among American Negroes." Woodson told an enthusiastic audience at Hampton Institute in Virginia in 1921 that "we are going back to that beautiful history and it is going to inspire us to greater achievements. It is not going to be long before we can so sing the story to the outside world as to convince it of the value of our history."

Philanthropic endorsement of his unremitting labors came at long last in the form of substantial, multiyear gifts from the Carnegie Corporation and the Laura Spelman Rockefeller Memorial Fund. The grants were sufficient to allow Woodson at forty-seven to retire from teaching and return to Washington. In the respectful judgment of W. E. B. Du Bois, Woodson was ready to "buckle up his belt, give up most of the things a man of his age would be looking forward to . . . choose his life's work, and never waver from it."[18]

In September 1922 Woodson found a permanent home for the Association for the Study of Negro Life and History, a three-story, 1880s Victorian-style row house at 1538 Ninth Street in the heart of the Shaw District of northwest Washington. He made a down payment of $10 on the purchase price of $2,750. On November 24, 2003, the U.S. Senate passed the Carter G. Woodson Home National Historic Site Act (H.R. 1012), sponsored by Rep. Eleanor Holmes Norton, designating the building, as well as three adjoining structures, as a National Historic Site in the District of Columbia. The National Park Service planned to rehabilitate the house, which was endangered and in serious disrepair, boarded up and vacant since the 1970s, and convert it into an interpretive museum, visitor center, and administrative headquarters for the Association for the Study of African American Life and History.[19]

Installed in the two-room apartment he took for living quarters on the third floor, Woodson settled down to a "Spartan-like" lifestyle that varied little during the next twenty-eight years of his life. He believed that "the servant of the people [should be] down among them, living as they live, doing what they do. . . . He should have more humility than those whom he serves." In that spirit of simplicity, Woodson rose early, dressed in suit and tie, and prepared a breakfast of fresh fruit juice that he drank while seated at a white enameled table in the kitchen. Promptly at nine o'clock, he descended to the second-floor office, expecting to find his assistant ready and waiting. Poet Langston Hughes, arriving in Washington at twenty-three "fresh from Europe and thoroughly broke" and living with his unemployed mother, suffered unsuccessful stints at a wet-wash laundry and an oyster bar before coming to work for Carter Woodson in 1925. His plain-spoken boss was not one for small talk. He greeted the obliging young man with little more than a "Good morning." Hughes swept and dusted the "musty" office, wrapped books and magazines for shipment, read *Journal* page proofs, and "banked the furnace at night" in the basement, which served as the store-

house for association publications. His major clerical task was to alphabetize more than thirty thousand names for inclusion in Woodson's current
massive research project, a compilation of *Free Negro Heads of Families in
the United States in 1830*. After several months of severe eyestrain, "although [he] realized what a fine contribution Dr. Woodson was making to
the Negro people and to America," Hughes took a job as a busboy in the
Wardman Park Hotel on Connecticut Avenue. In the new year 1926,
Langston Hughes's first book of poetry, *The Weary Blues*—"Droning a
drowsy sycopated tune, / Rocking back and forth to a mellow croon, / I
heard a Negro play"—was published by Alfred A. Knopf in New York
City.[20]

After a morning of fund-raising correspondence and dictation delivered
with nary a split infinitive, walking back and forth around the office, his
hands clasped behind his back, Woodson grabbed a handful of grapes for
lunch, then returned to the tasks at hand. If the weather was fine, he permitted himself a break in midafternoon to sit outside on the stoop in the
sun and laugh with the neighborhood children stopping by on their way
home from school. Later, in the course of a constitutional stroll, he
dropped off the day's parcels at the post office. Woodson frequented one of
two places for dinner in segregated Washington: Union Train Station,
where Negroes were permitted, or, more enjoyably, the new Phyllis Wheatley Residence for Women nearby, on the corner of Ninth Street at Rhode
Island Avenue. Built in 1920, organized by members of the Book Lovers
Club, and named in honor of America's first published black poet, this was
the city's first YWCA. After dinner, always the perfect gentleman—he neither drank nor smoked—Woodson "lingered in the lobby into the evening,
sitting and chatting with the young ladies as they tarried there . . . [enjoying] the richness and entertaining quality of his conversation." At a decent
hour he went home for a nostalgic snack of cornbread and buttermilk, and
then to bed.[21]

Possessed with prodigious energy and now living exclusively for "The
Cause," as he called it, during the first decade of his full-time immersion in
the work of the association, in addition to *Free Negro Heads of Families*,
Carter Woodson produced under the imprint of the Associated Publishers:
*Free Negro Owners of Slaves in the United States in 1830: Together with Absentee Ownership of Slaves in the United States in 1830; Negro Orators and Their
Orations; The Mind of the Negro as Reflected in Letters Written During the Cri-*

sis, (1800–1860); Negro Makers of History; African Myths: Together with Proverbs; The Negro as a Businessman (with John H. Harmon Jr. and Arnett G. Lindsay, his stellar M.A. student from the 1919–20 academic year at Howard); *The Negro Wage Earner* (with another bright protégé, Lorenzo Greene); and *The Rural Negro*.

In 1933 would come Woodson's hugely popular polemic, *The Mis-Education of the Negro*. The book's point of view from beginning to end was relentlessly consistent. Woodson contended that in all forms of American education—from grade school to schools of theology to schools of business administration to schools of journalism to trade schools—the Negro was bombarded with a mixed message. On the one hand, he was a part of the American body politic, but on the other hand, he was told to remember to "stay in his place." The "highly-educated" Negro was subject to condescension, well-intentioned charity, and missionary work. In fact he had not been educated at all and never would be—unless, and only unless, he regained contact with the masses of his own people, took pride in the historical tradition they shared, and, most important of all, seized control of the thrust of his own thinking. Still very much in print in the twenty-first century, with over four hundred thousand copies sold over seventy years, *The Mis-Education of the Negro* is regularly at or near the top of the *Essence* magazine Paperback Nonfiction Best-selling list.[22]

From this plethora of substantial, exhaustive (and, in a few unfortunate cases, tough-slogging) lineage of books, *The Negro in Our History* (1922) stood out as epitomizing Woodson's commitment to correcting "the monstrous binary distortion [of] the American narrative." The book was Woodson's systematic attempt, employing the rigorous scholarship of a "scientifically-trained Negro," to redress the "downgrading" of the race and its near-exclusion from the work of such Progressive historians as Frederick Jackson Turner, V. L. Parrington, and Charles and Mary Beard. John Hope Franklin, elder statesman of black American historians and author of *From Slavery to Freedom*, describes Woodson as the "dominant figure," and *The Negro in Our History* as the standard-bearer, the most important focal point for "the second generation of Negro historians"—worthy successors to George Washington Williams in 1882 and Booker T. Washington in 1909.[23]

Alrutheus Ambush Taylor, a Harvard Ph.D. with expertise in the Reconstruction period, was Woodson's research assistant for *The Negro in Our History*. His job title was "Associate Investigator." Taylor observed that his mentor's approach was studiously nonconfrontational. Determined to put forth a strong narrative as the foundation for a 525-page textbook priced at $3.15 and designed "for the average [college] reader," Woodson said that the betterment of the race would not be accomplished through "propaganda or fire-eating agitation." In an essay, "Some Things Negroes Need to Do" (". . . if they hope to enjoy the blessings of real democracy, if it ever comes") that appeared in the *Southern Workman* magazine less than two months before the first edition of *The Negro in Our History* was published, Woodson showed that even though he no longer was in the classroom every day, he was still a dedicated pedagogue. "We must have educational independence," he said, "for a man is educated when he can do without a teacher, when he can learn and will develop and grow without the stimulus of instruction . . . you will read the history of Africa, the history of our ancestors—people of whom you should be proud," he continued, addressing the younger generation directly and leading the way to the book's opening chapters.

"It is a wonderful tale," wrote an enthusiastic early reviewer in *America* magazine, "You must go back to the ancient world to get the effect of the Egyptian queen Nefertari, of ivory thrones, leopard skins . . . or the Negro poet Nossayeb of Damascus. . . . All kinds of adventures are there." The *American Historical Review* praised it as "highly valuable," and the *Mississippi Valley Historical Review* approved of Dr. Woodson's use of "the principles of historical investigation which safeguard accuracy, proportion, and judgment."[24]

The book explored, in Woodson's unhurried and systematic fashion, "the [heretofore] unknown African origin" of the Negro, with illuminating descriptions of rituals and structured ways characteristic of tribal life, revealing interpenetration with other sophisticated cultures within the vast continent as well as beyond. Undermining the received tradition of his subservience in America, the Negro was portrayed from the beginning of the book as a seminal, influential race. Woodson embarked upon an extended discussion of the pervasiveness of slavery in colonial times, and of the "Middle Passage," the long journey that brought slave cargo from West Africa to North America, South America, and the Caribbean. He dismissed the myth of the "ignorant Negro," displaying on almost every page portraits of noteworthy members of the race presented as in every respect equal to Emerson's distinguished, "representative men" of history. The dehumanization of the Negro by the "peculiar institution of slavery" was thrown into dramatic relief by repeated insistence upon his enduring attributes. Woodson presented slavery as the moral touchstone that ultimately "forced the irrepressible conflict" of the Civil War. "Under this exploitation system," he wrote, "the Negro race became an element with which the whites would not deal as man to man." The irony of the supposed "new social order" of postbellum Reconstruction, Woodson asserted bitterly, was that it precipitated a "stormy" and calamitous "abridgement of Negro rights" in a South resistant to social reform.[25]

The first edition of one thousand copies, bearing a striking block-print jacket graphic by James Lesesne Wells, was published in March 1922. A critical appraisal by Woodson's respected colleague, philosopher Alain LeRoy Locke, a cosmopolitan cultural pluralist and passionate collector of African art, was prophetic. Locke shared Woodson's admiration of Wells's modernist style with its powerful, primitive, sculptural edges. He further agreed with Woodson that Negro education must espouse aims that were "positive and compensatory. . . . [W]hen the record is finally balanced," Locke concluded his reasoned critique of *The Negro in Our History*, "the role of this book as the wedge of the entire movement will be apparent, and we shall then acknowledge that it belongs to that select class of books that have brought about a revolution of mind."

By the end of June 1923, *The Negro in Our History* had been adopted as a text in more than twenty schools and colleges and the *Journal of Negro History* was placed in hundreds of college and public libraries. Eleven subsequent editions followed, exceeding fifty thousand copies. After 1950 the book was greatly amplified, thanks to the efforts of two historians, Charles Harris Wesley, the first president of Wilberforce University in Ohio and Woodson's friend since 1916, and Rayford Whittingham Logan, author of *The Negro in American Life and Thought: The Nadir, 1877–1901*, and Woodson's research assistant in the early 1930s. In its final editions, *The Negro in Our History* approached nine hundred pages and included tributes to Lorraine Hansberry, James Baldwin, LeRoi Jones (before he became Amiri Baraka), and the civil rights legislative legacy of Lyndon Johnson.[26]

W oodson was pleased to report that the fiscally responsible years of the early 1920s were "the most prosperous in the history of the Association." To put this statement in perspective, the total annual operating budget for the Association for the Study of Negro Life and History, as of June 30, 1924, was $20,653.49, which included the executive director's salary of $1,833.35. "[C]alled to encourage a school or a club to do more for the study of Negro life and history," Woodson found it difficult to preserve his routine, hermetic lifestyle. His "field work" through the South and West aimed "to increase the income of the Association" by encouraging grass-roots, "rank-and-file Friends" groups to donate modest funds.

One such journey took him to the Stanton School, established by the Freedmen's Bureau in Jacksonville, Florida, as the first school for black children in the state. "Moving about very much like a skilled boxer, never hurried, never faltering, sparring skillfully for openings, driving home his blows deftly," Woodson, dressed impeccably as usual in a tweed suit, was speaking in the auditorium before an assembly for several minutes when he noticed one of the children was asleep. Agitated, Woodson pointed to the boy, his voice rising, "Wake him up, wake up that sleeping one!" Then, wheeling around to face the transfixed audience, he cried, "*This* is what we have been doing for decades: *sleeping*, sleeping away our rights!" The effect upon one sixth grader was "electric." He never forgot that day. Lawrence Dunbar Reddick went on to Fisk University and the University of Chicago. In 1937, in an essay called "A New Interpretation for Negro History," he noted the necessity to "awaken and educate" his race. In 1938, at the age of twenty-eight, Reddick succeeded the legendary Arthur Alfonso Schomburg as curator of the Division of Negro Literature, History, and Prints of the New York Public Library at 135th Street.[27]

The wake-up call to action was one of Woodson's favorite ideals, often stated in different ways—the marginalized Negro in his "sequestered sphere" needed to "wake up" to an understanding of his position and work hard to rectify it by "doing for self," in order to "elevate" himself. "Properly awakened," he wrote in *The Mis-Education of the Negro*, thinking of intellectual awakening, "the Negro can do the so-called impossible." Woodson quoted often and at length from the great abolitionist leader, suffragist orator and human-rights activist Frederick Douglass. "It is vain that we talk of being men, if we do not the work of men," Douglass wrote in 1852. "We must become valuable to society in other departments of industry than those servile ones from which we are rapidly being excluded. We must show that we can do as well as they." Eurocentric cultural history was overvalued in America while African history was devalued. With forceful, enriched consciousness of the Negro past, however, Woodson was certain that "the trend must start upward."[28]

"Negro History Week" was actually not a direct outgrowth of the popularity of *The Negro in Our History* and Woodson's speaking tours around the country. The idea had been coalescing in his mind for several years. In February 1920 Woodson gave a lecture to the Nashville chapter of Omega Psi Phi, a fraternity founded at Howard University in 1911. He encouraged his fraternity brothers to become more active in raising awareness of Negro history and culture. For the next six years until 1926, "Negro History and Literature Week" was presented as an Omega Psi Phi program until Woodson decided that the Association for the Study of Negro Life and History should take it on. He chose the second week of February in order to coincide with the birthdays of Abraham Lincoln and Frederick Douglass. Ten years later, at an ASNLH annual meeting, Woodson told the twenty-one-year-old John Hope Franklin that "he looked forward to the time when it would not be necessary to set aside a 'week' to call attention to the contributions of Negroes. [Woodson] fervently hoped," Franklin recalled, "that soon, the history of African Americans would be an integral part of American history . . . that Negro History Week would outlive its usefulness. . . . What we need," Woodson said, expanding the terrain, "is not a history of selected races or nations, but the history of the world, void of national bias, race hate and religious prejudice."

In preparation for the inaugural observation of Negro History Week, Woodson mailed a four-page grassroots "mission-statement" brochure to churches, colleges, schools, community centers, boards of education headquarters, libraries, labor unions, and literary societies, encouraging book displays, lectures, symposia, and other "living examples of Negro accomplishment. . . . Save the records of the Negro such as old newspapers . . . wills and the like," Woodson wrote in the flyer, encouraging respect for the documentary past. "Have the outstanding citizens of your community agree . . . to make the celebration reach all groups. Persuade your pastor to deliver an address on the Sunday beginning the celebration. Set aside one day as a Book and Picture Fund Day . . . [P]ersuade your public library to purchase these things . . . Promote the actual study of the Negro in a club or class. . . . [T]ell intelligently to children in schools and churches interesting stories of distinguished Negroes who have achieved things worth while." To meet demand the brochure was expanded into a "kit" distributed by the association. The kit in turn grew into the establishment of a Home Study Department through which the ASNLH offered correspondence curricula for classroom teachers, social workers, ministers, and businessmen desirous of enriching their knowledge of Negro history. These professionals could register for a roster of courses taught by distinguished scholars, including "The Problem of the Races," "General Anthropology," "Negro Economic History," and "The Negro in Recent Literature."[29]

In "The Propaganda of History," the brilliant summarizing chapter of *Black Reconstruction in America* (1935), W. E. B. Du Bois wrote passionately of the corrupt suppression of American historical memory and of the importance of reassessing black history, especially the bleak period between the end of the Civil War and the beginning of World War I. He paid tribute to Carter Woodson as the leader of "the new school of historians" and listed *The Negro in Our History* and *Negro Orators and Their Orations* as two "standard works" in a definitive "Bibliography" of approved texts. Five years later, in *Dusk of Dawn: An Essay Toward an Autobiography of a Race Concept*, Du Bois went further, calling the invention of "Negro History Week" the "greatest single accomplishment" of "the artistic movement among Negroes." Writing shortly after Woodson's death, Du Bois referred to Negro History Week as Carter Woodson's "crowning achievement. . . . I know of no one man who in a lifetime has, unaided, built up such a national celebration." During the nation's Bicentennial, by order of Pres. Jimmy Carter, the "Week" was expanded to all of February, and Black History Month was created.[30]

It was no coincidence that Negro History Week arrived at the peak of the Harlem Renaissance—an efflorescence of creativity in literature, music, and the arts in black America. In the Foreword to *The New Negro* (1925), his defining anthology overview of the movement, Alain Locke wrote of Negro life "finding a new soul. . . . There is a renewed race-spirit that consciously and proudly sets itself apart." He was speaking of the contours of the cultural landscape shaped by "the transformations of the inner life . . . of the Negro mind and spirit." Glorifying black artistic achievement, Alain Locke had written his Ph.D. dissertation at Harvard under the supervision of Josiah Royce (1855–1916), the foremost American idealist philosopher of his time. "Our ethical obligation," wrote Royce, "is to the moral order, and takes the form of loyalty to the great community of all individuals." Locke's sentiments echoed Carter Woodson's approach in his new book on *The Mind of the Negro as Reflected in Letters Written During the Crisis, 1800–1860*, in which he emphasized the "psychology of the Negro, which must be taken into consideration as an important factor in the study of history . . . [and] historical interpretation." Reminding his readers "what the free Negro [of the nineteenth century] was actually thinking and feeling," Woodson as a documentary historian brought forward statements from Negro everymen and -women to guide contemporary students toward a fairer perspective.[31]

At the June 1926 conference of the National Association for the Advancement of Colored People (NAACP) in Chicago, John Haynes Holmes, social activist and Unitarian minister, and one of the original founders of the NAACP in 1909, presented Carter Woodson with the organization's highest honor, the gold Spingarn Medal. In his introductory remarks, Reverend Holmes noted that "the eve of the Sesquicentennial of the signing of the Declaration of Independence" was a fitting moment to honor Dr. Woodson as one of the prime movers in the "spiritual emancipation" of "the New Negro." Holmes saluted Woodson, the twelfth recipient of the Medal—following in the distinguished footsteps of, among others, George Washington Carver, W. E. B. Du Bois, James Weldon Johnson, and Archibald Grimké, third president of the American Negro Academy—as "a scholar laboring year after year in the quiet seclusion of the laboratory, seeking no popularity, not caring for the applause of men, indifferent to reward, save the plaudit of his own heart and the joy of fresh discovery and knowledge."[32]

W oodson resisted bringing the Association for the Study of Negro Life and History into affiliation with an institution of higher learning, turning down overtures from Atlanta University, Tuskegee Institute, and Howard University, instead sticking stubbornly to the path of autonomy. Wary of the "strings attached" to institutional philanthropy, Woodson appealed to individual donors to continue the work of the association. He alienated some of his initial supporters and as he acerbically put it, "so-called 'traducers' of the Negro," and by the early 1930s, much of the association's foundation support had evaporated. The autocratic, Harvard-educated child of slaves and former coal miner did not affiliate himself with any political party and was suspicious of New Deal social welfare programs for blacks. However he agreed to serve as a consultant to an ambitious two-year Works Progress Administration project to photograph and interview former slaves across the South. He forged on with community outreach efforts, summer research trips to Europe, and a steady stream of publications, including *The Negro Professional Man* (1934), *The Story of the Negro Retold* (1935), *African Heroes and Heroines* (1939), and an edition of the works of Archibald Grimké's younger brother, Francis Grimké, pastor for sixty years of the Fifteenth Street Presbyterian Church in Washington, D.C.

In 1941 Woodson received an honorary Doctor of Laws from West Virginia State College, and after World War II he began to moderate his hardened views. In the prolific decade before his death on April 3, 1950, at the age of seventy-four, he produced more than fifty articles for *The Negro History Bulletin* and more than two hundred book reviews for his beloved *Journal of Negro History*.[33]

Carter Woodson's ideal, as well as his conflict, persist in our culture. His ideal as a populist intellectual was to clarify the narrative of black people in America. His conflict was how to situate the story of the disenfranchised into the dominant framework of white America. At dismal and angry times he delivered the narrative in intimidating and painful terms, complaining that the plot line was distorted by centuries of prejudice and bias. At assertive and uplifting times Woodson's tracts and speeches motivated blacks—especially the young—to do better, to live better, and, most of all, to *think* better. Woodson knew that the race question was his country's lasting national shame, but he never capitulated to it. He was not afraid to place the burden for the answer upon the shoulders of whites as well as blacks. Martin Luther King Jr. said, "Change the behavior and the heart will follow." Eighty years after the publication of *The Negro In Our History*, both sides continue searching for resolution.[34]

George C. Marshall

10

The Marshall Plan

Whether, in the next half-century, the United States will achieve a
more stable and effective balance of its self-interest with the universal
moral and ethical principles it has traditionally espoused depends,
ultimately, upon the character of the American people. . . . [They] have
shown an ability to grasp the hard realities of world leadership and yet
retain the moral enthusiasm nourished during isolation and innocence.
No people has had to grow so old so fast. The nation is still in transition.

—Robert Endicott Osgood,
Ideals and Self-Interest in America's Foreign Relations (1953)

True national security is achieved not just by military power—necessary
though that regrettably is—but by taking actions which subtract from
the number of our potential enemies and add to the number and
strength of our friends.

—Henry Cabot Lodge, Foreword,
The Marshall Plan, 1947–1951 by Theodore A. Wilson (1977)

The president had faith that the respected and popular new secretary
of state would deliver the right speech with the right measured, reassuring tone during a time of national anxiety. The secretary had
already expressed concern publicly in recent months that the United States
might "slip into a state of disinterested weakness" and fail to fulfill its economic responsibilities in a war-ravaged world. Military historians pointed
out that the distinguished secretary, a decorated army general called back
from retirement by his admiring commander-in-chief, possessed a knack for
"seeing time as a stream," applying battle-tempered experience to present-
day political exigencies.[1]

"I need not tell you, gentlemen, that the world situation is very serious," the low-key, soft-spoken secretary began eight minutes of unheralded policy remarks before a hushed crowd on a warm, glorious spring afternoon. "That must be apparent to all intelligent people. I think one difficulty is that the problem is one of such enormous complexity that the very mass of facts presented to the public by the press make it difficult for the man in the street to reach a clear appraisal of the situation. . . . It is logical that the United States should do whatever it is able to do to assist in the return of normal economic health in the world, without which there can be no political stability and no assured peace. . . . Political passion and prejudice should have no part in this effort. With a willingness on the part of our people to face up to the vast responsibilities which history has clearly placed upon our country, the great difficulties ahead can—and will—be overcome."[2]

The president was Harry S. Truman. The historians were Richard Neustadt and Ernest R. May. The sixty-seven-year-old secretary of state was George Marshall, veteran of two World Wars. His speech at Harvard on the afternoon of June 5, 1947, launched the "European Recovery Program." Six years later, on December 10, 1953, the self-effacing elder statesman became the first professional soldier to receive the Nobel Peace Prize. Marshall accepted the prize at Oslo with typical modesty, not for himself, but as "the representative of the American people, whose efforts and money made the Program a success." Franklin D. Roosevelt's secretary of war, Henry Lewis Stimson, said Marshall was "the finest soldier I have ever known. . . . In his presence, ambition folds its tent."[3]

The concluding story in our three-century journey reverses the geographical perspective. We first followed John Winthrop on a westward voyage of renewal to foreign shores. Now we turn to face Europe, depressed in the wake of a devastating war, a harsh winter, a summer of drought, and a sparse harvest. America's helping hand was extended to our "worn out friends" with the largest voluntary transfer of economic resources in history, not only billions of dollars in development loans as well as outright grants, but also machinery, raw materials, food—especially grain and fuel—especially coal. Foreign aid was leveraged to help remake the Old World in the likeness of the New. The Marshall Plan was a potent mixture at midcentury, planting the seeds for NATO and the European Union, linking the promise of economic well-being with the intent of widening America's sphere of influence and forestalling the advance of Soviet Communism.

The youngest of three children of Laura Bradford and George C. Marshall Sr., both originally of Augusta, Kentucky, George Catlett Marshall was born on December 31, 1880, in a two-story brick house on Federal Road in Uniontown, Fayette County, Pennsylvania, forty miles southeast of Pittsburgh. His mother, a sociable, even-tempered lady, who played piano and sang every evening, was an observant Episcopalian. His father, a successful coal manufacturer and local history and genealogy buff, instilled in the boy, nicknamed "Flicker," a lifelong interest in hunting, fishing, and gardening.

After an informal early education, George was unable to gain admission to West Point and so entered Virginia Military Institute in Lexington. Flourishing in the disciplined setting, he graduated in 1901 as senior first captain of the Corps of Cadets with a degree in civil engineering. The following year he married Elizabeth Carter Coles; they honeymooned at the new Willard Hotel in Washington. After service in Mindoro, the Philippines, the Oklahoma Territory, and at Fort Clark on the Texas-Mexico border, Marshall graduated with honors from the Infantry-Cavalry School at Fort Leavenworth, Kansas, and was promoted to first lieutenant in 1907. During the next decade, he distinguished himself in a variety of posts around the country, returned to the Philippines for three years, then helped to plan the war mobilization. He sailed aboard the *Tenadores* on June 14, 1917, as a captain and assistant chief of staff for the American Expeditionary Force, landing at St. Nazaire with the first troops to serve in France. Valued for his strategic brilliance and logistical expertise, Marshall did not receive a combat posting. He was retained on the First Division and General Headquarters (GHQ) planning staff for the duration of the war, then taken under the rigorous wing of General of the Armies John J. "Black Jack" Pershing. As one of three aides-de-camp, he remained with Pershing for five years, rose to the rank of lieutenant colonel, then shipped out to Tientsin, China, where he served until the summer of 1927 with the Fifteenth Infantry Regiment, guarding the railroad supply line to Peking. His beloved wife Elizabeth ("Lilly") died that fall. For the next five years, Marshall was assistant commandant of the Infantry School in Fort Benning, Georgia. During his tenure some "two hundred future generals passed through as instructors or students" and fell under the influence of Marshall's emphasis upon the virtues of "brevity and simplicity" in command. "Get down to the essentials," he told the men. "Make clear the real difficulties," he insisted, "and expunge the bunk, complications and ponderosities."

In the fall of 1930 Marshall remarried. His new wife, Katherine Boyce Tupper Brown, was a widow with three small children. He went on to streamline and reform the Illinois National Guard in Chicago. In 1936 he was made brigadier general and commander of the Fifth Brigade of the Third Division in Washington. In the spring of 1939, after less than a year in the War Plans Division of the War Department, Marshall was chosen by President Roosevelt to be the next chief of staff of the U.S. Army. He was sworn in on the morning of September 1, 1939, mere hours after news reached Washington of Germany's invasion of Poland.[4]

In the face of initial congressional and presidential reluctance, Marshall viewed his nonpartisan role for the next two years strictly as an advocate for preparedness: "If Europe blazes, we must put our house in order," he said, testifying forty-eight times before various House and Senate committees, appearing in civilian clothes rather than in uniform, and speaking in a calm and rational voice about the necessity for an "efficient" military, careful not to "wave the flag" overmuch. He did allow himself to lose his composure in private meetings with Roosevelt, who at the outset favored bolstering naval and air power over ground forces. Marshall eventually managed to drive the army budget upward and increase the level of personnel sevenfold until it became the largest military force in American history. Marshall's steady lobbying paralleled a string of incursions by Hitler's army pushing hard against Britain then shifting toward the east against Russia. By the fall of 1941 global tensions were at an unprecedented level, further exacerbated by instability in the Far East. As the American build-up in the Philippines accelerated, diplomatic relations between the United States and Japan deteriorated. Roosevelt provided matériel support for Britain and Russia in the cautious belief it might still be possible to avoid "full-scale belligerency." Then came the Pearl Harbor attack on the morning of December 7, 1941, and the United States entered the war.[5]

Marshall was a stalwart, reassuring presence at the major strategy conferences of World War II—Arcadia, Casablanca, Washington, Quebec, Cairo, Yalta, Potsdam. Despite the peripatetic demands of the job, General Marshall protested he was "no diplomat," preferring to portray himself as a straightforward thinker and practical planner. Behind the carefully cultivated mask of authority—the formal, unsmiling commander at his desk every day by 7:30 in the morning and expecting the same of his staff—were the checks and balances of an overarching mind. Even when engaged in disputes with Roosevelt and Churchill and juggling the constantly shifting demands of a vast global battleground with fronts in the Pacific, the Mediterranean, North Africa, Europe, and Russia, Marshall never lost sight of the primacy of the Anglo-American alliance, and never departed from his ardent "Germany-first" approach, advocating a preemptive Channel crossing early in the conflict, more than two years before "Operation Overlord." By the time that pivotal D day arrived in the spring of 1944, Marshall had become—in the eyes of the president—an indispensable mediator knitting together the entire war effort. Even so Roosevelt was willing to designate TIME magazine's "Man of the Year" as the supreme allied commander if Marshall stepped up and asked for it. Much as Churchill, Stalin, Roosevelt's entire cabinet, and even the American public assumed Marshall would take field responsibility for the European theater of operations, the general could not in good conscience express this long-held desire. He did not want to "embarrass the president one way or the other" by placing his career feelings ahead of the best interests of the country. The commander in chief must "deal in this matter with a perfectly free hand. . . . I would go whatever way he wanted me to go," Marshall recalled a dozen years later without a trace of bitterness.

"I feel I could not sleep at ease with you out of Washington," Roosevelt admitted, naming Marshall's protégé, Gen. Dwight D. Eisenhower, to the post. By the end of the summer of 1944, France was liberated and the Axis powers were staggering. Germany surrendered unconditionally weeks after the death of Franklin D. Roosevelt the following spring. Eleanor Roosevelt turned to Marshall, the army's first five-star general and her husband's closest adviser at the end, to be responsible for funeral and burial arrangements at Hyde Park. Marshall devoted increased attention to developing postwar occupation policy and to high hopes for a new organization, the United Nations. In the summer of 1945, having been a member of the combined Oversight Committee for Atomic Studies by American and British scientists, Marshall joined with Pres. Harry. S. Truman in unqualified approval of the use of the bombs at Hiroshima and Nagasaki to shorten the war and effect an enormous reduction in American casualties: "We had notified them of the bomb [by formal ultimatum]," Marshall said bluntly. "They didn't choose to believe that. And what they needed was shock action, and they got it."[6]

"Most of you know how different, how fortunate is America compared with the rest of the world," Chief of Staff Marshall observed in his farewell retirement speech at the Pentagon on November 26, 1945. "The world of suffering people looks to us for such leadership." The ordeal of the war just concluded—and the 1914–18 global conflict fresh in memory—convinced Marshall that the time for unilateralism was finished. America's moral perspective needed to be placed upon the world arena. "Along with the great problem of maintaining the peace we must solve the problem of the pittance of food, of clothing, and coal and homes. . . . They are directly related, one to the other." Here was a compassionate acknowledgement of international responsibility coming from a man who had presided over the largest military deployment of all time. "Neither of these problems can be solved alone," Marshall said, emphasizing that liberation must take tangible form if the cycles of European economic stagnation and political frustration characterizing the past three decades were to be broken.[7]

Much as Katherine Marshall looked forward to having her husband all to herself, his retirement was not to be. The day after the Pentagon ceremony, he received a call from the president, an even bigger admirer than Roosevelt had been. Until he met the general, "he [had] wondered if the 'modern times' were capable of producing a great man . . . The more I see and talk with him the more certain I am he's the great one of the age," Harry Truman wrote. "I am sure lucky to have his friendship and support." He asked Marshall to go to China as a mediating special presidential emissary with the rank of ambassador in order to forestall the growing civil war between the Nationalist Kuomintang government and the Communists.[8]

In the midst of testifying at daylong congressional hearings on the Pearl Harbor attack, Marshall had almost no time to prepare. Nevertheless, he responded, "undismayed and determined," with the usual taciturn alacrity. An initial cease-fire was reached in China in the new year, but was short-lived. Marshall's stay was extended several times; but by December 1946, visibly frustrated by the prospect of an all-out conflict, he was recalled by Truman, who nominated him on January 7, 1947, to become the next secretary of state. By the end of the day he was confirmed by the Senate Foreign Relations Committee under the aggressive leadership of Sen. Arthur Vandenberg, Republican of Michigan. Two weeks later Marshall took the oath of office.[9]

The train from Chicago pulled into the platform at Washington's Union Station. The general and his wife emerged. Standing in the windy, frigid cold, Marshall was resplendent in a beaver-trimmed camel's hair coat. Shoulders slightly stooped, he was a shade under six feet tall, ruddy and fit after a brief Hawaii vacation. His eyes were light blue, gray hair closely trimmed. Before heading to the swearing-in ceremony at the White House, he made a short statement to the clamoring crowd of reporters to put one particular gossip item to rest—George Marshall for president? "I think this is as good a time as any to terminate speculation about me in a political way," he said, speaking in a low, staccato voice that forced listeners to lean in toward him. "I am assuming that the office of secretary of state, at least under present conditions, is nonpolitical and I am going to govern myself accordingly. I will never become involved in political matters and therefore I cannot be considered a candidate for any political office."[10]

Marshall's first action as secretary of state was to drop in unannounced at the office of Under Secretary Dean Gooderham Acheson and ask him to stay on as chief of staff in a direct-reporting relationship, "coming to him when I needed help," Acheson wrote, "and his look indicated that that had better not be often." Tall and elegant, impeccably tailored and mustachioed, coming up by way of Groton, Yale, and Harvard Law School, Acheson had clerked for Justice Louis Brandeis at the Supreme Court and was a partner at the respected Washington firm of Covington & Burling before joining the State Department in 1941. The two men had already worked closely together. When Marshall was in China, Acheson had served as his hand-picked "rear echelon," the one person at headquarters he relied upon. "I shall expect of you," Marshall said on the brink of their new initiative, "the most complete frankness, particularly about myself. I have no feelings except those I reserve for Mrs. Marshall." In the opinion of his friend and colleague, Sir Oliver Franks, the British ambassador to Washington, Dean Acheson was "a pure American type of a rather rare species . . . a blade of steel." As such, and as a penetrating student of the human condition, he was the ideal foil to George Marshall.[11]

Marshall's first foreign policy challenge was the multifaceted "British problem" symptomatic of Europe's general malaise. Britain's Empire was loosening, her economy "sputtering" in disarray, unemployment surging, transportation in shambles, postwar loans drawing down at a precipitous rate. On February 21 the Foreign Office informed the State Department that the United Kingdom could no longer sustain the presence of occupying forces stationed in Greece since the German withdrawal in October 1944. By the end of the following month, Britain would have to pull out of that troubled land, where a full-scale guerrilla war raged between the Communist insurgent National Popular Liberation Army and the incumbent Royalists in Athens. "Was the U.S.," TIME magazine wanted to know, "ready to take Britain's place?"[12]

Marshall had been briefed on Britain's decision before he gave his first address as secretary of state at a Princeton convocation to commemorate the university's bicentennial on Washington's Birthday, February 22, 1947. His ominous sentiments spoken at the Senate Foreign Relations Committee the prior week resonated with his war's end Pentagon farewell. "The war years were critical, at times alarmingly so," Marshall told the students. "We are living today in a most difficult period. The problems are different [now] but no less vital to the national security than those during the days of active fighting. . . . [T]here is a natural tendency to relax and to return to business as usual, politics as usual, pleasure as usual," which is the wrong path. It was more imperative than ever, he said, making an impression upon the young audience, that "the students in every university, college, and high school in the United States" glean from history an awareness of the obligations of their country's new position in the world—geographically, financially, militarily, and scientifically. "In order to take a full part in the life which is before you," Marshall said, "I think you must in effect relive the past so that you may return to the present with deep convictions and an understanding of what manner of country this is for which men for many generations have laid down their lives."[13]

The dominant agenda item for the Moscow Conference of Foreign Ministers, scheduled to begin at the middle of March, was the future of Germany and Eastern Europe, where the Russian army, to the unease of the other Western Allied Powers, still remained since the end of the war. Marshall departed for the conference on the morning of March 5.

That same day another trusted member of his inner circle was headed in the opposite direction, removing himself from the pressure-cooker atmosphere of Washington to a ranch near Tucson, Arizona, with the intention "to let his mind roam over the big problems" facing the country—from a different angle of approach than Acheson's. William L. "Will" Clayton was a Mississippi-born high school dropout, master of cotton commodity brokerage and self-made millionaire who by the end of World War I stood out as a "humble" Democrat among corporate Republicans. "The modest magician," as Clayton's close friends liked to call him, was summoned away from Houston, Texas, and into government service by President Roosevelt as a "dollar a year" economic adviser. Named assistant secretary of state in 1944, he was promoted by President Truman to under secretary for economic affairs. As a practical businessman, Clayton advocated for free enterprise and low trade barriers as the most desirable correctives to the "disturbing world picture. . . . The preservation of world peace depends first of all upon the preservation of the integrity and independence of sovereign nations," he wrote in a memorandum that Clayton's biographer, Gregory Fossedal, says was delivered in the form of "talking-points" directly to Acheson. Such sovereignty would be guaranteed, not by military aid alone, but by a huge, well-publicized infusion of money beyond the "piecemeal" millions here and there since the end of the war. At least five billion dollars in foreign loans was called for, "as well as technical and administrative assistance."[14]

When Marshall touched down at Paris before going on to Berlin, he received the text of a dramatic, eighteen-minute speech the president intended to read before a joint session of Congress the following week. In what became known as "the Truman Doctrine," the president summarized the desperate situation in Greece and, by extension, in Turkey. Truman feared the domino effect of world-wide "confusion and disorder" if these governments should fall prey to a "second way of life" relying "upon terror and oppression." He did not mention the "unwelcome challengers" by name. The president asked for a four-hundred-million-dollar package "to aid free peoples who are resisting attempted subjugations by armed minorities or by outside pressure."[15]

Marshall read the speech—"a hanger with many hooks on which an array of global policies could be accommodated"—and was not pleased. The Soviet Union was not referred to explicitly, but it seemed to Marshall "that there was a little too much flamboyant anti-Communism." In this critique, he consulted closely with Charles "Chip" Bohlen, the charismatic special assistant for Soviet affairs accompanying him on the mission. Marshall was so impressed by Bohlen's professionalism and depth of knowledge in Russian language and culture that he soon promoted him to State Department counselor, an appointment requiring congressional approval. Bohlen, a Harvard man, had been in the Foreign Service since 1930. He served with George Kennan in the Moscow Embassy and in the Eastern European section of the State Department. Transferred to Tokyo in 1940, he was there at the time of the Pearl Harbor attack. He was then made assistant chief of the Russian department at the State Department. Bohlen was Roosevelt's interpreter at Yalta and Truman's at Potsdam. He agreed with Marshall that "Truman was using too much rhetoric." Marshall did not relish presidential saber rattling at such an inopportune moment so close to his Moscow destination. Listening to Bohlen in the customary careful manner, Marshall cabled their diplomatic concerns back to Washington, asking that the aggressive speech be "toned down." The reply was that "in the considered opinion of the Executive Branch, including the president, the Senate would not approve the doctrine without the emphasis of the Soviet danger."[16]

Six frustrating weeks of talks followed in Moscow among Secretary Marshall; Ernest Bevin, British secretary of state for foreign affairs; Georges Bidault, French foreign minister; and Soviet foreign minister Vyacheslav Molotov. The remainder of March was spent by the "big Four" trying to forge a balanced peace agreement on Germany and Austria. Discussions on economic reparations, war-zone territorial cessions, and the proposed composition of a central German government became bogged down in technicalities and "wrangling" among the occupying powers. A ninety-minute courtesy call on Generalissimo Stalin at ten o'clock on the night of April 18 only fed the atmosphere of willful confusion. While Marshall warned the Soviet leader that it was dangerous to leave Germany in an unresolved state, Stalin doodled with a red pencil in an indifferent posture of studied detachment. "Don't worry. . . . We may agree next time," he told Marshall, placing a comradely hand on his shoulder, "and if not, the time after that." If there were to be an economic collapse in Germany, Stalin seemed to believe, so be it.[17]

Marshall reluctantly concluded that the Soviet Union was not negotiating in good faith and that it was going to be difficult to induce them to cooperate in achieving European recovery. On the plane returning to Washington, "shaken by the realization of the seriousness and urgency of the plight in Western Europe," he drafted a talk for delivery on nationwide radio. In a "slow, grave voice," he informed the American public that "the recovery of Europe has been far slower than expected. . . . The patient is sinking while the doctors deliberate. So I believe that action cannot await compromise through exhaustion."[18]

The next morning, April 29, Marshall resumed his methodical, determined plan to reorganize the fragmentary "compartments" of the State Department into a coherent division of labors. He wanted to construct a small, confidential Policy Planning Staff (PPS), charged with the mission—in Acheson's words—of "looking ahead . . . beyond the smoke and crises of current battle." At the top of this intimate group, in the office adjoining his own, Marshall installed the brilliant career diplomat George Frost Kennan, plucking him away from his new job as first civilian deputy commandant at the new National War College. Joining the Foreign Service in 1926 fresh out of Princeton, Kennan was stationed at the first U.S. Embassy in Moscow from 1933 to 1937 under Ambassador William Bullitt and was in Berlin when the U.S. declared war on Nazi Germany. In 1945 he returned to Moscow as chargé d'affaires standing in for Ambassador Averill Harriman. In February of 1946, in response to a request from the State Department for an informed analysis of Soviet intentions, Kennan sent an eight-thousand-word "Long Telegram," refined in a memo a year later to Secretary of the Navy James Forrestal, the essence of which was published in the July 1947 issue of *Foreign Affairs* magazine as "The Sources of Soviet Conduct." Kennan soberly warned that the Communist Party line "messianic ideology" was a reaction against the perceived threat of "capitalist encirclement." Soviet expansion, Kennan said, could best be "*contained* by the adroit and vigilant application of counterforce at a series of constantly shifting geographical and political points." Counterbalancing the intermittently militant tone of the memorandum, Kennan concluded that the problem of Soviet antagonism should be approached "calmly and with good heart . . . with courage, detachment, objectivity and determination." Underplaying its impact, Kennan recalled a half century later that "for some reason [the document] struck this very responsive bell back in Washington and was circulated all around."

Saying he "just didn't want to accumulate any ordinary people," Marshall chose Kennan for his State Department brain trust: "I would rather have one good man than five mediocrities." The general was in a hurry for some results. "Fixing [Kennan] penetratingly over the rims of his glasses," and with raised eyebrows—"eyebrows before whose raising," Kennan recalled, "better men than I had quailed," Marshall told him curtly that "in a matter of two to three weeks at most . . . I want to know what this government should do about Europe." In parting, he added—"Avoid trivia."[19]

During an intense month of foreign policy jockeying, Dean Acheson claimed he was the first to "gallop" out of the starting gate. With the sanction of the president, who had a longstanding commitment to appear but could not attend, Acheson gave a keynote speech on May 8 to a convention of cotton growers in the sweltering gymnasium of Delta State Teacher's College in Cleveland, Mississippi, largely written by Joseph Marion Jones of the State Department's Office of Public Affairs, who had worked on early drafts for Truman's "Doctrine." Acheson told Jones he wanted all the "grisly facts" from Europe. For his part Jones felt strongly that "the right psychological tone" was required. "We have a great deal to gain by convincing the world that we have something positive and attractive to offer, and not just anti-Communism.

"European recovery cannot be complete until the various parts of Europe's economy are working together in a harmonious whole," Acheson said, reinforcing the connection between European health and American safety. "It is necessary if we are to preserve our own freedoms and our own democratic institutions." The speech was an important step toward the coalescence of the European Recovery Program, because it was the first sanctioned, public statement to reinforce Truman's plea to Congress. *The New Republic*, among many other publications, reacted favorably: "A major shift in emphasis has taken place in the State Department's strategy toward Russia." Acheson's words were similarly welcomed abroad. Winston Churchill referred a week later to the necessity of "a European solution for European problems."[20]

Next to concur was Will Clayton, sent to Geneva by President Truman to represent the United States at the first meeting of the United Nations Economic Commission for Europe and to "give it a closer look." After addressing the conference on May 2, Clayton set out on a tour of Western European capitals that left him "shocked" and troubled. On the flight back to Washington in mid-May, he churned out a "furiously-written" report for Marshall and Acheson, broadly circulated and discussed in the State Department between May 19 and 27. "We understood the physical destruction," an anguished Clayton told his colleagues, "but failed to take fully into account the effects of economic dislocation on production." Paul Nitze, deputy director of the Office of International Trade Policy in the State Department, met with Clayton at the Metropolitan Club for lunch and debriefing and found his friend "genuinely alarmed that Europe was on the brink of disaster. . . . Something had to be done to break the impasse [in Europe], to get industry and agriculture moving again. . . . It will be necessary for the President and the Secretary of State to make a strong, spiritual appeal to the American people," Clayton said.[21]

The last contributory element of the troika was the Policy Planning memorandum put forward by George Kennan and his staff—Joseph E. Johnson, Col. Charles Hatwell Bonesteel III, Jacques Reinstein, Ware Adams, and Carleton Savage. Ordered by Marshall at the end of April to "avoid trivia," Kennan presented "Certain Aspects of the European Recovery Problem from the United States Standpoint" on May 23, quick to admit the paper had been assembled in haste. Kennan's recommendations fell into short-term and long-term. For the former, a quick fix of industrial fuel to help step-up European coal production; for the latter—perhaps the most influential point of Kennan's thinking brought to bear upon Marshall's final synthesis—the policy group stressed the necessity to "distinguish clearly between a program for the economic revitalization of Europe on the one hand, and a program of American support for such revitalization on the other. . . . The program that this country is asked to support must be a joint one," Kennan's group wrote, ". . . not a series of isolated and individual appeals." The idea, they said, was to avoid divisive nationalism, and incline toward what was best for the entire continent. Following that line and recognizing the current appreciation of the United

Nations and its "predominant role in world affairs," Kennan advised that the Economic Commission for Europe be closely involved going forward in the administration of American aid. Accepting that the Russians would de facto have to be included, Kennan took a more moderate tone than he had in the "Long Telegram," preferring to call for an approach that would serve to "*create* strength in the West rather than *destroy* strength in Russia." Furthermore, he said, American support could not be open-ended. Whatever budget was drawn up needed to be finite: "The Truman Doctrine is not a blank check."[22]

On the morning of May 28, Marshall convened a meeting in his office of Acheson, Clayton, Kennan, Bohlen, and Benjamin Cohen, the State Department legal counsel. Clayton's memorandum and Kennan's report were on the table. Marshall asked for general comments. He listened courteously and expressionlessly, thanked the group, and dismissed everyone. Late that afternoon, at the prompting of Carl Hummelsine, director of the executive secretariat, anxious to pin down Marshall's pending calendar commitments, Marshall confirmed tentative acceptance of Harvard president James B. Conant's invitation to deliver brief remarks at the alumni meeting on the afternoon on June 5 at Cambridge, following the commencement ceremony at which Marshall also agreed, after first declining, to receive an honorary degree. Two days later he decided his Harvard remarks should take shape as a formal address. Marshall asked his special assistant, Gen. Marshall Carter, to "have someone consider the various suggestions as to talks that I might make and prepare a draft for a less than ten-minute talk by me at Harvard to the Alumni. . . . It is of tremendous importance," he wrote, "that our people understand the situation in Europe, the plight of the people . . . and particularly the dominant character of the economic factors. . . . Irritation and passion," Marshall cautioned, "should have no part in the matter." Carter had been on the Moscow foreign ministers' trip with Marshall and Chip Bohlen, and knew the general favored Bohlen's writing style. He sent Bohlen the Clayton and Kennan papers, asking Bohlen, as special assistant for Soviet affairs, to draw up the speech on Marshall's behalf under strict confidential orders that there be no advance publicity and no background guidance solicited from anyone else. The wheels were spinning rapidly. Bohlen had a draft in hand on June 2.[23]

All elements of the problem were held, as it were, in solution in his mind until it was ready to precipitate a decision. This is the essence and the method—or rather the art—of judgment in its highest form." Dean Acheson praised George C. Marshall as possessing "not merely military judgment, but judgment in great affairs of state, which requires both mastery of precise information and apprehension of imponderables. . . . When he was through, he was through—and off he went." Chip Bohlen agreed, "He would listen carefully to all sides of a question and then make up his mind. Once a decision was made, there was no turning back."[24]

In Marshall's opinion, the draft he received from Bohlen "wasn't at all finished." He edited the text in solitude on the plane ride to Boston on June 4. That evening at James Conant's home, he tinkered with it some more. One sticking point was that Bohlen wrote that America's "policy is directed not against any country or doctrine, and specifically not against *Communism.*" Marshall dropped the defensive-sounding reference to "Communism." He further decided to offer help to "*all* Europe, including the Soviet Union and her satellites," which Bohlen considered "a hell of a big gamble . . . if the Russians came in . . . there was no chance of congressional action [i.e., budgetary approval]." But Marshall was "adamant." He wanted to put the prospect of assistance out there and give the Soviets one more chance to join the community of nations. Marshall also insisted that the European countries do their own homework and "come clean—that they come up with a workable plan for recovery based on actual requirements, not what they thought the U.S. would give." Will Clayton felt that some measure of consulting advice might be appropriate, but Marshall was "almost arbitrary [and] military" in hewing to this "command." No one on the State Department staff was privy to the speech in its final form, and no press kit was created. The European powers were not consulted prior to Marshall's delivery of the speech. Neither was Senator Vandenberg of the Foreign Relations Committee, although he would become an invaluable ally.

On the morning of June 5, in the company of atomic physicist J. Robert Oppenheimer, literary critic I. A. Richards, poet T. S. Eliot, and eight others, Marshall received an honorary doctor of laws degree. "Just before" he stepped to the podium at 2:00 p.m. before the largest group of Harvard alumni ever assembled, Marshall realized how close to the vest he had kept his work in progress during the preceding several days: "[Truman] hadn't seen it" either.[25]

Playing with his reading glasses and staring down at the manuscript, Marshall touched upon the range of economic and political issues debated and discussed with his staff during the five months since he had taken office as secretary of state. The language of the speech reflected the blended labor of many hands, shaping a vivid and poignant picture of Europe in distress, the pressing need for change, the belief that the United States must step up "against hunger, poverty, desperation and chaos" and help shape a new economy to avoid the problems that plagued the West between the two World Wars. There was a veiled warning to "any government which maneuvers to block the recovery of other countries." There was a clear request for European "initiative," setting to rest any pretense of American unilateralism. Marshall's handwritten, extemporaneous flourish asserted that "the whole world of the future hangs on a proper judgment. It hangs, I think, to large extent on the realization of the American people."[26]

He ended masterfully with a series of compelling questions designed to appeal beyond the immediate audience to the moral and patriotic standards of American society. "What are the reactions of the people? What are the justifications of those reactions? What are the sufferings? What is needed? What can best be done? What *must* be done?" He called for the application of those standards when they mattered most—to the present moment of international tension. Linking America's interests with the interests of other countries, connecting America to a world community, predicating American prosperity upon global prosperity, Secretary of State Marshall showed himself to be an idealist—a pragmatic idealist—who understood that no benevolent program could survive if it seemed contrary to popular opinion. "Great changes in the way a nation thinks and acts come like the tide. . . . For the first time since the nation had become a world power," historian Robert Endicott Osgood wrote in his pioneering 1953 study, *Ideals and Self-Interest in America's Foreign Relations*, "the great majority of the American people understood that their everyday lives were seriously affected by what happened beyond the seas."[27]

When Marshall finished speaking, the applause was tremendous, but press coverage of the untitled address was thin. The next day a brief story in the *New York Times* was headed, "Mr. Marshall's Hint." The full text of the speech was not published until several days following. State Department policy makers were at a momentary loss—"Marshall 'Plan,'" Kennan wrote tentatively. "We have no plan." Economic staff assistant Ben Moore added, "The 'Marshall Plan' has been compared to a flying saucer—nobody knows what it looks like, how big it is, in what direction it is moving, or whether it really exists." The president's adviser, Clark Clifford, told Truman the "Plan" should be named in his honor, but Truman was too smart for that. Name it after "the greatest living American," he replied. Even the general alluded to his Harvard talk as "the so-called Marshall Plan," deeming it inappropriate to claim personal credit for a collective enterprise. With unsparing precision, journalist Walter Lippmann, writing in his "Time and Tide" column in the *New York Herald Tribune* while responding to George Kennan's "containment" piece in *Foreign Affairs*, correctly caught the general's intentions. The Harvard speech, Lippmann said, was sophisticated leverage, meant to show the European governments that America valued their independence, and likewise understood their interdependence, and was testing the abilities of the separate nations to come together and devise a comprehensive way to chart rehabilitation. Regardless of proper title, or nuance of interpetation, the immense challenge over the next twelve months was clear to Marshall—to "put the damned thing over."[28]

Ernest Bevin and Georges Bidault, the British and French foreign ministers, issued a broad communiqué in zealous reponse to Marshall that invited European nations to send representatives to the Grand Palais in Paris to begin the work of defining a stability plan under the umbrella of a new organization, the Committee of European Economic Cooperation (CEEC). The chairman was Dean Acheson's colleague, Sir Oliver Franks. American loans and matching grants would be requested for investment, reconstruction, and modernization, including technology transfer. America would provide "the lubricant in an engine—not the fuel—allowing a machine to run that would otherwise buckle and bind." Chip Bohlen viewed America's role as more biological than mechanical—"injecting a little economic blood into a system that had stopped functioning."

Vyacheslav Molotov arrived in Paris on June 26 with a party of over one hundred delegates, raising false hopes of an extension of Russia's pro-détente stance. But the meetings took a downward turn almost immediately thereafter as the sullen, "indelicate" Molotov, true to his reputation as "Mr. Nyet," struck a suspicious and uncompromising position. He refused to provide the United States, Britain, and France with privileged Soviet financial and investment data as the prerequisite for establishing a baseline for future support; and he balked at German inclusion in the plan unless Russia's extreme reparations demands were met.

Will Clayton connected peace with economic emancipation: "Enemies in the market place cannot long be friends at the conference table." Molotov walked out of the deliberations. The Soviet news agency, *Tass*, announced in early July that the satellite states of Poland, Yugoslavia, and Romania would not attend an expanded Paris conference. Bulgaria, Czechoslovakia, Hungary, Albania, and Finland followed suit. In the fall, the "Cominform," the Information Bureau of the Communist and Workers' Parties, was created at Belgrade as the official organization to coordinate actions under Soviet direction among all local Communist Parties. Standing in opposition to "United States imperialism," the Cominform publicized the dictum, sanctioned by Stalin and articulated by Politburo member and Leningrad party leader Andrei Zhdanov, that the Truman Doctrine and the Marshall Plan were evidence of America's subversive effort to initiate an economic hegemony under the guise of benevolent statesmanship, rewarding liberal and centrist European leaders and "split[ting] Europe into two camps."[29]

On September 21 the Committee of European Economic Cooperation sent a report tied up in red ribbon to the State Department. Ambitious goals for agriculture, manufacturing, shipping, mining, metals processing, and electricity output were put forth at a price tag of $19.2 billion over four years. Marshall and his team embarked upon a strenuous effort to take the concept of the European Recovery Program (ERP) to the country and encourage wide public discussion. To the general, "selling the ERP to the American people was an exacting task." The "campaign" took on a military character. "There's nothing so profound as the logic of the thing," Marshall recalled. "But the execution of it, that's another matter. . . . I flew thousands of miles a week . . . almost as if I were running for office." Marshall was the program's greatest asset, its living exponent. His name and reassuring image of rectitude had dominated the front pages since his return from

Moscow the preceding spring. Republican investment banker Robert M. Lovett, successor to retired Dean Acheson as under secretary of state, Will Clayton, Attorney General Tom Clark, Secretary of the Treasury Clinton Anderson, Chip Bohlen, assigned to take charge of public relations, and members of the State Department staff, all helped to push the program at home, fanning out to deliver speeches before nearly one thousand different audiences.

A "Citizens' Committee for the Marshall Plan" with headquarters in New York City was set up at the encouragement of retired secretary of state Henry L. Stimson. "Americans must now understand," wrote the elder statesman, "that the United States has become, for better or worse, a wholly committed member of the world community." The Citizens' Committee, composed predominantly of corporate executives and community leaders, produced newsreels and informational documentary films, distributed millions of informational packets and brochures, and took out full page advertisements in major newspapers placing emphasis upon the humanitarian dimension of the program.[30]

On the legislative front, Marshall was indefatigable, unfailingly courteous to lawmakers in Capitol Hill briefings, submitting to hours of questioning in open and closed sessions. With Lovett at his side, Marshall met early and often with Joseph Martin, speaker of the House of Representatives, and his staff. Martin took an active role, establishing "fact-finding" delegations to travel abroad, "stand amidst the rubble," and talk with "emaciated mothers and children." The House created a Select Committee on Foreign Aid to institutionalize its efforts in assessing the program. According to Marshall and Acheson, the deciding factor for European Recovery support resided in the "full partnership" and "genuine belief" of the internationalist, bipartisan consensus-builder extraordinaire, Sen. Arthur H. Vandenberg: "We could not have gotten much closer unless I sat in Vandenberg's lap or he sat in mine . . . ," Marshall said. The two men met frequently at Blair House. "He was marvellous to work with and fortunately he thought I was. . . . He was my right hand man and at times I was his right hand man. . . . He was just the whole show when we got to the actual movement of the [program]."[31]

Long before President Truman submitted the formal proposal for the European Recovery Program on December 19, 1947, Vandenberg realized that "our friend Marshall is certainly going to have a helluva time" faced with a

Republican Congress anxious to reduce taxes and trim government spending. The senator worked in tandem with the State Department staff to be sure that the program received a fair hearing. Vandenberg referred to the "'so-called Marshall Plan'" in a letter to Malcolm W. Bingay, columnist of the *Detroit Free Press*, as an assertion of "our concept of free men, free government, and a relatively free international economy." From January 8 to February 5, 1948, the Senate Foreign Relations Committee chaired by Vandenberg heard more than ninety witnesses and received seventy-six written statements on behalf of the program. During this time, there was a Communist coup in Czechoslovakia, adding urgency to the argument, such that when his colleagues began to talk about cutting the first twelve months' budget allocation, Vandenberg warned, "When a man is drowning twenty feet away, it's a mistake to throw him a fifteen-foot rope. . . . In the final analysis, peace is cheaper than war." On March 1 he rose before a capacity crowd in the Senate chamber to plead for passage of the Economic Cooperation Act of 1948. Vandenberg had worked on the speech for many weeks, "improving it one thousand percent on his own typewriter" and rewriting it seven times from top to bottom after some assistance from Robert Lovett. "Mr. President," Vandenberg declared, "this act may well become a welcome beacon in the world's dark night, but if a beacon is to be lighted at all, it had better be lighted before it is too late . . . The greatest nation on earth either justifies or surrenders its leadership. We must choose."

At five minutes past midnight on March 14, the Senate voted approval, 69 to 17. Soon thereafter, the House agreed to the major portions of the bill, 329–71, minor differences were resolved in conference, and Truman signed the bill into law on April 3, establishing the Economic Cooperation Administration (ECA) under the direction of Paul G. Hoffman, the former president of the Studebaker Corporation.[32]

During the next four years, $13.3 billion, between 1 and 2 percent of the gross national product for that period, and more than $100 billion in today's dollars, was disbursed in aid to more than 270 million people in sixteen countries of Western Europe. The preponderant portion of loans and grants during the first three years—in excess of 70 percent—went to restore transatlantic trade and halt inflation. Commodities were purchased by European managers from U.S. suppliers, who were paid in dollars credited against the proportion of funding allocated to each country. By the fourth year, in the words of ECA deputy administrator William C. Foster, the plan "doffed its overalls in favor of combat fatigues" in response to the outbreak of the Korean War, and the expenses shifted toward defense, under the slogan "Strength for a Free World." The president wrote in triumph; "In all the history of the world, we are the first great nation to feed and support the conquered."[33]

The eight-day voyage on board the *Andrea Doria* from New York via the southern route to Naples in November 1953 was cold and choppy. George C. Marshall, just released from Walter Reed Hospital where he was treated for the flu, intended to write his Nobel Prize remarks at sea. By the time he reached Paris, he had not composed one line and was still suffering from respiratory complications. He arrived exhausted at the residence of Gen. Alfred B. Gruenther, Supreme Allied Commander of Europe, and went immediately to bed. A NATO staff assistant, Col. Andrew J. Goodpaster, was assigned to help Marshall pull his thoughts together from a series of note cards and an hour and a half of dictation.

At the December 10 ceremony in Oslo, Marshall's lecture of acceptance was full of hope.

We must present democracy as a force holding within itself the seeds of unlimited progress by the human race. By our actions we should make it clear that such a democracy is a means to a better way of life, together with a better understanding among nations. Tyranny must inevitably retire before the tremendous moral strength of the gospel of freedom and self-respect for the individual. . . . In America we have a creed which comes to us from the deep roots of the past. It springs from the convictions of the men and women who founded this nation and made it great. . . . I am not implying in any way that we would attempt to persuade other people to adopt our particular form of government. I refer here specifically to those fundamental values on which our government, like many other democracies, is based. These, I believe, are timeless and have a validity for all mankind. These, I believe, will kindle the imagination and arouse the spirit.[34]

Marshall's words have poignant resonance. Here was a man who came up over the course of decades through the ranks of American military culture, took on the ultimate authority for its fighting army, and sanctioned the deployment of the original weapon of mass destruction. He was then called upon to transfer this immense inheritance into an utterly dissimilar arena. Employing an almost unimaginable degree of moral willpower, the global warrior during the greatest conflagration of the past century became a global humanitarian strategist. As secretary of state, his single-minded goal was to rebuild, not vanquish.

Marshall's transformation was legitimate, because he connected the use of American power with the nation's concomitant obligation to international responsibility. He would have been the last person to characterize himself as a philosopher in an isolated realm of thought. He was an activist who saw the mission of the Department of State—from within the structure of the American government outward—as a multilateral instrument with which to export the great usefulness of democracy as a tangible gift, not a grafted ideology.

"I don't believe there's a statue of General Marshall in Europe," said Alistair Cooke in his weekly BBC *Letter from America* on December 9, 2002. "There ought to be, as a reminder of the American aim to restore the fabric of European life."[35]

Afterword: A Sense of History

The most difficult part of my job as a historian, when I am literally surrounded on all sides by facts and anecdotes about the past and can no longer see the floor of my study because it is covered with books and papers, is the process of making choices in order to support my case. The closer I get to the current age of information and instant media, the more difficult those choices become. The American Revelation came to rest in the 1950s, because I needed clarifying space between my subject matter and my imagination. The '50s are at a comfortable and objective distance. They reside in my mind on that cusp at which journalism ends and history begins, a time when I can still recall watching some of the cast of characters on black and white television, hearing their voices on the radio during the evening news broadcast, and reading the names of others in block letter headlines on the front page of the newspaper.

Remember that these are ten ideals—not the ten ideals—that shaped our country, selected to create a cumulative portrait of America as a place to begin anew, an enlightened democratic experiment, an arena in which each individual should ennoble and serve the whole, a nation driven forward by expansive energy with an obligation to preserve the ties that bind it together, as well as with other societies. This book was intended to be a truthful portrait, and therefore it is an unvarnished one. The deeper I delved into the lives of the ten people about whom I chose to write, the more I became convinced of the consistency in their own minds—the purity of the original intentions that drove them. Each person's life was a dramatic prelude leading up to the moment when the ideal emerged into the culture of the era.

Arthur M. Schlesinger Jr. wrote recently in his Memoirs that "history is forever haunted by the crises and preoccupations of the age in which it is written." Historical objectivity, no matter how desirable the standard, is tempered and modified in subtle ways by the sentiments of the historian, who is, after all, only human. He wants to position his ideas in relation to all time, even as he must always accept in the end that he is fixed in a historical moment. This book is appearing in exceptionally turbulent times, but when we look back, it seems as if there have always been unusual times in America.

Where do we go from here? I have been engaged for many years in composing a cumulative biography of modern America. In past books I have told the absorbing stories of four complex and remarkable people who contributed to our collective contemporary life. My books on William Carlos Williams, Man Ray, Thomas Edison, and Henry Ford are about home-grown literature and art, invention, and entrepreneurial technology. I continue to believe that we must possess a firm grip on the past before we move ahead too quickly. Greater understanding of the value of shared history enables us to face the future with intelligence.

My concluding sentiment is hope—that the end of this book is not the end of the story but the beginning of the revelation that we need to start now to reconstruct within ourselves a redeeming image of America—the America we deserve.

Acknowledgments

As always, I begin with gratitude to the librarians and archivists who held the keys to many and various realms and permitted me generous and helpful access to their collections. At The New York Public Library, where I spent countless days and hours in blessedly anonymous research during the past three years, I thank Paul LeClerc, President; Beth Diefendorf, Chief of the General Research Division; Michael Terry, Dorot Chief Librarian, and Roberta Saltzman, the Jewish Division; William Stingone, Curator of Manuscripts, and Melanie A. Yolles, Manuscripts and Archives Division; Wayne Furman, Special Collections; and the reference staffs of the Performing Arts Research Center, the Schomburg Collection for Research in Black Culture, and the Science, Industry, and Business libraries.

Grateful thanks as well to Lee Arnold, Director of the Library, the Historical Society of Pennsylvania; India Artis, The Crisis magazine, NAACP; Jan Hilley and Becky Amato, Manuscripts Division, and the Library staff, the New-York Historical Society; Helen Beckert, Glen Ridge Public Library; Wendy E. Chmielewski, Curator, the Swarthmore College Peace Collection; John Y. Cole, Director, the Center for the Book at the Library of Congress; Brian Leigh Dunnigan, Curator of Maps, William L. Clements Library, University of Michigan, Ann Arbor; Mary Huth, Rush Rhees Memorial Library, the University of Rochester; Cornelia S. King and Philip Lapsansky, Reference Department, Library Company of Philadelphia; the staff of the Harry A. Sprague Library, Montclair State

University; Timothy D. Murray, Head, Special Collections, University of Delaware Library; Angelique Speight, the National Medical Association; and Suzi Waters, Journals Manager, University of North Carolina Press.

For scholarly advice and counsel, and for friendship and support in other valued ways, I thank Debra Bard; Larry I. Bland, Director, the George C. Marshall Foundation; Victoria Bissell Brown; W. Paul Coates, Director, Black Classic Press; Stella Connell; Gioia Diliberto; Rob Earp, Ingram Book Company; Jessica Hagedorn; Walter Isaacson; David Levering Lewis; Will Lippincott; Walter Mosley; Barbara Novak; Nathaniel Philbrick; Randall Rothenberg; Ellen Ryder and Matthew Venzon; Kenneth Silverman; Domna C. Stanton; Ronald Steel; Alberto A. Vitale; and Michael R. Winston, President, Alfred Harcourt Foundation.

Thanks to the Trident Media Group team for their professional representation: Robert Gottlieb, for his unique, unflagging enthusiasm and persistence; and John W. Silbersack, my serious, loyal, and encouraging agent, who is to be commended for never losing his patience. Thanks to John's vigilant assistant, Kate Scherler; and also to Kimberly A. Whalen, Melissa Flashman, Alex Glass, and Adrienne Jozwick.

My editor at St. Martin's Press, Diane Reverand, drew upon her eclectic knowledge to make this into a better book, from the moment we had our first ebullient conversation over lunch, until the last revisions came through and measured up to her high standard of satisfaction. Thanks also to Diane's assistant, Regina Scarpa, and to publicist Elizabeth Coxe.

My wife, Roberta, first reader for all my books, continues to be my most rigorous, unsparing critic—a thankless task, for which I embrace her nevertheless.

Notes

I. CITY ON A HILL

1. Dunn, "Winthrop's Journal," 185–86, 211.
2. Dunn, "Winthrop's Journal," 192.
3. I have used today's place names to clarify the seventeenth-century geography of New England. "Winthrop's Journal" 13–31; Bremer, 169, 188; Morison, ix, 79; Baritz, 8; Morgan, *Visible Saints*, 119–20. In my discussion of the Puritan world view, I have depended upon the writings of Samuel Eliot Morison, Edmund S. Morgan, and Perry Miller.
4. muweb.Millersville.edu/Winthrop/index.html; Dr. Francis J. Bremer, editor of the Winthrop Papers project (1929ff) of the Massachusetts Historical Society, is the author of the passionate scholarly biography, *John Winthrop: America's Forgotten Founding Father* (2003), of great help in shaping this chapter. See also Moseley, 3, 156; Dunn, "Winthrop's Journal," 188; Morison, 60–61.
5. Morison 52; Morgan, *Dilemma*, 5; Bremer, 79, n. 407.
6. Dunn, "Winthrop's Journal," 189.
7. Schweninger, 16–18; Morison, 60; Dunn and Yaendle, ixff.; Miller, *American Puritans*, 84–85, 230.
8. Miller, *American Puritans*, 265; Dunn and Yaendle, ix; Gray, 703–5; Morgan, *Dilemma*, 12; Atkins, 4, citing John Cotton, *Christ the Fountaine of Life*. On the Puritan insistence upon "balance between religious tradition and civic order," see Michael Knox Beran, "Sacred Texts, Used and Abused," *Wall Street Journal*, August 18, 2003.
9. Weber, 105; Gray, 693, 700; Bremer, xviii.
10. Miller, *American Puritans*, 1; Weber, 83–84.
11. Rutman, 51; Morgan, *Visible Saints*, 11, 14, 23 citing the works of Henry Barrow (1590) and John Field (1588); Morgan, *Dilemma*, 71; Elwood Johnson, 6ff; Morison, 58.

12. Bremer, 103–21.

13. Bozeman, "Errand," 245–46.

14. Bremer, 138; Dunn and Yaendle, ix; Miller, *Puritans*, 36; Morgan, *Dilemma*, 40ff; Baritz, 7–8; Rutman, 23, 34, 41, 87; Morison, 65.

15. Rutman, 30, 32; Morgan, *Visible Saints*, 33, 63–64; Baritz, 39; Miller, *Puritans*, 3; Bremer, 199, and n. 437, citing Winthrop essay, "Reformation Without Separation."

16. Moseley, 34–35; Miller, *Errand*, 114; Rutman, 15, 41, 88.

17. Bremer, 155, 164; Miller, *Errand*, 4; Rutman, 43, 51, 52; Dean and Yeandle, x.

18. Miller, *Puritans*, 36.

19. Dunn, "Winthrop's Journal," 190; Bremer, 163–164.

20. Morgan, *Dilemma*, 40ff; Bremer, 169.

21. *An Early Puritan Commentary by John Cotton*, (Harvard Library 1584–1652), www.hds.Harvard.edu/library/exhibit.html; Miller, *Prose and Poetry*, 171; Dawson, 225, citing note in *Winthrop Papers*, 2:240; Schweninger, 41; Miller, *American Puritans*, 171; Cressy, "Vast and Furious Ocean," 516–17, 528–30.

22. Gray, 699; Bercovitch, 9; Johnson, 196; Bremer 175; Morison, 71–72.

23. Text of "The Humble Request" with accompanying editorial commentary by John Beardsley, www.winthropsociety.org/doc_humble.php; Bremer, 188; Dawson, 224, 227; Dunn and Yeandle, 15–16, citing "Winthrop's Journal"; Miller, *Errand*, 9.

24. Morgan, "Modell," 145, and note 10, 150–151; Dunn and Yeandle, ix; Dawson, 219; Miller, *American Puritans*, 78–79. The definitive dating of the composition and delivery of "A Model of Christian Charity" is Hugh Dawson (1991), 219ff.; see also Dunn and Yeandle, x; Miller, ibid.; Morgan, "'Modell'" (1987); Miller, *Responsibility of Mind*, 145; and Schweninger, 44. My explanation of the sermon refers to the authoritative text edited by Dunn and Yeandle (1996), 1–11.

25. Johnson, "Economic Ideas," 244.

26. Gray, "Political Thought of JW," *New England Quarterly*, 689–91; Bozeman, "Errand," 239.

27. Bremer, 176, 385; Schweninger, 42–46; Baritz, 25; Gray, 681, 685, 694; Morgan, "'Modell'" 145–50; Johnson, 37, 62; Johnson, "Economic Ideas," 247, 249.

28. Miller, *Errand*, 5; also, ibid., 137, with his reference to "my friend Richard Niebuhr," for which see Niebuhr's 1954 essay, "The Idea of Covenant and American Democracy," 129–30. The essay was originally read as a lecture before the American Studies section of the American Historical Association in Chicago on December 28, 1953; Dunn and Yeandle, op.cit., 3–9; Johnson, 37.

29. Johnson, 37–40; Morgan, *Dilemma*, 70, 82; Miller, *Errand*, 90; Niebuhr, 134–35.

30. www.mindprod.com/kjv/Matthew/5.html; bibletools.org/index.cfm; Dunn and Yeandle, op. cit., 9–11; Miller, *Errand*, 5, 11–12; Morgan, *Dilemma*, 12; Baritz, 17; Bercovitch, 39; Bozeman, "Errand," 233.

31. Baritz, 17; John Milton (1643) cited in Bercovitch, 39; Dunn and Yeandle, ibid., 10.

32. www.Antioch.com.sg/gi-bin/bible.pl; Bercovitch, 40; Weber, 112; Moseley, 44; Schweninger, 46; Baritz, 31; Miller, *Errand*, 113.

2. COMMON SENSE

1. Conway, 338–39, 347; Keane, 40, 98, 156, 371, 467; Williamson, 48.

2. For the biographical facts of Thomas Paine's life from birth through arrival in Lewes, I am indebted to the chronologies and accounts provided by Conway (1892, 1977), Kramnick, (1976), Foner, *Collected Writings* (1995), and Keane (1995).

3. *The Life of Thomas Paine*, by Francis Oldys (pseud. George Chalmers, 1791), cited in Hawke, *Paine*, 13, 231–232, and notes, 408, 439.

4. Contemporary account of Headstrong Club activities: Paine's friend and early nineteenth-century biographer, the poet Thomas "Clio" Rickman, cited in Conway, 10; and Williamson, 20, 40, quoting Rickman's interview with "a Mr. Lee, who was often present" at the White Hart. William Lee was publisher of the town's weekly newspaper, *Lewes Journal*, per Keane, 67; Gordon S. Wood, 27ff.

5. Dyck, 50; Ayer, 5; Williamson, 50; Keane, 73 and fn 550.

6. Kramnick, 26–27; Foner, 834–35; Conway, 13–15; Keane, 77; Williamson, 50–56.

7. Paine, Letter to the Hon. Henry Laurens, January 14, 1779; Williamson, 62. For the details here and through the rest of this chapter regarding the gradual build-up of tensions between England and America in the decade leading to the Declaration of Independence, I am grateful for the scholarship of Bernard Bailyn, Gordon S. Wood, and Edmund S. Morgan.

8. Franklin, note, 205.

9. Wood, 48–51.

10. Franklin correspondence referenced from the ten-volume *Writings* VI, ed. Albert Henry Smyth (1905–7), in Van Doren, 479–484, and notes, 785, 798–99, also, Morgan, Foreword (2003) to Franklin, *Autobiography*, 3, 5, 6.

11. Van Doren, notes, 810, 828; Conway, 16; Hawke, 25. The chronology of Franklin's difficult final year in London is derived from Franklin, *Autobiography*, 309ff.

12. Paine, *The American Crisis*, no. 7 (November 11, 1778), also "The Forester's Letter," III (April 22, 1776); Letter to Hon. Henry Laurens, January 14, 1779; Letter to Benjamin Franklin, March 4, 1775; Conway, 330.

13. Paine, *The American Crisis*, no. I, (December 19, 1776); Morgan, Foreword citing Franklin, *Autobiography*, 3; and *Chronology*, 308; Bailyn, 149.

14. Foner, 68–69; Bridenbaugh, 29; Bailyn, 1; Wood, 131; McCullough, *John Adams*, 81; Conway, 19; Keane, 92.

15. Bridenbaugh, 79, 126; Conway, 17; Hawke, 26.

16. Italics are Paine's. Text of essay: www.thomaspaine.org/archive/mag.html.

17. Keane, 23, 95; on increased magazine circulation, Hawke, 29–30 and note 410, letter from Thomas Paine to Benjamin Franklin, March 4, 1775; Kramnick, Editor's Introduction, 28.

18. Paine, *The American Crisis*, no. 2, (January 13, 1777); Szmyd, 218; Hawke, 403; Conway, 17; Williamson, 13, 52; Dyck, 3.

19. Dyck, 26; description of Washington in John Adams letter to Abigail Adams, June 17, 1775, cited in Hawke, 37.

20. Wilson, 13, 14; Wood, 52ff; Foner, 73–74.

21. Hawke, 41; Williamson, 78; Paine, *The American Crisis*, no. 3 (April 19, 1777); Letter from Paine to Laurens, op. cit., January 14, 1779; Aldridge, 35; Conway, 27, citing letter from Benjamin Rush to James Cheetham, ca. 1809.

22. Conway, 27–28, citing Robert Bell's laudatory description of himself in a "contemporary leaflet" Kramnick, 28; Keane, note 57, 555, led me to a summary of Thomas Reid's common sense school of philosophy, his reliance upon ordinary language, and the role of causation and free will in defining human nature: *The Stanford Encyclopedia of Philosophy*, www.plato.Stanford.edu/entries/reid. For the "inevitability" in *Common Sense*, see Joseph Ellis, *Founding Brothers*, 5.

23. Conway, 27, citing Paine, *Pennsylvania Journal*, April 10, 1776.

24. Williamson, 36, 40; Conway, 24.

25. Conway, 25; Paine to Laurens, January 14, 1779. My analysis below of *Common Sense* refers to the text in Kramnick, ed. (1976, 1986), 61–128; Paine's critical references to the king's speech: Appendix to *Common Sense*: Kramnick, 113.

26. Williamson, 284; Paine to Laurens, ibid.; Conway, 27; Hawke, 45.

27. Williamson, 9, 284; Kramnick, 122.

28. Wilson, 128; Kramnick, 63.

29. Parrington, Vol. I, 335–36; Bailyn, 285; Szmyd, 220; see also Paine, "The Forester's Letter," III (April 22, 1776).

30. Williamson, 40; Ayer, 187; Kramnick, 82–87, 92, 99, 120.

31. Ayer, 187; Kramnick, 122; Bailyn, 142–43; Parrington, Vol. I, 346; Foner, 75; see also Paine's draft of the "Rules for the Philadelphia Philosophical Society," February 1787, in Conway, 92, note 2.

32. For the tenor of the Second Continental Congress, see especially Bailyn, *Ideological Origins*, 142ff; Paine to Laurens, ibid; Kramnick, Introduction, 8, citing Franklin; Conway, 25, 26, 84, citing George Washington, Benjamin Rush, Edmund Randolph; Page Smith, *A New Age Now Begins*, 682, citing Washington; Foner, 86, citing Washington and Joseph Hawley.

33. Paine, "The Forester's Letter," II (April 10, 1776) and Paine to Henry Laurens, January 14, 1779; Wood, 55–56; Keane, 128, and Note 558 citing the *Papers of General Charles Lee* I, 312ff.

34. Italics are Paine's; Bailyn, 285; Wood, 56; Szmyd, 208.

35. Williamson, 45, 76; Wilson, 28. Citations from *The Forester's Letters* in Paine (1995), 60–90.

36. McCullough, citing Adams to Abigail, February 1776: 75, 97; Hawke, 48–49, and note 413, citing John Adams correspondence, April and May 1776.

37. Bailyn, 175, 288; Kramnick, 30; Conway 124, citing Adams's *Works* III, 189; Hawke, 7; McCullough, 102, citing Adams's debt to the philosopher James Harrington.

38. Wood, 56; Aldridge, 46; Hawke, 57.

3. E PLURIBUS UNUM

1. Bernstein, 44–45.

2. Deutsch, 387; Patterson and Dougall, 6; Morgan, Franklin *Chronology*, 314; Van Doren, 549.

3. Patterson and Dougall, 10, 13, citing Edmund C. Burnett, ed., *Letters of the Members of the Continental Congress* II (1963), 8; Sifton, 8, 11; Donaghy, iv.

4. Donaghy, 1–4; Orosz, "Pioneer" 8; Orosz, *Eagle* 51; Bridenbaugh, 95, 354; Peter Force Collection, Library of Congress, Memorandum Book, dated ca. 1784, *Sketch of the Plan of a Work intended to illustrate the Revolution in North America . . . from the first Settlement, down to the Declaration of Independence;* Du Simitière Letter Books, Library of Congress, Letter to Augustin Provost, Esq., May 28, 1784, ". . . [I have] prevail'd so far with [my landlord] to persuade him to wait some time longer for his payment . . . it is a melancholy truth that by a variety of unfortunate circumstances . . . [I am] reduced to distress. . . .

5. Du Simitière Memoranda Books, Peter Force Collection, Library of Congress; Library Company, *Descriptive Catalogue*, 161 ff.; Bridenbaugh, 90, 163; Donaghy, 6–7; Orosz, "Pioneer" 8–9; Alan Riding, "British Museum Takes an Enlightened Look Back," *New York Times*, March 31, 2004.

6. See for example Du Simitière Letter Books, Library of Congress, Letters from du Simitière to Robert Aitken, August 7, 1782, and ff., ". . . your personal regard for me, and the desire you have always shown to assist in enriching my collection of American national and artificial Curiosities. . . ."

7. Sifton, 8ff; Orosz, "Pioneer," 10; Potts, 356ff; *Pennsylvania Magazine*, bound Volumes I and II, collection of the Library Company of Pennsylvania, April 1776 issue, 184; see also, Coolie Verner, "The Aitken Map of Virginia," *Imago Mundi* XVI, Amsterdam (1962), 152–56.

8. Potts, 359; Huth, 325, citing letter from George Washington to the Reverend William Gordon, March 8, 1785.

9. Orosz, *Eagle*, 39, citing Adams Family Correspondence, Vol. II, June 1776–March 1778; Huth, 322, notes 23 and 24; see also http://www.historicalartmedals.com.

10. Donaghy, n.p.; Patterson and Dougall, 12–13, citing Boyd, ed., Jefferson *Papers* I, 482; Huth, 322–23; http://memory.loc.gov/cgi-bin/query: Image 656 of 1487, Thomas Jefferson Papers, Manuscript Division, Library of Congress, Series 1. General Correspondence, 1651–1827, Description and Sketch of Virginia Coat of Arms, P. E. Du Simitière, August 1776.

11. McCullough, *John Adams*, 146, 150; Charles Francis Adams, ed., *Familiar Letters of John Adams and His Wife Abigail Adams during the Revolution* (New York: Hurd & Houghton, 1876), 210ff.

12. Patterson and Dougall, 14, note 18, referencing Julian P. Boyd, "'Bradshaw's Epitaph': The Source of 'Rebellion to tyrants is obedience to God,'" in *The Thomas Jefferson papers*, I. Appendix, 677ff., 1950. See also http://etext.lib.virginia.edu/etcbin/foley, *The Jefferson Cyclopedia*.

13. Charles Francis Adams, 1876, ibid.; Patterson and Dougall, Franklin mss. note, n.d. [August 1776], 14, note 17, referencing Thomas Jefferson Papers, Manuscript Division, Library of Congress.

14. Adams, 1876, ibid.; see also *The Jefferson Cyclopedia,* ibid., Letters from Jefferson to J. Evelyn Dennison, 1825; and Stephen McNallen, *Hengist, Horsa and Thomas Jefferson*, http://www.runestone.org/jef.html. For "common law," see Thomas Jefferson, Letter to Thomas Cooper, February 10, 1814.

15. Adams, 1876, ibid.

16. See Adams, 1876, ibid.; and Patterson and Dougall, 15. Also Anthony Hicks's liner notes for Georg Frideric Handel's 1750 cantata, *The Choice of Hercules*, Hyperion Records, 2002.

17. Grateful acknowledgement to Gordon S. Wood, *The American Revolution*, 99, for the elegant concept of "neoclassical dreams"; the Hercules legend provenance is recounted in Hicks, ibid.

18. Adams, 1876, ibid.

19. Sketch and proposal in the Thomas Jefferson Papers, Manuscript Division, the Library of Congress, http://lcweb.loc.gov/exhibits/us.capitol/eleven.jpg; manuscript of Proposal for United States Coat of Arms, dated in header "September 20, 1776"; Patterson and Dougall, narrative transcription of Du Simitière text, 19, 20.

20. Du Simitière papers, Library Company of Philadelphia, *Descriptive Catalogue*. Two expert sources concur that Du Simitière "first introduced" the Eye of Providence into American iconography: Patterson and Dougall, 22; as well as Louis Jordan, *The Eye of Providence*, an essay published by the Numismatic Endowment of the University of Notre Dame, Department of Special Collections. On the Masonic connection, see also Robert Hieronimus, *America's Secret Destiny* (Rochester, Vermont: 1989), 48ff., and Issac Kramnick, ed., Introduction, *The Enlightenment Reader*, ix.

21. Deutsch, 391–92.

22. Patterson and Dougall, 23–24.

23. Thomas Keymer, Introduction, *The Gentleman's Magazine in the Age of Samuel Johnson, 1731–1745*, Sixteen Volumes (London: Pickering & Chatto, 1998).

24. Deutsch, 392. The first twenty volumes of the magazine have been digitized and placed online by the Bodleian Library, Oxford University: The *Gentleman's Magazine* 2 (December 1732), title page, http://bodley.ox.ac.uk/cgi-bin/ilej/image.

25. Sifton, 400, 485; Donaghy, 14.

26. Patterson and Dougall, 24–25.

27. Worthington Chauncy Ford, and Gaillard Hunt, eds., *Journals of the Continental Congress, 1774–1789* (Washington, D.C.: Library of Congress, 1904–37), in thirty-four volumes, Volume V, 689, 691.

28. Isaacson, *Benjamin Franklin*, 299–300; Wood, 141; McCullough, *John Adams*, 147.

29. Bailyn *Ideological Origins*, 323–24; Bernstein, 44–45, 53, *Resolution of Congress*, May 15, 1776, broadside.

30. Bernstein, ibid.; Wood, 70ff.

31. Patterson and Dougall, 27–44.

32. Patterson and Dougall, 44–71; Deutsch, 388.

33. Bridenbaugh, 26, 304; Hutson, 49; Patterson and Dougall, 71.

34. Tuveson, *Redeemer Nation*, 111–19; Patterson and Dougall, 74–88; http://www.techtours.washington.com/seal; and see also Linda Hales, "Out of Many Symbols, One Nation's Great Seal," *Washington Post*, Friday, July 4, 2003, C1. The classical explanations derive from Meyer Reinhold, *Classica Americana: Virgil in the American Experience*, chapter 9 (Wayne State University Press: 1984), and Forrest McDonald, *Novus Ordo Seclorum: The Intellectual Origins of the Constitution* (University Press of Kansas: 1986).

35. Harriet P. Culley, ed., *The Great Seal of the United States*, Bureau of Public Affairs pamphlet, United States Department of State. Washington, D.C. (July 1980), 3–9; Patterson and Dougall, chapter 7, "The Die of 1782," 111–28 and 514.

36. Potts (1889), 352; Orosz (1985), 15, citing the "exhaustive" research of Paul Sifton, op. cit.; Donaghy, 53, citing Du Simitière, Letter to the President of Congress, July 20, 1780.

4. SELF-RELIANCE

1. Miller, *Transcendentalists*, 416.

2. Emerson, *Journals and Miscellaneous Notebooks*, hereafter *JMN*, I, xxxvi and ff; Mattheissen 64–65; 627.

3. Details of Emerson Chronology from Joel Porte, ed., Ralph Waldo Emerson: *Essays and Lectures*, 1, 25–27; and Lawrence Buell, "The Infinitude of the Private Man," *Harvard Magazine* 105, no. 5 (May–June 2003).

4. Porte, ed., *Chronology*, 1,127; for insights into Emerson's religious conflict, Frank Schulman, "Ralph Waldo Emerson," *Dictionary of Unitarian and Universalist Biography*, Unitarian Universalist Historical Society, 2003; Whicher, ed., 11; Rusk, 170.

5. *JMN*, (September 1, 1833) in Whicher, ed., 13; Emerson letter to Mary Moody Emerson, December 10, 1829, in Nicholas Halmi et al, eds., *Coleridge's Poetry and Prose* (New York; W. W. Norton, 2004), 665; Mathiessen, 64ff.

6. Francis Jeffrey, ed. *Edinburgh Review*, to Carlyle, 1828; *JMN* III: 131, in Paul, 197; also, Paul, 211; Harris, 8.

7. Riley, 159; Harris, 42ff.

8. *JMN*, VI, 252–53, Emerson's list of "Thomas Carlyle's Writings."

9. Harris, 16–17, 30–31; Parrington, *Main Currents* II, "The Genesis of Transcendentalism," 376–77; Ameriks, ed., 8–9, and Charles Larmore in Ameriks, 153–154; see also Ralph Barton Perry's definitive "Introduction" to *Kant* (n.p.: Harvard Classics, 1909–1914).

10. Harris, 10–11, 17; 161; Bryan Hileman, "Emerson and Thomas Carlyle," on the American Transcendentalism Web: www.vcu.edu/engweb/transcendentalism/roots/rwe-tc; Whicher, 13; *JMN* VI, xx; see also the brilliant Introduction to *Basic Writings of Kant*. Edited by Allen W. Wood (New York: Modern Library, 2001): vii–xxv and 40–41.

11. Italics Coleridge's, and see *Biographia Literaria*, chapter 13.

12. Porte, ed., *Chronology*, 1,127–28; *JMN* VI, *Chronology*, xix–xx; Parrington, Volume II, op. cit., 378ff., places emphasis upon the transformative importance of Emerson's "momentous" European trip, as does Miller, *American Transcendentalists*, Foreword, and 171ff.

13. James Eliot Cabot, *A Memoir of Ralph Waldo Emerson* (Boston: Houghton Mifflin, 1888), 244; Orestes Brownson, in Miller, *Transcendentalists*, 208; John Updike, "Ralph Waldo Emerson Turns Two Hundred," *New Yorker* (August 4, 2003).

14. Matthiessen, 8; Emerson, *Essays and Lectures*, 7–8.

15. Whicher, ed., "First Fruits," 12–21.

16. Leslie Perrin, "New England Transcendentalism," *Concord Magazine* (November 1998); Emerson, *Essays and Lectures*, "Nature," 7, 43. Miller, *Transcendentalists*, 10,

115, 494, stresses the pivotal importance of "the year 1836" when *Nature* was published in understanding the development of American transcendentalism. For a caveat issued by the transcendentalists, eloquently insisting they were a non-"movement," see Margaret Fuller and Ralph Waldo Emerson, "The Editors to the Reader," *Dial*, no. 1 (July 1840): 1–4.

17. JMN V: xviii, 497; Allen, 309; Robert Sattelmeyer, review of Albert J. von Frank, chief editor, with an "Historical Introduction" by David M. Robinson, *The Complete Sermons of Ralph Waldo Emerson* (University of Missouri Press, 993), www.textual. org/text/reviews/sattelme.htm.

18. Rusk, 267; Van Leer, 72ff; Emerson, *Essays and Lectures*, 52ff.; Richard Higgins, "Remembering the Emerson Who Sought God," *Harvard Divinity Bulletin* (June 2003).

19. Parrington, Volume II, 380.

20. JMN V: xv, 457, 465; Rusk, 267; Van Leer, 73–76; Allen, 316; JMN V: xv, 465, 467; JMN VII, Journal "D," 34–35; David M. Robinson, in von Frank, op. cit., Volume I, 14.

21. JMN V: 357, 470, 479, 487; JMN VII, Journal "D": 112; on Emerson's growing resolution of will in the months before the Harvard "Address," see also Van Leer, op. cit., 76; Henry James, *American Writers*, 1883, 252–253.

22. JMN VII, Journal "D," entry for "10 July," 1838.

23. Rusk, 268; Allen, 316; Miller, *Responsibility of Mind*, 192.

24. Henry James, (1883) op. cit., 253; Complete text of "Divinity School Address": Emerson, *Essays and Lectures*, 75–92.

25. Emerson to Carlyle, *Correspondence*, 174; Dyck, *Legacy of Thomas Paine*, 141–42, and fn. 148, citing Ralph Rusk, ed., *Letters of Emerson* I, 148n; Emerson, JMN VII: 52–53.

26. Harris, op. cit., 24; Matthiessen, 61; JMN, VII: 118, 124.

27. JMN VII: xi, 63, n.174; for complete text of Norton article, see Miller, *Transcendentalists*, 193–96; also, Miller, 198; Emerson *Letters*, ed. Myerson, to Henry Ware Jr., July 28 and October 8, 1838, 186, 190, and to Mary Moody Emerson, September 1, 1838, 186–87.

28. Paul, 155; JMN V: xv–xvi, citing Emerson Journal entry of April 1840; JMN, VII, xii, 50, 60–70; 145, 181 n. 534; Allen, 341; Whicher, ed., "Society and Solitude," 122ff.

29. *Cambridge History of English and American Literature*, *1907–1921* XVI, "Divines and Moralists, 1783–1860," brief essays on "Andrews Norton" and "Opposition to Transcendentalism"; Norton's text excerpted in Miller, *Transcendentalists*, 210–13.

30. Lopez, 23–24, is pertinent on the long tradition of "condescending to Emerson"; Paul, 79, 81, 190; JMN, "D," 1838, 64.

31. JMN V: 494. Emerson and Carlyle, *Correspondence*, May 21, 1841, 326–27; Lopez, ibid., 83, 113 observes that Emerson's mind, "more than any other American writer's, is characterized by its restless need for an antagonism by which to define itself." See also Miller, *Responsibility of Mind*, 32.

32. Emerson, *Essays*, ed. Porte, *Chronology*, 1,129; JMN, VII (November 1839), 297: "Strike the hardest blow . . . labor;" Miller, ibid., biographical details on Fuller, 331–34; and 247–51, "The Editors to the Reader," *Dial* (July 1840): I, 1–4.

33. JMN VII, 376–77; Woodbridge Riley, *American Thought*, 169, "Emerson's temperament sweetened the strain of idealism handed down from Puritan days."

34. Rusk, 279; *JMN* VII, 393, 498, 521.

35. *Letters*, Emerson to Carlyle, February 28, 1841; Rusk, 278; Lemon, *Philosophy of History*, 174ff; Allen, 518, *JMN*, VII, 92; *Essays* 268.

36. Parrington, 382–83; Whicher, ed., 8, citing Emerson *Journal* entry of September 27, 1830; *Essays*, 271, 272; Matthiessen, 627.

37. Lopez, 145, 161; Cawelti, 86, 98; Paul, 172; *Essays*, 281–82.

38. Emerson, *Essays*, 237ff.

5. MANIFEST DESTINY

1. Hudson, 50, for magazine circulation figures; Pratt, 1927, 797, and 1933, 221–22; Graebner, 15ff, citing "The Great Nation of Futurity."

2. Webster's *Spelling Book*, 1845 edition (n.p.); "eloquently . . . schemer," Julian Hawthorne, cited in Pratt, 1933, 219.

3. Julian Hawthorne, cited in Pratt, 1933, 219; also Pratt, 1933, 216–17; Widmer, 31–33: Edward L. Widmer's *Young America: The Flowering of Democracy in New York City* (Oxford University Press, 1999) is an important new corrective to the scholarship on the American Renaissance; Sampson, 3–4: I am also indebted to Robert D. Sampson's fascinating *John L. O'Sullivan and His Times* (Kent State University Press, 2003), the first full-length scholarly treatment of O'Sullivan's life.

4. Pratt, 1933, 217, 228–34; Merk, 27; Julian Hawthorne, cited in Schlesinger, 371; Sampson, 5, 127.

5. Miller, 11.

6. Pratt, 1933, 218–20; Fresonke, 5, 91; Widmer, 34–35; Stephanson, 39; Sampson, 8; Schlesinger, 372.

7. "The Democratic Principle—The Importance of Its Assertion, and Application to Our Political System and Literature," *United States Magazine*, I. no. 1 (October 15, 1837). See also James Buchanan, "Party Competition and the Rise of the Whigs" (1840), Gilder Lehrman Collection, Document Number GLC 2919, The New-York Historical Society.

8. Emphasis O'Sullivan's.

9. Widmer, 81, 92; Julian Hawthorne, cited in Pratt, 1933, 218–19; Johannsen, 11; *United States Magazine* VI, no.23 (November 1839); Schlesinger, 369–74, 388; Miller, 110–11.

10. Merk, 39; Hudson, 46; Miller, 109, 127, quoting Charles Frederick Briggs and Cornelius Mathews; Parrington, Volume II, *Main Currents in American Thought: The Romantic Revolution in America*, 233, 238; Jonathan A. Glickstein, review of Edward Widmer's *Young America* in *Journal of American History*, 87 no. 1 (Summer 2000); and Widmer, 14, 57.

11. Kasson, in Scheiber and Elliott, eds., 187; Widmer, 59; Merk, 40, 53, citing the *Boston Times* December 11, 1844.

12. Miller, *Transcendentalists*, 188–89; Johannsen 12; Graebner 3; Emerson, *JMN* VIII, 521, referring to "Mr. OS;" and Ralph Rusk, ed. *Letters*, III, 146–47.

13. Emerson, *Essays and Lectures*, 213–30; Harris, *Carlyle and Emerson* 134; Sherman Paul, *Emerson's Angle of Vision*, 227; also, John Q. Anderson, "Emerson's 'Young American' as Democratic Nobleman," *American Transcendental Quarterly*, no. 9 (Winter 1971): 16–20.

14. *United States Magazine* XVI (June 1845): 589–602. Collection the New-York Historical Society.

15. Emerson, *Essays: Second Series,* 602–3. For an overview of Bishop Berkeley's life and work: *The Internet Encyclopedia of Philosophy,* www.utm.edu/research/iep/b/ berkeley.html. Berkeley's poem is in the *Faber Book of America,* 397. For two illuminating discussions of Leutze's painting, see Jochen Wierich, "Struggling Through History: Emmanuel Leutze, Hegel, and Empire," *American Art* XV, no.2 (Summer 2001) and Roger Cushing Aikin, "Paintings of Manifest Destiny: Mapping the Nation," *American Art* XIV, no. 3 (Fall 2000); also, Boime, 43–45; Paul, 225; De Tocqueville cited in Turner, op. cit., 153.

16. O'Sullivan, Editorial, "Democracy," *United States Magazine* VII (March 1840): 215–29; see also "The Great Nation of Futurity," op. cit, (November 1839) and "The Democratic Principle," op. cit. (October 1837); Turner essay, "The Old West," *Proceedings of the State Historical Society of Wisconsin* (1908) reprinted in *The Frontier in American History,* 67–127.

17. Seigenthaler, *Polk* "Milestones," 168–72; Widmer, 264, Note 3; Graebner, xxvii; Pletcher, 139.

18. Pratt, 1933, 222; Schlesinger, 65, 431–36; Pletcher, 145–46; Seigenthaler, 65, 78–85; Graebner, xxxiv.

19. Graebner, xxiii; Sampson, 155; Seigenthaler, 99; Miller, 110; Polk, *Diary,* Quaife, ed. Volume I, 23; and Volume IV, 446 and 476ff., provide evidence of O'Sullivan's access to the president, who refers often throughout his term to unofficial, confidential "private . . . after noon" and "after night" meetings with O'Sullivan, beyond formal office hours.

20. Seigenthaler, 100; Graebner, xxxv; Merk, 28, citing *Congressional Globe,* January 27, 1845, 200; Pletcher, 577; O'Sullivan editorial, "The Popular Movement," *New York Morning News,* May 24, 1845, cited in Merk, 22–23; Pletcher, 577.

21. Pratt, 1927, 797, and 1933, 222; Merk, 45–62, 77; Pletcher, 269–272.

22. John L. O'Sullivan, "Annexation," *United States Magazine and Democratic Review,* (July 1845): 5–10, Collection The New-York Historical Society; Pratt, 1927, 798; Weinberg, 111; Adams, 93. See also Merk, 29, citing *Congressional Record* of January 10, 1846, when Indiana representative Andrew Kennedy echoed O'Sullivan's "population explosion" fear: "How long, under this process of multiplication, will it take to cover the continent with our posterity, from the Isthmus of Darien to Behring's [sic] Straits?"

23. De Voto, 9.

24. http://xroads.virginia.edu/MAO1/Lisle/dial/bancroft.html; Schlesinger, 374; Brock, 213; Jochen Wierich, op. cit.

25. Charles G. Sellars, *Polk,* Volume II, 1966, 213; Graebner, xlii.

26. Weinberg, 21–22, 53; 132; Graebner, 91, 102–9.

27. *New York Morning News,* editorial, October 13, 1845, cited in Weinberg, 25, note 3; Pletcher, 301–3.

28. Weinberg, 142; Seigenthaler, 126; Pratt, 1927, 798; and 1933, 223; Pletcher, 320–22.

29. *New York Morning News,* December 27, 1845. Collection, The New-York Historical Society; Pratt, 1927, 795, 798; and Pratt, 1933, 224, 225.

30. De Voto, 25–26, citing Polk, *Diary*, ed. Milo Quaife, Volume I, 155; *New York Morning News*, Monday, January 5, 1846, "A Splendid New Year's Compliment," by John L. O'Sullivan. Collection, The New-York Historical Society.
31. Tuveson, ix, 7–10 and 90ff; "When Did Destiny Become Manifest?" Sampson, 129; Weinberg, 3.
32. De Voto, 125ff; Thomas R. Hietala, in Johannsen, *et. al.*, 48–51; see also interviews with Professors Sam W. Haynes and Robert W. Johanssen, "Manifest Destiny" and "A Go-Ahead Nation," www.pbs.org/kera.
33. Graebner, "Introduction," li; Pletcher, 581; Scheiber and Elliott, eds. 282; Weinberg, 161–66; *United States Magazine* VI (November 1839): 426–30; *United States Magazine* XVII (October 1845); *Morning News*, January 5 and May 26, 1846; Tuveson, 131; Horsman, 221.
34. Johannsen, 9; Sampson, 207; Pratt, 1933, 225, citing F. L. Mott, *A History of American Magazines, 1741–1850*, 677–84; Brock, 100.
35. Matthiessen, *American Renaissance*, 635; Boime, 170–171.
36. Sampson, 208; Pratt, 1933, 226–34; Brock, 59; Miller, 349; Sampson, 237.

6. PROGRESS AND POVERTY
    1. There are three biographies of Henry George. The first is worshipful, warm, and detailed, filled with excerpts from Henry George's journals and correspondence, *The Life of Henry George*, by his son and eldest child, Henry George Jr. (1900); followed a half-century later by *Henry George, Citizen of the World*, an affectionate memoir by his second daughter, Anna Angela George de Mille, edited by Don C. Shoemaker with an Introduction by George's granddaughter, choreographer Agnes de Mille (1950); and the most recent study (1955) is a lengthy and scholarly account, *Henry George*, by Charles Albro Barker, who was a professor of history at Stanford University and Johns Hopkins University. Background information herewith on Henry George's early years is selectively drawn from George Jr., 1–40; and Barker, 3–30; as well as from the introductory "Biographical Sketch" to the *Henry George Papers Finding Aid* in the Manuscripts and Archives Division of the New York Public Library, adapted for www.nypl.org by curator Melanie Yolles (1996).
    2. George Jr., 2–3, 32–148; Barker, 31–62; poverty anecdotes and self-betterment resolutions, 63–66. Also Milton Rugoff biographical essay on Henry George, in *America's Gilded Age*, chapter 9, "Critics and Cassandras" (New York: Henry Holt, 1989).
    3. George Jr., 149–77; Barker; 63–105.
    4. "What the Railroad Will Bring Us," *Overland Monthly* 1. no. 4, (October, 1868); also on the Web at www.cooperativeindividualism.org/george_railroads.html; Kris Feder, *Progress and Poverty Today*, introduction to the new abridged version of *Progress and Poverty* (New York: Robert Schalkenbach Foundation, 1997); George's "paradox," in Andelson, ed., 31ff; "the new elite," Phillips, 43, makes pointed reference to *Progress and Poverty*.
    5. "Big manufactories" and wire service observations, HG correspondence to Charles A. Sumner, managing editor, and John Nugent, publisher, *San Francisco Herald*, January and April 1869, cited in George Jr., 181–85; also, HG journals and pocket diaries, January–April, 1869, Manuscripts and Archives Collections (microfilm), The New

York Public Library; NYC impressions, Henry George, *Social Problems*, chapter 7, "Is It the Best of All Possible Worlds?" 58–69. Note: Henry George employed the phrase "how the other half live" (64) in a series of essays in *Frank Leslie's Illustrated Newspaper* (Spring and Summer 1883) seven years before the publication of Jacob Riis's classic, *How the Other Half Lives*. HG to the Reverend Dawson, in George Jr., 192–93, 367. See also George, *Science of Political Economy*, 201.

6. Allan Nevins entry, "Horace Greeley," in *Dictionary of American Biography* 7: 528–34.

7. Young, *Men and Memories*, 417–18; also Rose, 37

8. Rose, 37; George, Jr., 196–97; George, *Science of Political Economy*, Book II, chapter vii, 200–1; HG pocket diary entries, April 2 and 3, 1869.

9. *Principles* took eighteen months to write. J.S. Mill, ed., Riley, Introduction, vii, xviii–xix; Rose, 42; "Mill's Principles of Political Economy," *North American Review* 98, no 202 (January 1864), 270–73, praised it as "a work of immense practical importance [to] the progress of liberalism;" W.J. Ashley, 1909 "Introduction" to the 1870 Seventh Edition; Heilbroner 133.

10. Ashley, ibid.; Heilbroner, 134; Sowell, 117, 209.

11. Schumpeter, 543; Ashley ibid.

12. Sowell, 21, 257 n. 47; Rose, 42; F. Y. Edgeworth, "Mill, John Stuart," in Palgrave, *Dictionary of Political Economy*, 756–63.

13. *New-York Daily Tribune*, May 1, 1869, microfilm, Collection of the New-York Historical Society. F. Y. Edgeworth, ibid., 760, discusses Mill's "wages-fund theory" and his subsequent recantation. Mill to HG, October 23, 1869, in George Jr., 198–200. Note: In the same issue of the *Tribune*, Horace Greeley jumped upon the economics bandwagon, advocating stringent protection of homeland markets in the first article of a series "written for the common people." Greeley's collected *Essays Designed to Elucidate the Science of Political Economy* were published the following December 1 as a book through Fields, Osgood & Company of Boston.

14. Rose, 47; George Jr., 219–20; Wenzer, ed., ix, "Prefatory Note" by HG Jr., December 1900, and 235 n. 1; Heilbroner, 131.

15. Emerson, "The Young American," February 7, 1844, in Graebner, ed., 7; Sam Houston, *New York Herald*, January 30, 1848, in Weinberg, *Manifest Destiny*, 508 n. 134; George, "Land," in Wenzer, ed., 14; also see Parrington, Book 3, 128.

16. All italicized emphases are HG's. F. Y. Edgeworth, ibid., 758–59, is a clear analysis of Mill's *Principles* relating to the matter of "private property"; Adelson, ed., 236; HG, "Land," as quoted in George Jr., 233–34; Wenzer, ed., 1–93, provides the complete text of "Our Land and Land Policy," elucidated by excellent end notes, 236–42.

17. George Jr., 236–51; Barker, 168; HG manuscripts for *Progress and Poverty* and other works, microfilm, NYPL.

18. George Jr., 249; George, *Science of Political Economy*, 201.

19. Rose, 53; Andelson, ed., 15; Wenzer, ed., "Land," 95–108, Notes, 242–43.

20. Rose, 53; George Jr., 283; Wenzer, ed., "Land," 109–28, Notes, 243–48; and Wenzer, ed., *Anthology*, "Exhortative Works," 10–14, notes, 45. The text for "The American Republic" became Book X, chapter 5 of *Progress and Poverty*.

21. HG, *Progress and Poverty* manuscript and notebooks, February 1877–January 1879,

NYPL; Barker, 252–54; Kenneth M. Johnson, "Progress and Poverty—A Paradox," *California Historical Society Quarterly* (March 1963).

22. Heilbroner, 187; Andelson, ed., 30, 38; Parrington, Volume 3, 132–36; *P&P*, Book III, chapters 1–5, and Book IV, chapter 4; "knight-errant," Parrington, op. cit., 135; *P&P*, Preface to Fourth Edition, [xi]–xiii; Peter Barnes, "Reconsiderations: Progress and Poverty," *New Republic* (December 11, 1971).

23. John K. Whitaker, "Henry George and the Classical Growth Theory" (January 2001); Riley, ed., *Principles*, J.S. Mill, xi; Teilhac, *Pioneers*, chapter 3, 114ff; also, Samuel Belcher Clarke in defense of HG, "piercing the crust of usage and causing traditionary ideas to be scrutinized and tested," and acknowledging the Physiocrats as his forerunners, in "The Single Tax and the *Impot Unique*," *Quarterly Journal of Economics* (1891).

24. Schumpeter, *History*, (1954), 865; HG journal entries cite readings in Spencer and Buckle, for example, February 26 and March 29, 1877, NYPL; Francis Neilson, "Henry George, the Scholar," (1940); Lukacs, *End of an Age*, 151; J. B. Bury, *The Idea of Progress* (1930), especially the overview in chapter 19, "Progress in the Light of Evolution." On Henry George and Rousseau, see Teilhac, 149–56, 160, and Lemon, *Philosophy of History*, 179.

25. George, *The Condition of Labour*, 61; Marx to Sorge, June 30, 1881; White, *Metahistory*, esp. chapter 8, "Marx: The Philosophical Defense of History in the Metonymical Mode," 284–88, 292–93; Wheen, *Karl Marx*, esp. chapter 3, "The Grass-eating King," 70–74; Parrington, 34; www.geocities.com/marx_henrygeorge.html; see also Friedrich Engels, *The Condition of the Working Class in England* (ed. 1958) 355–56.

26. Young, op. cit., 418–19; George Jr., "Introduction" to P&P 25th Anniversary edition ix–x; George, *Science of Political Economy*, 201–3; Kenneth M. Johnson, op. cit; Hofstadter, 62–63.

27. Rose, 92; John Dewey, *Appreciation of HG*, October 1927; HG nomination speech, *New York Tribune*, October 6, 1886, in the New-York Historical Society.

28. HG, *The Single Tax* (1890); on Shearman's career, see C.B. Fillebrown at www.cooperativeindividualism.org.

29. George, *Science*, "Preface," vii–viii; George Jr., 593–611; Rose, 151–62.

30. See Parrington, 132, "that men might plot a fairer course for society;" Barker, 620–35; *Progress and Poverty*, cited in Hofstadter, et. al., *Great Issues*, 63; Young, op. cit., 426.

7. THE SPHERE OF ACTION

1. Addams, Jane, *Papers*. Microfilm edition, Reel 4, Collection, NYPL.

2. James, "Chronology," *Writings*, ed. Gerald E. Myers, 1161; also, Perry, *Thought and Character*, 247–63.

3. Biographical details of JA's early life: Tims, *Jane Addams*, 2, "The Father God," 17–25; Lasch, *The New Radicalism*, 1, "Jane Addams: The College Woman and the Family Claim," 5–10; and Fischer, *On Addams*, "Biography," 1–2; ". . . build her own fire," Addams, *Twenty Years*, 63.

4. On Addams and Ruskin, see Anne F. Scott, ed., xii, citing Jane Addams's letter to Ellen Gates Starr, November 22, 1879; Davis, *American Heroine*, 51; Brown, *Education*, 69; and Farrell, *Beloved Lady*, 38. Also, Ruskin, essays in *Political Economy*, 118ff, and 250ff.

5. Tims, 25.
6. Lasch, *New Radicalism*, 15–17; 23; Tims, "Shares and Delusions," 29–33; Addams, *Twenty Years*, cited in Brown, ed., Introduction, 8.
7. Addams, ed. Brown, *Twenty Years*, 74, and "Tolstoyism," 148ff; and Brown, *Education*, 164, note, 351, pinpointing JA's reading of Tolstoy as fall 1886, and note, 369, regarding the Hapgood version; Farrell, 141, citing Addams, "A Book That Changed My Life," October 13, 1927.
8. Brown, *Education*, 170–71; Addams, "Introduction," *What Then Must We Do?* cited in 1935 Aylmer Maude translation, xvi–xvii; Maude, Editor's Note, vii–viii; Tolstoy, *What Then*, 94–97, 315–23; Diliberto, *Useful Woman*, 120–22.
9. Chronology for JA and Sarah Anderson traveling to Toynbee Hall, from Brown, *Education*, 185–200.
10. Addams, ed. Brown, *Twenty Years*, 56; Himmelfarb, *Idea of Poverty*, 235, citing Toynbee, "Progress and Poverty," *A Criticism of Mr. Henry George*; and 275, citing Toynbee, *Industrial Revolution*; see also Carson, *Settlement Folk*, note 2. p. 201, pertaining to Himmelfarb's assessment of the doctrine in late Victorian England in *Idea of Poverty* that "consensus prevailed that poverty was a major social problem and . . . fundamentally a *moral* problem." Emphasis Carson's.
11. Himmelfarb, *Poverty*, 241–43; Farrell, *Beloved Lady*, 49; Carson, *Settlement Folk*, 197; Letter from JA to Alice Haldeman, June 14, 1888, cited in Crunden, *Ministers*, 25, and Davis, *Heroine*, 50; Letter from Ellen Gates Starr to her sister, Mary Starr Blaisdell, February 23 [1889], cited in Himmelfarb, Note, 241.
12. Addams, ed. Brown, *Twenty Years*, "The Snare of Preparation," 78; McCree Bryan, "First Year," 101–3; Scott, ed., "Introduction" to Addams, *Democracy*, xlv.
13. Farrell, *Beloved*, 52–56, citing previous Letter from EGS to sister Mary Blaisdell, February 23 [1889]; Diliberto, *Useful Woman*, 136–43.
14. JA to Anna Haldeman Addams, May 9, 1889, and EGS to Mary Blaisdell, February 23 [1889], cited in Mary Lynn McCree Bryan, "First Year," 102–6; also, Farrell, 57.
15. Tims, *Jane Addams*, 43–45; McCree Bryan, 107–9; Dorothea Moore, "A Day at Hull-House," (1897), 629.
16. Moore, "A Day," (1897), 631; Letter from JA to Alice Haldeman, October 8, 1889, cited in McCree Bryan, "The First Year," 110; Diliberto, 159; Farrell, 60–61; Addams, ed. Brown, *Twenty Years*, 84, 87; Robert Kiely, ed.; *Romola*, "Introduction," xiii–xxii.
17. McCree Bryan, "The First Year of Hull-House," 110–14, citing letters from JA to Alice Haldeman, October 8, 1889, and December 22, 1889, to George Haldeman, November 24, 1889, and to Helen Culver, March 7, 1890, and Ellen Gates Starr to her parents, November 3, 1889.
18. Addams, ed. Brown, *Twenty Years*, Related Documents, appendix 1, "Hull-House Weekly Program," March 1, 1892, 207–18.
19. Contemporary anecdotal and on-site descriptions of Hull-House daily activity drawn from Dorothea Moore, "A Day at Hull-House," (1897), 629–42.
20. Excerpt of Letter from JA to Alice Haldeman, October 8, 1889, and brief biographical summaries of Hull-House leadership derived from Davis, *Heroine*, "Early Years at Hull-House," 69–82; also, Farrell, 65, 68, note 42; and Deegan, *Chicago School*, note 29, citing Lionel Lane.

21. Addams, "How Would You Uplift the Masses?" (1892), 118–21.

22. Addams, ed. Brown, *Twenty Years*, "Chronology," 254; Brown, *Education*, 213; and Addams, ed. Seigfried, *Democracy*, xxxv, note 12. Professor Seigfried emphasizes Addams's deliberate testing of theory in the arena of communal practice; Fischer, *Addams*, 15–17; and Addams, complete text of "The Subjective Necessity for Social Settlements," in Elshtain, ed. 14–28. The "subjective necessity" was building up within the mind of the author herself.

23. www.csiss.org, Center for Spatially-Integrated Social Systems, at University of California, Santa Barbara, "Florence Kelley, Slums of the Great Cities Survey Maps, 1893," by Nina Brown; Florence Kelley, "The Sweating System," *HHMP*, 12; Farrell, 66–67, discusses Kelley's "withering disdain" for bleeding-heart liberalism.

24. *HHMP*, "Prefatory Note," vii–viii; Addams, ed. Brown, *Twenty Years*, 110; Himmelfarb, 7, 79; www.cssis.org, "Charles Booth, Mapping London's Poverty, 1885–1903," by David Fearon. Booth's reference to the "poverty line," Fearon observes, was "tied to qualitative factors of food, clothing and shelter and relative deprivation."

25. *HHMP*, Contents, and 12ff; Scott, xxxviii; "Settlers in the City Wilderness," *Atlantic*, (January 1896), review of *Hull-House Maps and Papers*, 118–23.

26. Brown, ed., *Twenty Years*, 19; Carson 335–36, 122; "American Social Workers in Session at the Hull-House," *Commons Magazine* IV no. 2 (June 1899): 7, 9–13; Sharon Harr, "Location, Location, Location: Gender and the Archaeology of Urban Settlement," *Journal of Architectural Education* 55, no. 3 (1999): 154.

27. Crunden, *Ministers of Reform*, 80–83; Mary Jo Deegan's important essay, "The Feminist Pragmatism of Jane Addams," in Mary Ann Romano, ed., *Lost Sociologists*; also see Deegan's superb study, *Jane Addams and the Men of the Chicago School*, 7–13 and 323–26; Farrell, 67 and 68, note 40; Wendy E. Chmielewski, Curator, Swarthmore College Peace Collection, personal communication to the author, March 8, 2004; Victoria Bissell Brown, personal communication to the author March 20, 2004; Tims, 13; Addams, ed. Scott, xliii; Jane Addams, syllabus pamphlet, "Democracy and Social Ethics," JAPP Microfilm Edition, Collection NYPL, reel 30, filmed from the Anita McCormick Blaine Papers, State Historical Society of Wisconsin. Hereafter referred to as "DSE syllabus."

28. Diliberto, *Useful Woman*, 255, and note 288, citing Letter from JA to MRS, July 28, 1899; DSE syllabus, 5; Addams, ed. Brown, *Twenty Years*, 50; Addams, intro. Commager, *Twenty Years*, 169–70; Seigfried, Introduction, xl; Mazzini, *An Essay on the Duties of Man Addressed to Workingmen* (New York: Funk & Wagnalls, 1898), 62.

29. DSE syllabus, 6–7.

30. DSE syllabus, 7–8; Addams, ed. Scott, lvi; Addams, ed. Seigfried, xxv; on HH as "ideal community," see Dewey, *The School as Social Centre* (1902), cited in Seigfried, "Socializing Democracy," 213; Carson, 228, note 7, and Farrell, 68, note 41, describe John Dewey's enthusiastic reaction to JA.

31. Davis, *Heroine*, 141ff.; Addams, ed. Brown, *Twenty Years*, 161; Addams, ed. Lasch, *Social Thought*, 84, citing WJ to JA, December 13, 1909, and 183ff; James, "Chronology," *Writings*, 1159; see also Merle Curti, "Jane Addams," 245, on JA's "desire for action to fulfil social obligation."

32. DSE syllabus, 8–9.

33. DSE, Bibliography, 2, and syllabus, 9–10.
34. DSE syllabus, 11–12, 13–14; Sklar, *Hull House*, 671–72, and note 38; Elshtain, ed., 52, 60–61, note 2.
35. Elshtain, "Bibliography," 450–52; Brown, "Jane Addams," in *Women Building Chicago, 1790–1990*, 14–22; Link, *Progressivism*, 24; Rader, *Academic Mind*, 115–16; DSE manuscript ancillary correspondence, JAPP, Reel 4, Microfilm Collection, NYPL: Addams often complained that she was "swamped with work" and wrote "slowly and painfully." See Ely to Addams, "January 1901," Addams to Ely, May 18, 1901; Addams to Florence Kelley [July 1901]; Addams to Ely, November 11, 1901; Ely to Addams, January 28, 1902, Ely to Addams, October 31, 1902.
36. JAPP microfilm, NYPL, reel 4, Macmillan Company to Addams, May 24, 1902, and Ely to Addams, October 31, 1902; Lasch, *Social Thought* (1965), 62–63; Link, *Progressivism*, 72–74; Addams, cited in Deegan, *Chicago School*, 230–33 and 323–26. Also Kathryn Kish Sklar's excellent essay, "Hull-House in the 1890s" (1985), 658–77.
37. Addams, ed. Scott, 273–74.
38. www.nobel.se/peace/laureates/1931/press.html. Copyright 2002, The Nobel Foundation.

8. THE MELTING-POT

1. Joseph H. Udelson, *Dreamer of the Ghetto*, 196; Joseph Leftwich, *Israel Zangwill*, 148–49.
2. Michael Terry, Dorot Chief Librarian, the Jewish Division, NYPL, personal communication to the author, April 23, 2004; Udelson, 110; Leftwich, 108–111; Adams, 19.
3. Rochelson, 10ff; Wohlgelertner, 24ff; Leftwich, 21; Adams, "Chronology," xv.
4. For an introduction to the Wanderers of Kilburn, www.jewishmuseum.org.uk/exhibit; also, Leftwich, 53; and Udelson, 271, note 3.
5. Louise Mayo, 41, 46–47; Zangwill, "The Position of Judaism," *North American Review* (April 1895): 425–39 online at www.cdl.library.cornell.edu; Udelson, 193, cites a subsequent Zangwill essay, "Two Opposing Forces at Work on the Jew" (1903) employing the gaberdine metaphor; mezuza anecdote, see Leftwich, 177.
6. *The Poetical Works of Henry Wadsworth Longfellow, with Bibliographical and Critical Notes III* (Boston and New York: Houghton Mifflin, 1890), 33–36; Zangwill, ed. Maurice Simon, *Speeches*, 11–12, 29.
7. Isaac M. Fein, "Zangwill," 16ff.; Udelson, 81, 83; Simon, ed., 41; Adams, 52ff.
8. The authoritative essay on *Children of the Ghetto* is Meri-Jane Rochelson's Introduction to the 1998 Wayne State University Press reprint of the 1895 American edition. Isaac M. Fein's "Zangwill," is a fascinating survey with well-selected highlights of the voluminous 1892–1923 Sulzberger-Zangwill correspondence in the Central Zionist Archives, Jerusalem. The letters cited herewith are dated May 3, 1892; September 30, 1892; September 12, 1893; and July 6, 1900; also, Zangwill, "Tribute to Sulzberger," in Simon, ed., 143ff.
9. Wohlgelertner, 149–150, citing Herzl's diary entry for November 21, 1895; Leftwich, 181, citing *Theodore Herzl, a Biography* by Joseph Fraenkel (Second Edition, London, 1946); Hertzberg, on Nordau, 233–34; Mendes-Flohr and Reinharz, Introduction to

"Zionism" section, 529–31; Herzl, "A Solution to the Jewish Question," 1896, excerpted in Mendes-Flohr and Reinharz, 533–38.

10. Mendes-Flohr and Reinharz, ibid.; Wohlgelertner, 152; a cogent overview of the range of Zionist philosophies will be found at www.israel.org/mfa.

11. Regarding Zangwill's "propriety," see Leftwich, 181, "I was the first person that Dr. Herzl came to in London. . . . I worked for him loyally as a perfect slave for a great many years, so it is not true that I am an obstinate person and cannot work with anybody." Wohlgelertner, 152; Zangwill, "Zionism," (October 1899) in Simon, ed., 156ff.

12. Wohlgelertner, 152–54; Zangwill's moving eulogy for Herzl, July 1904, in Simon, ed., "Tribute to Herzl," 131ff.; Zangwill's (lightly fictionalized) eyewitness account of the first Zionist Congress, written later in 1897 and early 1898, provided the details here: Dreamers of the Ghetto, "Dreamers in Congress," 430–40.

13. Zangwill, in Simon, ed., "Zionism," 152; "Dreamers in Congress," 438; Gottheil, "The Aims of Zionism" (1898/1899), cited in Hertzberg, 84 and 495–500.

14. On Tolstoy, Zangwill lecture of September 8, 1898, cited in Wohlgelertner, 193–95; first impressions of America, Zangwill, in Simon, ed., "The New Jew"; Garland on Zangwill, in Adams, 19–20, 155, notes 6 and 7, citing Hamlin Garland, November 1899 and June 1930.

15. Zangwill, in Simon, ed., "Send-Off to Dr. [Solomon] Schechter," 64, 69; "The New Jew," October 1898, 54–63; and "Zionism," October 1899, 155.

16. Roth, Now and Forever, epigraph/frontispiece; Zangwill, Blind Children, 103, 130–31; Adams, textual survey of Blind Children, including Zangwill's translations, 133–42; Udelson, 148–52; Wohlgelertner, 25; Leftwich, 102.

17. Rochelson, "Introduction," Children of the Ghetto, 13; Wohlgelertner, 25; Udelson, 205; Edith and Israel Zangwill, correspondence, 1904–1914, Annie Russell (Yorke) Papers, box 3 (folders 5 and 6), Manuscripts and Archives/Special Collections, NYPL.

18. Udelson, 289, note 24, citing Zangwill in Chicago Sentinel, February 15, 1924; Leftwich, 102–3, reporting his conversation with Mrs. Zangwill and her response to a comment by Jacob de Haas, editor of the Boston Jewish Advocate and an early Zionist.

19. Zangwill to Sulzberger, June 23, 1903; and September 11, 1903, in Fein, 20–21; Zangwill, "A Manifesto," Jewish Chronicle (August 25, 1905), cited in Mendes-Flohr and Reinharz, 550–51; Zangwill, April, 1905, cited in Speeches, 204; Adams, 23; Hertzberg, 41, 202–3.

20. Zangwill to Sulzberger, July 8, 1904 (Herzl died on July 3), in Fein, 22; Mann, 105; Zangwill, "The East Africa Offer," in Simon, ed., 198–227; Zangwill, "A Manifesto," 551; Zangwill, "What is the ITO [Jewish Territorial Organization]?" (London: ITO Pamphlet, no. 1, 1905), Collection of the Jewish Division, NYPL; see also Cyrus Adler's letters to Zangwill, opposing his new organization, November 1 and December 31, 1905, in Ira Robinson, ed., 116–17, 124–26.

21. Naomi W. Cohen, "The American Solution: The Galveston Plan," in her definitive biography, Jacob H. Schiff, A Study in American Jewish Leadership, 159–68; Hertzberg, 41; Isaac Fein, ed.: Letters from Schiff to Zangwill, October 17 and November 21, 1905; Zangwill to Schiff, November 3, 1905; Zangwill to Daniel Guggenheim and Oscar Straus, April 24, 1906; Schiff to Zangwill, August 24 and September 21, 1906; Zangwill to Schiff, September 14, November 8, and November 9, and Oscar Straus,

September 28, 1906; Schiff to Zangwill, October 25, 1906; Schiff to Cyrus Sulzberger, December 3, 1906; Zangwill to Schiff, April 5, 1907.

22. Zangwill, "Afterword," *The Melting-Pot*, edition of 1926, 199; Zangwill, "Send-off to Dr. Schechter," in Simon, ed., 64ff; Zangwill, "A Land of Refuge," December 8, 1907, in Simon, ed., 237; Zangwill, "The Third Birthday of the ITO," August, 1908, in Simon, ed., 285; Leftwich, 239. Note: April 7, 1907, remains the single most populous day in American immigration history.

23. Zangwill letter to George C. Tyler, April 18, 1908, cited in entirety by Walker Whiteside in "The Story of a Play, being a narrative of the steps in the production of *The Melting-Pot* from the time Israel Zangwill outlined the theme in a letter, to the winning of decisive success on the Chicago stage," *Chicago Record Herald*, January 24, 1909, in the NYPL, Billy Rose Theatre Collection, Robinson Locke Scrapbook Collection (microfilm), "Melting-Pot Programme, Chicago 1908–1909;" Biographical Note, Liebler and Company Records, 1890–1930, the Billy Rose Theatre Collection, NYPL.

24. Zangwill to Tyler, April 18, 1908; Zangwill to Mary Berenson, July 15, 1908, cited in Udelson, 288, note 9.

25. NYPL, Robinson Locke Scrapbook Collection (microfilm), "Walker Whiteside Wins a Real Triumph," the *New York Telegraph*, September 19, 1909; Whiteside, "The Story of a Play" narrative, columns 2 and 3.

26. Zangwill, *The Melting-Pot*, Schiff Collection, The Jewish Division, NYPL, 1–3, 11–12, 37, 59, 101ff, 184–85; Zangwill, quoted in Leftwich, 151: "I do not know exactly when America began to call herself 'God's own country,' but her national anthem, 'My Country,'Tis of Thee,' [i.e., "America," by Rev. Samuel Francis Smith] dating from 1832, fixes the date when America consciously felt herself as a Holy Land."

27. Zangwill interview, "America—'The Melting-Pot,'" in Chicago *Inter Ocean*, December 6, 1908; Zangwill, "The East Africa Offer," 223; and *The Melting-Pot*, p.v., 33, 208; see also David to Quincy, Act II, 86–87: "[I am] a Jew who knows that your Pilgrim Fathers came straight out of the Old Testament"; Zangwill, *The Melting-Pot*, Act I, 18, typewritten prompt book with ink notes handwritten by Zangwill, and pencil blocking notes by stage manager, in the Billy Rose Theater Collection, the Liebler Collection, the NYPL; Letter from Esther Zangwill to Annie Russell, January 21, 1909, NYPL: "We have been almost snowed up with proofs. Israel's Melting-Pot is to be published"; Leftwich, 253; Higham, *Send These to Me*, 124, 238–39, stresses the play's "permanent" influence in "dominating assimilationist thinking."

28. *The Melting-Pot* critique by Ryan Walker in the *New York Review*, n.d., NYPL; Walker Whiteside, "The Story of a Play," columns 2 and 3; *The Melting-Pot* prompt book, typescript inserted page "30(a)," Act III, rewritten and expanded David Quixano monologue, as per pages 155–57, p.v.; Mann, 100, quotes Roosevelt as writing to Zangwill that he was "stirred" by the play; Letter from Edith Zangwill to Annie Russell (Yorke), October 7, 1908, NYPL. Liverpool-born Annie Russell (1869–1936) was a stage actress from the age of fourteen. She and her husband, the actor Oswald Yorke, became close friends with the Zangwills after their critically acclaimed appear-

ances on Broadway in Zangwill's play *The Jinny* in the spring of 1905. The following year, George Bernard Shaw selected Annie to create the title role of *Major Barbara*; Mann, *The One and the Many*, 100.

29. Walker Whiteside, "The Story of a Play," column 3; review clippings sequence in Robinson Locke Scrapbook Collection (microfilm), NYPL, 1908–11; NYPL Manuscript Division, Letters from Edith Zangwill to Annie Russell, January 21, 1909; August 12, 1911; and February 4, 1914: "Walker Whiteside has come over . . ."; for the history of Walker Whiteside's Broadway and screen performances in *The Melting-Pot*, 1908–15 inclusive, see www.ibdb.com and www.afi.com.

30. Magnes, *Emanu-El Pulpit*, II, 1–10 and III, 10, "A Republic of Nationalities," February 1909, cited in Higham, 203, and in Goren, 4–5; Levin, cited in Sorin, 234; see also Howe, 411–13.

31. Arthur Mann, "The Melting-Pot—Protean Appeal," 109–15, provides a good overview of the critical reponse to the play's first several seasons in America.

32. Zangwill, *The Melting-Pot*, 215–16; and see Hans Kohn on "The Melting-Pot as a fundamental trait of American nationalism," cited in Gleason, "The Melting-Pot," op. cit., and Mann, op. cit., 47, 68.

33. Stephan Thernstrom, in Tamar Jacoby, ed., 48; Seymour Martin Lipset, "Equality and the American Creed," Progressive Policy Institute (Washington, D.C.) *Backgrounder* (June 1, 1991); Forrest Church, "The American Creed," *Nation* (September 16, 2002); Peter D. Salins, in Jacoby, ed., 100–101.

34. Dinesh D'Souza, *What's So Great About America*, 95–99; Herbert J. Gans, in Jacoby, ed., 33.

35. Myrdal, *American Dilemma*, esp. Chapter I, "American Ideals and the American Conscience."

9. THE NEGRO IN OUR HISTORY

1. Carter Woodson, cited in Alvin L. Williams, Dissertation, 2, 19; Woodson, "And the Negro Loses His Soul," *Chicago Defender*, June 25, 1912; Woodson, Letter to Jesse E. Moorland, May 22, 1920, cited in Winston, "Prophet," 460; Woodson, "My Recollections of Veterans of the Civil War," 104ff.

2. Jessica M. Fair, "Thurmond, The Rise and Fall of a Coal City," *West Virginia Historical Society Quarterly* XIV, no. 3 (June 2000): www.wvculture.org/history; Williams, Dissertation, 19, citing Charles R. Long, "Woodson, Educator and Prophet," (Washington, D.C.: Associated Publishers 1989), 1; Woodson, "My Recollections," 115–16; Rayford W. Logan, "Carter Godwin Woodson," (1950) 344; and Scally, *Bio-Bibliography*, 5.

3. Rayford W. Logan, "*Phylon* Profile VI" (1945) 319; Carter Woodson, "My Recollections," 115–16; see also the Academic Affairs Library at the University of North Carolina at Chapel Hill online bibliographic project, *Documenting the American South* (DAS), www.docsouth.unc.edu/dasmain.html.

4. Logan and Winston, eds., *Dictionary*, 665ff; Scally, *Bio-Bibliography*, "Chronology," xv; Scally, "The Philippine Challenge," 16; Jacqueline Goggin, *Carter G. Woodson: A Life in Black History*, 16–17, is the first book-length scholarly treatment of the life and mission of CW; Woodson, *Mis-Education*, 151.

5. Scally, *Bio-Bibliography*, 6–7; Scally, "The Philippine Challenge," 16–17; Woodson, *Mis-Education*, 151–55; also see Web site of Jose Rizal University in Mandaluyong City, www.rizalweb@jru.edu.

6. Scally, "The Philippine Challenge," 17–18; Logan, "Carter Godwin Woodson," (1950), 344; Goggin, *Carter G. Woodson*, 21, note 51.

7. Thomas C. Holt, "African American History," in Foner, ed., 311; Russell L. Adams, "Black History as a Weapon of Intellectual and Political Struggle," *The Black Collegian* (February, 2000); John Hope Franklin, "The New Negro History," 93; David Levering Lewis, *W.E.B. Du Bois* I, 168–74.

8. Williams, Dissertation, 32, note 80, citing Alfred Young, "The Educational Philosophies of Booker T. Washington and Carter G. Woodson," with reference to Lorenzo Greene (Unpub. Ph.D. dissertation, Syracuse University, 1977); Winston, "Carter Godwin Woodson," 462.

9. No byline, "Carter G. Woodson: Father of Black History," *Ebony* (February 2004); No byline, "Louis Mehlinger—Secretary-Treasurer of the Association for the Study of Negro Life and History," *Negro History Bulletin* (October 1951): 18–19.

10. Impressions and memories of Woodson as a high school teacher drawn from Goggin, *Carter G. Woodson*, 30; Logan, "Carter G. Woodson" (1945), 320, and "Carter G. Woodson," (1973), 8–9; Williams, Dissertation, 6–7, citing personal communication with Mary Dougherty, CGW former secretary, on January 30, 1992, and Willie M. Miles of the Associated Publishers, on April 27, 1992; and Montague Cobb, "Carter Godwin Woodson, PhD," (September 1970), 389.

11. Roman, cited in Logan, "Carter G. Woodson," (1973), 8; Logan, ibid., 13; Sister Mary Anthony Scally, "Woodson and the Genesis of the ASALH," 653.

12. James E. Stamps, "Fifty Years Later, A Founding Associate Reminisces," *Negro History Bulletin* (November 1965), 31; Scally, "Genesis," 654; Janken, *Rayford W. Logan*, 85; John Hope Franklin, "The Place of Carter G. Woodson," *Negro History Bulletin* (May 1950): 174–75; Charles H. Wesley, "Carter G. Woodson," *Journal of Negro History* (January 1951): 18–19.

13. W. E. B. Du Bois, Editorial, "Journal of Negro History," *The Crisis* (December 1916): 61; Scally, "Genesis," 655; Wesley, "Carter G. Woodson," 19; Kate Tuttle, entry in Appiah and Gates, eds., *Africana*, "W.E.B. Du Bois," 635–36; *The Journal of Negro History* I, no. 1 (January 1916). The *Journal*, published without interruption for nine decades, is now under the editorship of Dr. V. P. Franklin and known as *The Journal of African American History*.

14. Woodson, "The Negro in Literature and Art," *JNH* (July 1918): 329–30; Scally, "The Carter Woodson Letters in the Library of Congress," *Negro History Bulletin* (June–July 1975): 420, citing Letter from Edward Channing to Woodson, July 30, 1917. The letter is in the five-thousand-item Woodson repository, *Collection of Negro papers and related documents, 1803–1936*, LC Control Number MM 76046342. The Library of Congress also holds the *Papers of Carter G. Woodson and the Association for the Study of Negro Life and History, 1915–1960*, edited by Jacqueline Goggin with Randolph H. Boehm, LC Control Number 99016370. Woodson's personal library, more than sixty-five boxes of books, pamphlets, periodicals, and print ephemera, was

acquired from the Association for the Study of African American Life and History in the spring of 2004 by the Special Collections & Archives Division of Emory University library.

15. "The Great Migration" (unbylined) entry in Appiah and Gates, *Africana*, 869–72; Goggin, *Carter G. Woodson*, 202–204; Woodson, *A Century of Negro Migration*, 43ff, 95.

16. Caryle Murphy, "Charter Seeks to Buy Historic School Site/Armstrong Building Closed Since '96," *Washington Post*, March 25, 2004, DZ03; Meier and Rudwick, *Black History and the Historical Profession, 1915–1980*, 8.

17. Arnett G. Lindsay, "Dr. Woodson as a Teacher," *Negro History Bulletin* (May 1950): 183, 191; Lorenzo D. Turner, [Untitled brief memoir of Woodson at Howard], *Negro History Bulletin* (July 1965); see also Carter Woodson, "Negro Life and History in Our Schools," *JNH* (July 1919): 273–80.

18. Charles H. Wesley, "Carter G. Woodson" (1951), 20; F. J. C. Sumner, book review, "The History of the Negro Church," *JNH* (April 1922): 223–24; Hampton Institute speech cited in Meier and Rudwick, chapter 1, "Carter G. Woodson as Entrepreneur," 9; Rayford Logan, "Carter Godwin Woodson" (1950), 346; Janken, *Rayford Logan*, 88–89; W. E. B. Du Bois, "A Portrait of Carter G. Woodson," *Masses & Mainstream* (June 1950): 21–22.

19. Goggin, *Carter G. Woodson*, 66. See also Ronald Roach, "Keeping a Legacy from Crumbling," *Black Issues in Higher Education* (February 13, 2003); and Rudi Williams, "'Father of Black History' House Named National Historic Site," February 3, 2004, www.newsblackhistory.htm.

20. "Spartan-like existence" see Rayford Logan, *Carter G. Woodson* (1945), 320–21; "servant of the people": *Mis-Education of the Negro*, 131; Langton Hughes, "When I Worked for Dr. Woodson," *Negro History Bulletin* (May 1950): 188; Arnold Rampersad, *The Life of Langston Hughes* I, 100–101, 140; and Rampersad, "Langston Hughes in Washington, D.C.," National Portrait Gallery *Profile* (Winter 2001).

21. Woodson dictation style: Hank Chase, "Carter G. Woodson's Home," *American Visions* (February 2000), citing interview with former CGW secretary, Mary Pearl Dougherty; Williams Dissertation, 43–44, citing Alexander L. Jackson, "Greetings to the Association of the Study of African American Life and History on its Golden Anniversary," 1999, 14; (Tribute from the residence of the Phyllis Wheatley YWCA), "The Death of the Founder," *Negro History Bulletin*, Editorial (May 1950); 170 and 176; for background on the Phyllis Wheatley YWCA (originally the Colored Young Women's Christian Association) see Sandra Fitzpatrick and Maria R. Goodwin, *The Guide to Black Washington*, revised edition (New York: Hippocrene Books, 1999).

22. Citations drawn from Scally, *Bio-Bibliography*, 12; *Mis-education of the Negro*, 2–6, 54–56.

23. David Levering Lewis, *W. E. B. Du Bois* II, 356–57; Peter Novick, *That Noble Dream*, 76, 475–76; John Hope Franklin, "On the Evolution of Scholarship in Afro-American History," in Darlene Clark Hine, ed., *The State of Afro-American History: Past, Present, and Future* (1986), 13–15.

24. Goggin, *Carter G. Woodson*, 69; Williams, Dissertation, 110, note 265; Meier and

Rudwick, 10–12; Woodson, "Some Things Negroes Need to Do," in James L. Conyers, Jr., ed., *Historical Reader*, 133–36; Associated Publishers promotional brochure for *The Negro in Our History*, [iv].

25. *The Negro in Our History*, 1–474 passim.

26. Goggin, *Carter G. Woodson*, 69, note 8; Williams, Dissertation, 110; Alain Locke, "The Negro in Our History," *Journal of Negro History* (January 1927): 99–101; *The Negro in Our History*, 802–803.

27. Woodson, "Annual Report of the Director," 1922–23 and 1923–24, *JNH* (October 1923) and (October 1924); L. D. Reddick, "As I Remember Woodson," *The Crisis* (February 1953): 75–80; Charles Whitaker, "Schomburg Celebrates Its 75th Anniversary," *Ebony* (November 2000).

28. Woodson, *Mis-Education*, 187, 109–110. See also Woodson, introductions to each chapter of *Negro Orators and Their Orations* (1925); and Molefi Kete Asante's attribution of Woodson's direct influence in "The Afrocentric Idea in Education," *Journal of Negro Education* 60, no.2 (1991): 170–180.

29. Carter G. Woodson, "Negro History Week," *JNH* (April 1926): 238–42; John Hope Franklin et al., "Black History Month," *Journal of Blacks in Higher Education*, no. 18 (Winter, 1997–1998): 87–92; Meier and Rudwick, 10; Letitia W. Brown, "Why and How the Negro in History," *Journal of Negro Education* (Autumn, 1969): 447–52; Williams, Dissertation, 37–38, 102–5, citing Patricia W. Romero, "Carter G. Woodson: A Biography," (Unpub. Dissertation, Ohio State University, 1971), 148–50; and "Bulletin of General Information, Home Study Department of the Extension Division of the ASNLH Associated Publishers (n.d.); L. D. Reddick, "Twenty-Five Negro History Weeks," *Negro History Bulletin* (May 1950): 178–79, 188.

30. W. E. B. Du Bois, ed. David Levering Lewis, *Black Reconstruction*, 724, 735; Du Bois, *Dusk of Dawn* (1940), 702; David W. Blight, "W.E.B. Du Bois and the Struggle for American Historical Memory," in Genevieve Fabre and Robert O'Meally, eds., *History and Memory in African-American Culture* (1994), 45, 63; Du Bois, "A Portrait of Carter G. Woodson," *Masses & Mainstream* (June 1950): 23. See also John Hope Franklin's tribute to Woodson in "The New Negro History," *JNH* 42 no. 2 (April 1957): 89–97.

31. Alain Locke, ed., *The New Negro* (1925, 1992), with an Introduction by Arnold Rampersad, ix, xi, xxv–xxvii, 3–4. Grateful acknowledgment to Dr. Michael Winston for his advice in steering me to the important essay by Benjamin Quarles, "Black History's Diversified Clientele," in *Black Mosaic* (1988): 204–205, 212–13. Biographical essay and bibliography on Alain Locke, www.africawithin.com/bios/alain_locke.html; Carter G. Woodson, *The Mind of the Negro* 2, 159.

32. John Haynes Holmes, "On Presenting the Spingarn Medal," *The Crisis* (September 1926): 231–34.

33. Darlene Clark Hine, "Carter G. Woodson, White Philanthropy and Negro Historiography," *The History Teacher* XIX no. 3 (May 1986): 406, 409 412–13, 416; Janken, *Rayford Logan*, "Bad Negro with a Ph.D.," 89; "traducers," see Charles H. Wesley, "Carter G. Woodson—as a Scholar," 23; Scally, *Bio-Bibliography*, 14–19; Logan, "Carter Godwin Woodson" (1950): 347; on the 1936–38 WPA project, see George P. Rawick, ed., *The American Slave: A Composite Autobiography* (Westport, Connecticut:

Greenwood Press), 1972–1979; Jacqueline Goggin, *Carter G. Woodson*, Epilogue, "His Cause Was the Presentation of the Truth," 208.

34. Prof. Richard A. Goldsby, quoting Martin Luther King Jr. in a symposium sponsored by the *Journal of Blacks in Higher Education* (October 18, 2004), "Gunnar Myrdal's *An American Dilemma: Do Whites Still Wish That Blacks Would Simply Go Away?*"

10. THE MARSHALL PLAN

1. Neustadt and May, *Thinking in Time*, 247–48.
2. George C. Marshall Foundation brochure, *The Marshall Plan Speech*, n.d.
3. Stimson, cited in Alistair Cooke, "Letter from America"; Marshall, "Nobel Prize Acceptance Speech," www.nobel.se/peace/laureates/1953.
4. For details of George Marshall's life and military career ascendancy, I am grateful to two sources: Forrest C. Pogue, *George C. Marshall, Interviews and Reminiscences*; and Larry I. Bland's biographical narrative, "Early life and background, education, influences," George C. Marshall Foundation Web site, www.marshallfoundation.org/about_gcm/secy_of_state.html; for "worn out friends," see Kennan, *Memoirs 1925–1950*, 351.
5. Mark A. Stoler, *George C. Marshall*, provides a lucid treatment of the shifting military and political dynamics in the World War II years before and after America joined the conflict. See Stoler, 70ff., and his judicious citings from Bland, ed., *Marshall Papers* II.
6. Larry I. Bland, biographical narrative; Forrest C. Pogue, *Interviews and Reminiscences*, responses by GCM, November 15, 1956, 343–45, and February 11, 1957, 424–25; Stoler, *George C. Marshall*, 89, 109–12, and 212, note 35, citing Robert E. Sherwood, *Roosevelt and Hopkins, an Intimate History* (1949), 803; also, Pogue, *George C. Marshall: Statesman*, 21–23.
7. Drew Middleton, Foreword, in Pogue, *George C. Marshall: Statesman*, x; Tony Judt's insightful Introduction to Martin Schain, ed., *The Marshall Plan*, 2–3, 9: "In the light of the European continent's rather uncertain trajectory since 1989, one thing is clear," Judt writes. "Western Europe in 1947 had a stroke of extraordinary good fortune."
8. Katherine Marshall's bitter remarks, Pogue, *Marshall: Statesman*, 29–30; David McCullough, *Truman*, 141, 533–35.
9. Larry I. Bland, *Marshall Narrative*, 7ff.
10. McCullough, *Truman*, 533–34; Pogue, *Marshall: Statesman* 144–45.
11. Dean Acheson, *Sketches from Life*, 153–54; and *Present at the Creation*, 140–42; James Chace, "An Extraordinary Partnership," *Foreign Affairs* (June 1997).
12. Tony Judt, in Schain, 3–5; Imanuel Wexler, *The Marshall Plan Revisited*, 4–6; Scott Jackson, "Prologue to the Marshall Plan," *Journal of American History* (March 1979): 1047–49 and note 16.
13. Jackson, ibid.; text of February 22, 1947, Princeton speech, in Pogue, *Marshall: Statesman*, Appendix, 523–25.
14. Gregory Fossedal and Bill Mikhail, "A Modest Magician: Will Clayton and the Rebuilding of Europe," *Foreign Affairs* (May/June 1997); Gregory Fossedal, *Our Finest Hour: Will Clayton, the Marshall Plan, and the Triumph of Democracy*, 216–19.

15. Thomas G. Paterson, *Soviet-American Confrontation*, 3, 26–28; NATO "Update" Web site, www.nato.int/docu/update/45-49/1947e.htm; Ferald J. Bryan, 491–92.

16. For the enlightening "hanger with many hooks" metaphor, I am indebted to Thomas G. Paterson, ibid., 28; Walter Isaacson and Evan Thomas, *The Wise Men*, 96, 411–13; Charles Bohlen, "Marshall, an Outstanding Secretary," *Witness to History*, 258–61, 268, 271: "[Marshall] gave a sense of purpose and direction. He had a power of command that I have never seen equaled," wrote Bohlen. "It is he whom I remember with the greatest admiration."

17. Gregory Fossedal, *Our Finest Hour*, 220; Bohlen, *Witness to History*, 262–63; Acheson, *Sketches from Life*, 156; Joseph Marion Jones, "The Lessons of Moscow," *The Fifteen Weeks*, 214–23.

18. Roy E. Foulke, typescript memorandum of interview with General Marshall, October 30, 1952, item 1, www.trumanlibrary.org/whistlestop/study_collections/marshall/large/folder7/mpgl, in the digitized manuscript collections of the Truman Presidential Museum and Library; Pogue, *Marshall: Statesman*, xi; Kennan, *Memoirs 1925–1950*, 325; Jones, ibid., 223.

19. Foulke memorandum of Marshall comments, ibid., item 4: "I took only a few intimate advisors into my confidence during the preparation of the European Recovery Program plan"; Pogue, *Interviews and Reminiscences*, GCM comments, 561–63, November 20, 1956; Ferald J. Bryan, "GCM at Harvard," *Presidential Studies Quarterly* (Summer, 1991), 490–91; summary analysis of Kennan's February 1946 "Long Telegram" in Ronald Steel, *Walter Lippmann*, 433, 443–45; Kennan, *Memoirs 1925–1950*, 325–326, 347, 356; Kennan, "Mr. X Speaks," May 1999 interview with Bob Guldin, *Foreign Service Journal* (February 2004). 14, 18–20. "If I have any hero," the ninety-five-year-old Kennan said in the course of the conversation with Guldin, "it was George Marshall."

20. Acheson, *Present at the Creation*, 227; Paterson, *Soviet-American Confrontation*, 28; Jackson, "Prologue to the Marshall Plan," 1056–58; Joseph Marion Jones, "Design for Reconstruction," May 20, 1947, and "Memorandum," July 2, 1947, Collection of the Truman Library, op. cit.; Fossedal, *Our Finest Hour*, 221–22; Bonds, *Bipartisan Strategy*, 19.

21. Fossedal, *Our Finest Hour*, 223–28, citing Ross J. Pritchard, "William L. Clayton," Ph.D. thesis, Fletcher School of Law and Diplomacy, 1955, 296–98; Wexler, *Marshall Plan Revisited*, 4.

22. Kennan, *Memoirs, 1925–1950*, 328–41, 352; "*create . . . destroy . . .* ," emphasis Kennan's, in the second (1950–1963) volume of his *Memoirs*, 90.

23. Bonds, *Bipartisan Strategy*, 20–21; Acheson, *Present at the Creation*, 231; Kennan, *Memoirs, 1925–1950*, 342; Bohlen, *Witness to History*, 263–64; Jones, *The Fifteen Weeks*, 254; Roy E. Foulke, Truman Library Interview with GCM, op.cit.; Pogue, *Marshall: Statesman*, 209–10.

24. Acheson, *Present at the Creation*, 141, and *Sketches from Life*, 159; Bohlen, *Witness to History*, 268.

25. Bohlen, *Witness to History*, 265; Acheson, *Sketches from Life*, 157; regarding the intention of Marshall's advisory staff to "correct . . . the misimpressions that had been created in connection with the Truman Doctrine," see Kennan, *Memoirs, 1925–1950*, 341; Ar-

mand Cleese and Archie Epps, eds., *The Fortieth Anniversary of the Marshall Plan*, 20; Foulke memorandum of interview with GCM, Truman Presidential Library Archives, October 30, 1952, op. cit.; Forrest C. Pogue, *GCM Interview*, November 20, 1956, 559–60: GCM said, "Will you stop the machine" [tape recorder]! Pogue: "Here he said turn it off and then said: 'I made the speech without telling the president. . . .' Of course he knew what we were doing and we were thinking along the same line . . ." See also John Bledsoe Bonds, *Bipartisan Strategy*, 21–24, citing Bohlen's "Oral History" in Truman Presidential Library; on Marshall neglecting to brief Truman beforehand and his subsequent apology to the president: National Archives document RG59, 711.00/6–1947, "Memorandum of Interview with the President" by GCM dated June 16, 1947.

26. Charles P. Kindleberger, "Memorandum for the files: origins of the Marshall Plan," July 1948, in *Marshall Plan Days*, 25–26; Walt W. Rostow, "Lessons of the [Marshall] Plan," *Foreign Affairs* (May/June, 1997): 205–6. Text of "The Marshall Plan Speech," published by the George C. Marshall Foundation, Lexington, Virginia, n.d.

27. Osgood, *Ideals and Self-Interest*, 429 39, 450. For a contemporary approach to the issues broached by Osgood, see Isaacson and Thomas, *The Wise Men*, 407; and on "pragmatic idealism," see Robert Kagan, *Of Paradise and Power*, 76–79, 95.

28. For audience response, see Laird Bell ('04), president of the Harvard Alumni Association, cited in John T. Bethell ('54), "The Ultimate Commencement Address," *Harvard Magazine* (May–June 1997); Fossedal, op. cit., "Summer 1947, From Marshall's Speech to a Plan"; Pogue, *Interviews and Reminiscences*, vii, and taped remarks of November 19, 1956, 527; Isaacson and Thomas, op. cit., 410; Larry I. Bland, Marshall biographical narrative at www.marshallfoundation.org; Walter Lippmann's fourteen-article series of "Cold War" columns ran in September and October 1947 and may be found at www.academic.brooklyn.cuny.edu/history/johnson/lippcoldwar.htm.

29. Introduction, "For European Recovery: The Fiftieth Anniversary of the Marshall Plan," Library of Congress Exhibition, 1997; "technology transfer," Charles S. Maier, "From Plan to Practice," *Harvard Magazine* (May–June 1997); "lubricant" also per Maier, cited in David Reynolds, "The European Response," *Foreign Affairs* (May–June 1997); Hadley Arkes, *Bureaucracy, The Marshall Plan, and the National Interest*, 42, 135; Bohlen, *Witness to History*, 266; on American "hegemony," see Harry B. Price, *Marshall Plan*, 5, and Maier, *In Search of Stability: Explorations in Historical Political Economy*, 148–49, and, citing Will Clayton, 122, note 3; Scott Parrish, "Soviet Reaction to the Marshall Plan: Opportunity or Threat?" in *Problems of Post-Communism* (September–October 1995); Bonds, "Europe Responds," *Bipartisan Strategy*, 37–42.

30. GCM to Forrest Pogue, *Interviews and Reminiscences*, November 19, 1956, 527; GCM in Foulke memorandum, October 30, 1952; Charles L. Mee Jr., *The Marshall Plan*, 236; Harry R. Price, *Marshall Plan and Its Meaning*, 327, 408; Bonds, *Bipartisan Strategy*, 26–30.

31. Isaacson and Thomas, op. cit., 399; Bohlen, op. cit., 267; Bonds, ibid., 32; Pogue, ibid., 527, and Foulke memorandum; Acheson, op. cit., 223.

32. Harry B. Price, *Marshall Plan and Its Meaning*, 61–63; Arthur H. Vandenberg Jr. with the collaboration of Joe Alex Morris, "The Marshall Plan," *The Private Papers of Senator Vandenberg*, 373 98.

33. Price, ibid., 223–25; William C. Foster, quoted in United States Economic Coopera-
    tion Administration booklet, *Three Years of the Marshall Plan*, 1–3; GNP statistics
    from Charles S. Maier, "Plan to Practice," 4; Otto Zausmer, *The Marshall Plan*, 4–6;
    McCullough, *Truman*, 583, and 1033 note citing *Off the Record, the Private Papers of
    Harry S. Truman*, 133.

34. Pogue, *Marshall: Statesman*, 505–6; Andrew J. Goodpaster, "George Marshall's World,
    and Ours," *New York Times* Op-Ed page, Thursday, December 11, 2003. General
    Goodpaster, chairman emeritus of the George C. Marshall Foundation, was supreme
    allied commander of NATO from 1969 to 1974; "George C. Marshall—Essentials to
    Peace," in Frederick W. Haberman, ed., *Nobel Peace Lectures, 1951–1970*, Amster-
    dam, 1972.

35. Alistair Cooke, *Letter from America*, Monday, December 9, 2002, "The Marshall
    Plan," www.news.bbc.co.uk/1/hi/world.

Bibliography

Paying close attention to the most recent scholarship in the ten ideals and their proponents, I also took great pleasure in tracking down vintage works of history, Enlightenment, and Victorian antiques. Isaac Newton wrote in 1676 to the experimental biologist Robert Hooke: "If I have seen further than others it is because I have stood on the shoulders of giants." This is how I feel about the multitude of distinguished writers represented in this Bibliography, lengthy for a book of moderate size. It is offered as a launching platform for further exploration into the lessons of our past for the meanings of our present.

Acheson, Dean. *Present at the Creation: My Years in the State Department.* New York: W. W. Norton, 1969.

———. *Sketches from Life of Men I Have Known.* New York: Harper, 1961.

Adams, Elsie Bonita. *Israel Zangwill.* New York: Twayne English Authors Series, 1971.

Adams, Ephraim D. *The Power of Ideals in American History.* New Haven: Yale University Press, 1913.

Addams, Jane. "The College Woman and the Family Claim." *Commons,* no. 29 (September 1898).

———. "Comment on 'How Would You Uplift the Masses?'" Ladies Night, Forty-second meeting of the Sunset Club, Chicago, February 4, 1892. *Sunset Club Yearbook, 1891–1892.* Chicago: Privately printed, 1892.

———. *Democracy and Social Ethics.* Edited and with an introduction by Anne Firor Scott. Cambridge: A John Harvard Library Book, Belknap Press of Harvard University Press, 1964.

———. *Democracy and Social Ethics.* Edited and with an introduction by Charlene Haddock Seigfried. Urbana and Chicago: University of Illinois Press, 2002.

———. *Democracy and Social Ethics: A Syllabus of a Course of Twelve Lectures.* Chicago: pamphlet, State Historical Society of Wisconsin, Anita McCormick Blaine Papers, 1899.

———. (Joint author with "Residents of Hull-House, a Social Settlement") *Hull-House Maps and Papers: A Presentation of Nationalities and Wages in a Congested District of Chicago, Together with Comments and Essays on Problems Growing Out of the Social Conditions.* New York: Thomas Y. Crowell, Library of Economics and Politics, 1895.

———. *The Long Road of Woman's Memory.* Urbana and Chicago: University of Illinois Press, 2002.

———. *The Spirit of Youth and the City Streets.* Urbana: University of Illinois Press, 1972 edition of 1909.

———. *Twenty Years at Hull-House.* Edited with an introduction by Victoria Bissell Brown. Boston and New York: Bedford/St. Martin's, 1999.

———. *Twenty Years at Hull-House.* New York: Signet Books, 1961.

Adiv, Udi. "The Jewish Question and the Zionist Movement." Return Magazine, no. 5 (December 1990).

Adler, Cyrus. *Selected Letters, Volume One.* Edited by Ira Robinson. Philadelphia: Jewish Publication Society of America, 1985.

Aldridge, Alfred Owen. *Man of Reason: The Life of Thomas Paine.* Philadelphia and New York: J.B. Lippincott, 1959.

Allen, Gay Wilson. *Waldo Emerson: A Biography.* New York: Viking Press, 1981.

Ameriks, Karl, ed. *The Cambridge Companion to German Idealism.* New York: Cambridge University Press, 2000.

Andelson, Robert V., ed. *Critics of Henry George: A Centenary Appraisal of Their Strictures on Progress and Poverty.* New Jersey: Associated University Presses, Cranbury, 1979.

Anderson, John Q. "Emerson's 'Young American' as Democratic Nobleman." *American Transcendental Quarterly,* no. 9 (Winter 1971).

Appiah, Kwame Anthony, and Henry Louis Gates Jr., eds. *Africana: The Encyclopedia of the African and African American Experience.* New York: Basic Civitas Books, 1999.

Arkes, Hadley. *Bureaucracy, The Marshall Plan, and the National Interest.* Princeton: Princeton University Press, 1972.

Ashley W. J. "Introduction to John Stuart Mill." *Principles of Political Economy.* 7th ed. Edgbaston, September 1909.

Atkins, Scott. *The Puritan Tradition and American Memory.* The Capitol Project, American Studies Group, University of Virginia. http://xroads.virginia.edu/Cap/Puritan.html.

Ayer, A. J. *Thomas Paine.* Chicago: University of Chicago Press, 1990.

Bailyn, Bernard. *The Ideological Origins of the American Revolution.* Cambridge: Harvard University Press, 1992.

———. *On the Teaching and Writing of History.* Hanover, New Hampshire: University Press of New England, 1994.

Baritz, Loren. *City on a Hill: A History of Ideas and Myths in America.* New York: John Wiley & Sons, 1964.

Barker, Charles Albro. *Henry George.* New York: Oxford University Press, 1955.

Barnes, Peter. "Reconsiderations: Progress and Poverty." *New Republic* (December 11, 1971).

Beard, Charles and Mary, and their son, William Beard. *New Basic History of the United States.* New York: Doubleday, 1944, 1960.

Bercovich, Sacvan. *The American Jeremiad*. Madison: University of Wisconsin Press, 1978.

Berger, Peter L. *Invitation to Sociology: A Humanistic Perspective*. New York: Anchor Books, 1963.

Bernstein Richard B., with Kym S. Rice. *Are We to be a Nation? The Making of the Constitution*. New York: Harvard University Press, Cambridge and London, in cooperation with The New York Public Library, 1987.

Bethell, John T. "The Ultimate Commencement Address: The Making of George C. Marshall's 'Routine' Speech." *Harvard Magazine* (May–June 1997).

Birnbaum, Jeffrey H. "A Mideast Marshall Plan?" *Fortune* magazine. (October 13, 2002).

Blaug, Mark. *Henry George, 1839–1897*. Aldershot, Hants., England: E. Elgar Publishers, 1992.

Bloom, Harold. *The American Religion*. New York: Simon & Schuster, 1992.

Bohlen, Charles E. *Witness to History: 1929–1969*. New York: W. W. Norton, 1973.

Boime, Albert. *The Magisterial Gaze: Manifest Destiny and American Landscape Painting, 1830–1865*. Washington: Smithsonian Institution Press, 1991.

Bonds, John Bledsoe. *Bipartisan Strategy: Selling the Marshall Plan*. Westport: Praeger, 2002.

Boorstin, Daniel I., ed. *An American Primer*. New York: Meridian Books, 1995.

Bozeman, Theodore Dwight. "The Puritans' 'Errand into the Wilderness' Reconsidered." *New England Quarterly* 59, no. 2 (June 1986): 231–51.

Bremer, Francis J. *John Winthrop: America's Forgotten Founding Father*. New York: Oxford University Press, 2003.

Bridenbaugh, Carl, and Jessica. *Rebels and Gentlemen: Philadelphia in the Age of Franklin*. New York: Oxford University Press, 1962.

Brock, William R. *Conflict and Transformation: The United States, 1844–1877*. New York: Penguin Books, 1973.

Brooks, Albert N. D. "Dr. Woodson the Inspiration." *Negro History Bulletin*, (December 1956).

Brown, Gordon. "The Marshall Plan for the Next 50 Years." *Washington Post*, December 17, 2001.

Brown, Letitia W. "Why and How the Negro in History." *Journal of Negro Education*, XXXVIII, no. 4. (Autumn 1969).

Brown, Victoria Bissell. *The Education of Jane Addams*. Philadelphia: University of Pennsylvania Press, 2004.

———. "Jane Addams" in Rima Lunin Schultz and Adele Hast, eds. *Women Building Chicago 1790–1990*. Bloomington and Indianapolis: Indiana University Press, 2001.

Bryan, Ferald. "George C. Marshall at Harvard: A Study of the Origins and Construction of the 'Marshall Plan' Speech." *Presidential Studies Quarterly* XXI, no. 3 (Summer 1991).

Bryan, Mary Lynn McCree. "The First Year of Hull-House, 1889–1890, in Letters by Jane Addams and Ellen Gates Starr." *Chicago History Magazine*. I (Fall 1970).

———. et al. *The Jane Addams Papers: A Comprehensive Guide*. Bloomington: Indiana University Press, 1996.

———. *The Jane Addams Papers, 1860–1960*. Ann Arbor, Michigan: University Microfilms International, 1984. Collection of The New York Public Library.

"Building Countries, Feeling Generous." *Economist* 363, issue 8279 (June 29, 2002).

Burke, Edmund. Isaac Kramnick, ed. *The Portable Edmund Burke*. New York: Penguin Books, 1999.

Bury, J. B. *The Idea of Progress*. London: Macmillan, 1920.

Carlyle, Thomas and Ralph Waldo Emerson. *Correspondence, Volume I*. Boston: James R. Osgood and Company, 1883.

Carson, Mina. *Settlement Folk: Social Thought and the American Settlement Movement, 1885–1930*. Chicago and London: University of Chicago Press, 1990.

Cawelti, John G. *Apostles of the Self-Made Man: Changing Concepts of Success in America*. Chicago: University of Chicago Press, 1965.

Charles Booth (1840–1916), a Biography. London School of Economics Library, www.booth.lse.ac.uk/ststic/a/2.html.

Chase, Hank. "Carter G. Woodson's Home." *American Visions* (February 2000).

Clarke, Samuel Belcher. "The Single Tax and the Impôt Unique: Comment." *Quarterly Journal of Economics* 3 (April 1891): 57–59.

Clesse, Armand, and Archie C. Epps, eds. *Present at the Creation: The Fortieth Anniversary of the Marshall Plan*. New York: Harper & Row, 1990.

Cobb, Montague. "Carter Godwin Woodson, PhD, 1875–1950: The Father of Negro History." *Journal of the National Medical Association* 62 (September 1970).

Cobb, William Jelani. "Heavy Lifting as We Climb." www.africana.com/articles/daily/index. (February 1, 2001).

Cohen, Naomi W. *Jacob H. Schiff: A Study in American Jewish Leadership*. Hanover and London: Brandeis University Press/University Press of New England, 1999.

Conway, Moncure D. *The Life of Thomas Paine*. New York: Arno Press, 1977 edition of 1892.

Conyers Jr., James L., ed. *Carter G. Woodson: A Historical Reader*. New York and London: Garland Publishing, 2000.

———. "A Tribute to Carter G. Woodson." *Black Issues in Higher Education*. n.p., February 13, 2003.

Cooke, Alistair. "The Marshall Plan." *Letter from America*. BBC, December 9, 2002. news.bbc.co.uk/1/hi/world/letter_from_america.

Cressy, David. "The Vast and Furious Ocean: The Passage to Puritan New England." *New England Quarterly* 57, no. 4 (December 1984): 511–32.

Cristensen, John. "Black History Month Edges into the Mainstream: Carter G. Woodson's dream continues to grow." CNN Interactive. www.cnn.com/specials/1999/blackhistory/overview.

Crunden, Robert M. *Ministers of Reform: The Progressives' Achievement in American Civilization, 1889–1920*. Urbana and Chicago: University of Illinois Press, 1984.

Curti, Merle. "Jane Addams on Human Nature." *Journal of the History of Ideas* (April–June 1961): 240–53.

Darlington, Sonja. "Who Was Jane Addams?" *Beloit College Magazine* (Spring 2003).

Davis, Allen F. *American Heroine: The Life and Legend of Jane Addams*. Chicago: Ivan R. Dee, 1973, 2000.

Dawson, Hugh J. "John Winthrop's Rite of Passage: The Origins of the 'Christian Charitie' Discourse." *Early American Literature* XXVI, no. 3 (1991): 219–31.

Day, Aidan. *Romanticism*. London and New York: Routledge, 1996.

Decker, Jeffrey Louis. *Made in America: Self-Styled Success from Horatio Alger to Oprah Winfrey*. University of Minnesota Press, Minneapolis: 1997.

Deegan, Mary Jo. "The Feminist Pragmatism of Jane Addams." Edited by Mary Ann Romano. *Lost Sociologists Rediscovered*. Lewiston, New York: Edwin Mellen Press, 2002.

———. *Jane Addams and the Men of the Chicago School, 1892–1918*. New Brunswick, New Jersey: Transaction Books, 1986.

Delbanco, Andrew. *The Real American Dream: A Meditation on Hope*. Cambridge and New York: Harvard University Press, 1999.

Descriptive Catalogue of the Du Simitière Papers in the Library Company of Philadelphia. Philadelphia: Historical Records Survey, Division of Professional and Service Projects, Works Projects Administration, April 1940.

Detwiler, Donald S. "The Definitive Biography of George C. Marshall." *Journal of Military History* 53 (July 1989).

Deutsch, Monroe E. "E Pluribus Unum." *Classical Journal* XVIII (April 1923): 387–407.

De Voto, Bernard. *The Year of Decision: 1846*. Boston: Little, Brown, 1943.

Dewey, John. *An Appreciation of Henry George, October 1927*. www.cooperativeindividualism.org/dewey_on_henry_george.html.

Diamond, Sigmund, ed. *The Nation Transformed: The Creation of an Industrial Society*. New York: George Braziller, 1963.

Diliberto, Gioia. *A Useful Woman: The Early Life of Jane Addams*. New York: A Lisa Drew Book/Scribner, 1999.

Donaghy, Elisabeth. *Pierre Eugène du Simitière, Unsuccessful Civil and Natural Historian in Revolutionary America*. Unpublished MA Dissertation, University of Delaware, Newark, 1970.

D'Souza, Dinesh. *What's So Great About America*. New York: Penguin Books, 2003.

Du Bois, W.E.B. *Black Reconstruction in America: 1860–1880*. Introduction by David Levering Lewis. New York: Free Press, 1992 edition of 1935.

———. *Dusk of Dawn: An Essay Toward a Biography of a Race Concept*. (New York: Harcourt, Brace, 1940). In *Writings*. Library of America, 1986.

———. "The Journal of Negro History." Editorial. *The Crisis* XIII (December 1916).

———. "A Portrait of Carter G. Woodson." *Masses & Mainstream* III, (June 1950).

Duignan, Peter, and Lewis H. Gann. "The Marshall Plan." Hoover Institution. *Hoover Digest*, no. 4 (1997).

Dulles, Allen W. Edited and with an introduction by Michael Walla. *The Marshall Plan*. Providence: Berg, 1993.

Dunn, Richard S. "John Winthrop Writes His Journal." *William and Mary Quarterly* 3rd Series. Vol. 41, no.2 (April 1984): 185–212.

Dunn, Richard S., and Laetitia Yeandle, eds. *The Journals of John Winthrop, 1630–1649*. Cambridge: Harvard University Press, 1996.

Dyck, Ian, ed. *Citizen of the World: Essays on Thomas Paine*. New York: St. Martin's Press, 1988.

Eagleton, Terry. *Ideology*. New York and London: Verso Books, 1991.

Economic Cooperation Administration. *Three Years of the Marshall Plan*. Washington, D.C., 1951.

Eliot, George. *Romola*. New York: Modern Library, 2003 edition of 1878.

Ellis, Joseph J. *Founding Brothers: The Revolutionary Generation*. New York: Alfred A. Knopf, 2000.

Ellwood, David. "You Too Can Be Like Us." *History Today* 48, Issue 10 (October 1998).

Elshtain, Jean Bethke, ed. *The Jane Addams Reader*. New York: Basic Books, 2002.

Emerson Ralph Waldo. *Essays and Lectures*. New York: Library of America, 1983.

————. *Journals and Miscellaneous Notebooks of Ralph Waldo Emerson, Volume V: 1835–1838*. Edited by Merton M. Sealts Jr. et al. Cambridge: Belknap Press of Harvard University Press, 1965.

————. *Journals and Miscellaneous Notebooks of Ralph Waldo Emerson, Volume VI: 1824–1838*. Edited by Ralph H. Orth, et al. Cambridge: Belknap Press of Harvard University Press, 1966.

————. *Journals and Miscellaneous Notebooks, Volume VII, 1838–1842*, edited by William H. Gilman, Alfred R. Ferguson, et al. Cambridge: Belknap Press of Harvard Univeristy Press, 1969.

————. *Journals and Miscellaneous Notebooks, Volume VIII, 1841–1843*, edited by William H. Gilman, J. E. Parsons, et al. Cambridge: Belknap Press of Harvard Univeristy Press, 1970.

The European Reconstruction, 1948–1961, a Bibliography on the Marshall Plan and OEEC. Organization for European Economic Cooperation, Paris, 1996.

Fabre, Genevieve, and Robert O'Meally, eds. *History and Memory in African-American Culture*. New York: Oxford University Press, 1994.

Farrell, John C. *Beloved Lady: A History of Jane Addams' Ideas on Reform and Peace*. Baltimore: Johns Hopkins University Press, 1967.

Fein, Isaac M. "Israel Zangwill and American Jewry." *American Jewish Historical Quarterly*, LX, no. 1 (September 1970).

Fein, Leonard. "One Big Step for Diversity." *The Forward*. Op-Ed page. (February 7, 2002).

Fiennes, Lord Charles, and/or Lady Arbella Fiennes Johnson. The Humble Request. Signed April 7, 1630 at Yarmouth, England. http://www.winthropsociety.org/doc_humble.php.

Fischer, Marilyn. *On Addams*. Toronto: Wadsworth Philosophers Series, 2004.

FitzGerald, Frances. *America Revised: History Schoolbooks in the Twentieth Century*. New York: Vintage Books, 1980.

Foner, Eric. *Tom Paine and Revolutionary America*. New York: Oxford University Press, 1976.

————. *Who Owns History?* New York: Hill and Wang, 2002.

————, ed. *The New American History*. Philadelphia: Temple University Press, 1997.

Fonseca, Goncalo L., and Leanne J. Ussher, eds. New School History of Economic Thought Web Site: www.cepa.newschool.edu/het/.

Fontaine, William T. "'Social Determination' in the Writings of Negro Scholars." *American Journal of Sociology* (January 1944).

Fossedal, Gregory. *Our Finest Hour: Will Clayton, The Marshall Plan, and the Triumph of Democracy*. Stanford: Hoover Institution Press, 1993.

Foulke, Roy E. "Interview with General George C. Marshall, 30 October 1952." www.trumanlibrary.org/study_collections/marshall.

Franklin, Benjamin. *The Autobiography of Benjamin Franklin*. Edited by Leonard W. Laba-
    ree, Ralph L. Ketcham, et al. Foreword by Edmund S. Morgan. New Haven: Yale Uni-
    versity Press, 2003.

Franklin, John Hope. "The New American History." *Negro Digest* (February 1967).

———. "The New Negro History." *Journal of Negro History* XLII, no. 2 (April 1957).

———. "On the Evolution of Scholarship in Afro-American History." In Hine et al.,
    1986.

———. "The Place of Carter G. Woodson in American Historiography." *Negro History
    Bulletin* (May 1950).

———, et al., "Black History Month: Serious Truth Telling or a Triumph in Tokenism?"
    Journal of Blacks in Higher Education, no. 18 (Winter 1997–8).

Franklin, Vincent P. "Changing Historical Perspectives on Afro-American Life and Edu-
    cation." In Franklin and James D. Anderson, eds. *New Perspectives on Black Educational
    History*. Boston: G. K. Hall, 1978.

Fresonke, Kris. *West of Emerson: The Design of Manifest Destiny*. Berkeley: University of
    California Press, 2003.

Gaddis, John Lewis. *The Landscape of History*. New York: Oxford University Press, 2002.

George, Henry. *The Condition of Labour*. New York: Robert Schalkenbach Foundation,
    1935.

———. *Progress and Poverty: The Remedy*. New York: Doubleday, Page, 1879.

———. "What the Railroad Will Bring Us." *Overland Monthly*, I, no. 4 (October 1868).

———. "The Chinese in California." *New-York Daily Tribune*, May 1, 1869, 1–2.

———. *Moses and the Crime of Poverty*. New York: International Joseph Fels Commission,
    1918.

———. *Our Land and Land Policy*. Edited by Kenneth Wenzer. Lansing: Michigan State
    University Press, 1999 edition of 1871.

———. *Science of Political Economy*. New York: Robert Schalkenbach Foundation, 1962
    edition of 1897.

———. "The Single Tax: What It Is and Why We Urge It." *Christian Advocate* (1890).

———. *Social Problems*. New York: Doubleday, Page, 1883.

———. *Testimony Before the Senate Committee on the Relations Between Labor and Capital*
    Washington, D.C.: 1883: www.progress.org/archive/hginter1–4.htm.

———. *Throwing His Hat in the Ring: Henry George Runs for Mayor*. Acceptance speech for
    the United Labor Party, Cooper Union, New York City, October 5, 1886: www.histo-
    rymatters.gmu.edu/d/5321.

George Jr., Henry. *The Life of Henry George*. Garden City, N.Y.: Doubleday, Page & Com-
    pany, 1911.

Gide, Charles. "The Single Tax and the Impôt Unique." *Quarterly Journal of Economics* 4
    (July 1891): 494–95.

Gimbel, John. *The Origins of the Marshall Plan*. Stanford: Stanford University Press, 1976.

Glazer, Nathan, and Daniel Patrick Moynihan. *Beyond the Melting-Pot: The Negroes, Puerto
    Ricans, Jews, Italians, and Irish of New York City*. Cambridge, Massachusetts: MIT Press
    and Harvard University Press, 1963.

Gleason, Philip. "The Melting-Pot: Symbol of Fusion or Confusion?" *American Quarterly*,
    XVI, no. 1 (Spring 1964): 20–46.

Goggin, Jacqueline. *Carter G. Woodson: A Life in Black History*. Baton Rouge and London: Louisiana State University Press, 1993.

Goodpaster, Andrew J. "George Marshall's World, and Ours." *New York Times*, Op-Ed page, December 11, 2003.

Goren, Arthur A. *New York Jews and the Quest for Community: The Kehillah Experiment, 1908–1922*. New York and London: Columbia University Press, 1970.

Graebner, Norman, ed. *Manifest Destiny*. New York: Bobbs-Merrill, 1968.

Gray, Stanley. "The Political Thought of John Winthrop." *New England Quarterly* III (1930): 681–705.

Grose, Peter, ed. "Marshall Plan Commemorative Section: The Marshall Plan Reconsidered." *Foreign Affairs* (May/June 1977).

Guldin, Bob. "Mr. X Speaks: An Interview with George Kennan." *Foreign Service Journal* no.13 (February 2004).

Habegger, Alfred. *My Wars Are Laid Away in Books: The Life of Emily Dickinson*. New York: Modern Library, 2002.

Halmi, Nicholas et al., ed. *Coleridge's Poetry and Prose*. New York: W. W. Norton, 2004.

Harris, Kenneth Marc. *Carlyle and Emerson: Their Long Debate*. Cambridge: Harvard University Press, 1978.

Hawke, David Freeman. *Paine*. New York: W. W. Norton, 1974.

Haynes, Sam W. and Christopher Morris, eds. *Manifest Destiny and Empire: American Antebellum Expansion*. College Station: Texas A&M University Press, 1997.

Heilbroner, Robert L. *The Worldly Philosophers: The Lives, Times and Ideas of the Great Economic Thinkers*. Updated and Revised 7th ed. New York: Touchstone/Simon & Schuster, 1999.

Herberg, Will. *Protestant Catholic Jew: An Essay in American Religious Sociology*. Chicago: University of Chicago Press, 1955.

Hertzberg, Arthur, ed. *The Zionist Idea*. Philadelphia: Jewish Publication Society, 1997.

Higham, John. *From Boundlessness to Consolidation: The Transformation of American Culture, 1848–1860*. Ann Arbor: University of Michigan, William L. Clements Library, 1969.

———. *Send These to Me: Jews and Other Immigrants in Urban America*. New York: Atheneum, 1975.

———. *Strangers in the Land: Patterns of American Nativism, 1860–1925*. New Brunswick: Rutgers University Press, 1955.

Himmelfarb, Gertrude. *Poverty and Compassion: The Moral Imagination of the Late Victorians*. New York: Vintage Books, 1992.

Hine, Darlene Clark. "Carter G. Woodson, White Philanthropy and Negro Historiography." *History Teacher* XIX, no. 3 (May, 1986).

———, ed. Introduction by Thomas C. Holt. *The State of Afro-American History: Past, Present and Future*. Baton Rouge and London: Louisiana State University Press, 1986.

Hitchcock, William I. *The Struggle for Europe*. New York: Anchor Books, 2003.

Hofstadter, Richard. *The Age of Reform*. New York: Vintage Books, 1955.

———. *The American Political Tradition and the Men Who Made It*. New York: Random House, 1948, 1973.

———, Clarence L. Ver Steeg, and Beatrice K. Hofstadter, eds. *Great Issues in American History, 1584–1776*. New York: Vintage Books, 1958, 1982.

Hogan, Michael J. *The Marshall Plan: America, Britain, and the Reconstruction of Europe, 1947–1952*. Cambridge: Cambridge University Press, 1987.

Holmes, John Haynes. "On Presenting the Spingarn Medal." *The Crisis* XXXII, (September 1926).

Holt, Thomas C. "African American History." In Eric Foner, ed., *The New American History*. Philadelphia: Temple University Press, 1997.

Horsman, Reginald. *Race and Manifest Destiny: The Origins of American Racial Anglo-Saxonism*. Cambridge: Harvard University Press, 1981.

Howe, Irving. *World of Our Fathers: The Journey of the East European Jews to America and the Life They Found and Made*. New York and London: Harcourt Brace Jovanovich, 1976.

Hudson, Linda S. *Mistress of Manifest Destiny: A Biography of Jane Mc Manus Storm Cazneau, 1807–1878*. Austin: Texas State Historical Association, 2001.

Hughes, Langston. "When I Worked for Dr. Woodson." *Negro History Bulletin* (May 1950).

Huntington, Samuel P. "The Hispanic Challenge." *Foreign Policy*. Washington, D.C.: Carnegie Endowment for International Peace (March/April 2004).

Huth, Hans. "Pierre Eugène Du Simitière and the Beginnings of the American Historical Museum." *Pennsylvania Magazine of History and Biography*, LXIX (October 1945): 315–25.

Hutson, James H. *Religion and the Founding of the American Republic*. Washington, D.C.: University Press of New England/Library of Congress, 1998.

Isaacson, Walter. *Benjamin Franklin: An American Life*. New York: Simon & Schuster, 2003.

———, and Evan Thomas. *The Wise Men: Six Friends and the World They Made*. New York: Simon & Schuster, 1986.

Jackson, Alexander L. "Carter D. Woodson." *Negro History Bulletin* (July 1965).

Jackson, Scott. "Prologue to the Marshall Plan." *Journal of American History*, no. 65 (1979): 1043–68.

Jacoby, Tamar, ed. *Reinventing the Melting-Pot: The New Immigrants and What It Means to Be American*. New York: Basic Books, 2004.

James, Henry. "Ralph Waldo Emerson," in *Literary Criticism: American Writers*. New York: Library of America, 1984.

James, William. *Writings, 1878–1899*. New York: Library of America, 1992.

Janken, Kenneth R. "Rayford Logan: The Golden Years." *Negro History Bulletin* (July–December 1998).

———. *Rayford W. Logan and the Dilemma of the African-American Intellectual*. Amherst: University of Massachusetts Press, 1993.

Johannsen, Robert, W., et. al. *Manifest Destiny and Empire: American Antebellum Expansion*. Arlington: Texas A&M University Press, 1997.

Johnson, Edgar A. J. "Economic Ideas of John Winthrop." *New England Quarterly* 3, no. 2 (April 1930): 235–50.

Johnson, Elwood. *The Pursuit of Power: Studies in the Vocabulary of Puritanism*. New York: American University Studies Series VII, Peter Lang Publishing, 1995.

Johnson, Kenneth M. "Progress and Poverty: A Paradox." *California Historical Society Quarterly* (March 1963).

Jones, Joseph Marion. "'Design for Reconstruction,' Proposed Address for Secretary Marshall, June 1947, drafted May 20, 1947." Collection Truman Presidential Museum and Library. www.trumanlibrary.org/study_collections/marshall.

———. *The Fifteen Weeks: An Inside Account of the Genesis of the Marshall Plan.* New York: Harcourt Brace, 1955.

———. "Memorandum: Secretary of State's Harvard Speech of June 1947, filed July 2, 1947." www.trumanlibrary.org/study_collections/marshall.

Kagan, Robert. *Of Paradise and Power: America and Europe in the New World Order.* New York: Alfred A. Knopf, 2003.

Kahn-Paycha, Daniele. *Popular Jewish Literature and Its Role in the Making of an Identity.* Lewiston, N.Y.: Edwin Mellen Press, 2000.

Kallen, Horace M. *Culture and Democracy in the United States.* New York: Boni and Liveright, 1924.

———. "The Issues of War and the Jewish Position." *The Nation* (November 29, 1917).

Kammen, Michael. *Mystic Chords of Memory: The Transformation of Tradition in American Culture.* New York: Random House, 1991.

Keane, John. *Tom Paine: A Political Life.* New York: Grove Press, 1995.

Kennan, George F. *Memoirs, 1950–1963.* London: Hutchinson, 1973.

———. *Memoirs, 1925–1950.* Boston: Little, Brown, 1967.

Kennedy, Lisa. "Persistence of Memory: Scholars Create an African-American Canon." *Village Voice Literary Supplement* (April 2001).

Kindleberger, Charles P. *Marshall Plan Days.* Boston: Allen & Unwin, 1987.

Kohn, Hans. *American Nationalism: An Interpretative Essay.* New York: Macmillan, 1957.

Kramnick, Isaac, ed. *The Portable Enlightenment Reader.* New York: Penguin Books, 1995.

Kurata, Phil. "Congressmen Propose Marshall Plan for Middle East." United States Department of State Communique, July 24, 2002.

Landes, David S. *The Wealth and Poverty of Nations: Why Some Are So Rich and Some So Poor.* New York: W. W. Norton, 1999.

Lasch, Christopher. *The New Radicalism in America, 1889–1963: The Intellectual as a Social Type.* New York: Alfred A. Knopf, 1965.

———, ed. *The Social Thought of Jane Addams.* New York: Bobbs-Merrill American Heritage Series, 1965.

Lears, T. J. Jackson. *No Place of Grace: Antimodernism and the Transformation of American Culture, 1880–1920.* New York: Pantheon Books, 1981.

Leftwich, Joseph. *Israel Zangwill.* New York and London: Thomas Yoseloff, 1957.

Lemon M. C. *Philosophy of History.* London and New York: Routledge, 2003.

Lengermann, Patricia Madoo, and Jill Niebrugge-Brantley, eds. *The Women Founders: Sociology and Social Theory.* Boston: McGraw-Hill, 1998.

Lewis, David Levering. *W. E. B. Du Bois: Biography of a Race, 1868–1919.* New York: Henry Holt, 1993.

———. *W. E. B. Du Bois: The Fight for Equality and the American Century, 1919–1963.* New York: Henry Holt, 2000.

Lewis, R. W. B. *The American Adam: Innocence, Tragedy and Tradition in the Nineteenth Century.* Chicago: University of Chicago Press, 1955.

Lindsay, Arnett G. "Dr. Woodson as a Teacher." *Negro History Bulletin* (May 1950).

Link, Arthur S., and Richard L. McCormick. *Progressivism.* Wheeling, Illinois: Harlan Davidson, 1983.

Lippmann, Walter. "The Cold War." Reprint of excerpts from "Today & Tomorrow" series of fourteen articles, September–October 1947, in *Foreign Affairs* 65, no. 4 (Spring 1987).

———. *Drift and Mastery.* Englewood Cliffs, New Jersey: Prentice Hall, 1914, 1961.

Locke, Alain. Edited and with an introduction by Arnold Rampersad. *The New Negro.* New York: Simon & Schuster, 1992 edition of 1925.

———. Review of "The Negro in Our History." *Journal of Negro History* XII, no. 1, (January 1927).

Locke, Robinson. Scrapbooks 483 (microfilm), and ser. 2, vol. 311. The New York Public Library, Billy Rose Theatre Collection.

Logan, Rayford W. "Carter G. Woodson: Mirror and Molder of his Time, 1875–1950." *Journal of Negro History* LVIII, no. 1 (January 1973).

———. "Carter Godwin Woodson." *Journal of Negro History* XXXV, no. 3 (July 1950).

———. "The Death of the Founder." *Negro History Bulletin* (May 1950).

———. "*Phylon* Profile VI: Carter G. Woodson." *Phylon* VI, no. 4 (1940–56, Fourth Quarter, 1945).

———, ed., with Michael R. Winston. *Dictionary of American Negro Biography.* New York: W. W. Norton, 1982.

Lopez, Michael. *Emerson and Power: Creative Antagonism in the Nineteenth Century.* De Kalb: Northern Illinois University Press, 1996.

Lougee, Wendy et al., eds. "The Nineteenth Century in Print: The Making of America in Books and Periodicals." Consortium of Library of Congress, University of Michigan Library, and Cornell University Library. www.memory.loc.gov/ammem/ndlpcoop/moahtml/ncpabout.html.

Lowenberg, Bert James. *American History in American Thought: Christopher Columbus to Henry Adams.* New York: Simon & Schuster, 1972.

Lukacs, John. *At the End of an Age.* New Haven: Yale University Press, 2002.

———. *Historical Consciousness: The Remembered Past.* New Brunswick, N.J.: Transaction Publishers, 1985.

Lyles, Dorothy E. "Carter Godwin Woodson: Father of Black History." A *Bio-Bibliography.* The Vivian G. Harsh Research Collection of Afro-American History and Literature, Chicago Public Library, Woodson Regional Library, February 2000.

Mac Einri, Piaras. "States of Becoming: Is there a 'here' here and a 'there' there?: Some reflections on home, away, displacement and identity." Irish Centre for Migration Studies, University College Cork (December 2002), www.migration.ucc./ie.

Maier, Charles S. *In Search of Stability: Explorations in Historical Political Economy.* New York: Cambridge University Press, 1987.

Mann, Arthur. *The One and the Many: Reflections on the American Identity.* Chicago and London: The University of Chicago Press, 1979.

Marr II, Warren. "Black History." *The Crisis* (April 1975).

Marshall, George C. *The Marshall Plan Speech, June 5, 1947*. Lexington, Virginia: George C. Marshall Foundation, n.d.

Matthiessen, F. O. *American Renaissance: Art and Expression in the Age of Emerson and Whitman*. New York: Oxford University Press, 1941.

Mayo, Louise A. *The Ambivalent Image: Nineteenth-Century America's Perception of the Jew*. Rutherford, New Jersey: Fairleigh Dickenson University Press, 1988.

Mays, Benjamin E. "I Knew Carter G. Woodson." *Negro History Bulletin* (January–March 1981).

McCullough, C. Behan. *The Truth of History*. London and New York: Routledge, 1998.

McCullough, David. *John Adams*. New York: Simon & Schuster, 2001.

———. *Truman*. New York: Simon & Schuster, 1992.

Mee, Jr., Charles L. *The Marshall Plan: The Launching of the Pax Americana*. New York: Simon & Schuster, 1984.

Meier, August, and Elliott Rudwick. *Black History and the Historical Profession, 1915–1980*. Urbana and Chicago: University of Illinois Press, 1986.

Mendes-Flohr, Paul, and Jehuda Reinharz, eds. *The Jew in the Modern World: A Documentary History*. New York and Oxford: Oxford University Press, 1995.

Merk, Frederick. *Manifest Destiny and Mission in American History*. Cambridge: Harvard University Press, 1963.

Mill, John Stuart. Edited by Jonathan Riley. *Principles of Political Economy*. New York: Oxford University Press, 1994.

———. *North American Review*. "On Liberty." [review] 97, no. 200 (July 1863).

———. *Principles of Political Economy*. [review] 98, no. 202 (January 1864).

Miller, Perry. *Errand into the Wilderness*. Cambridge: Harvard University Press, 1956, 1984.

———. *The Raven and the Whale: Poe, Melville, and the New York Literary Scene*. Baltimore: Johns Hopkins University Press, 1997.

———. *The Responsibility of Mind in a Civilization of Machines*. Amherst: University of Massachusetts Press, 1979.

———. *The Transcendentalists: The Classic Anthology*. Cambridge: Harvard University Press, 1950.

———, ed. *American Thought, Civil War to World War I*. New York: Holt, Rinehart and Winston, 1954.

———. *The American Transcendentalists: Their Prose and Poetry*. New York: Doubleday Anchor Books, 1957.

———. *The American Puritans: Their Prose and Poetry*. New York: Doubleday Anchor Books, 1956.

Miscamble, Wilson D. "Generation 'X.'" *Wall Street Journal*, February 24, 2004.

Moore, Dorothea. "A Day at Hull-House." *American Journal of Sociology* II, no. 5 (March 1897).

Morgan, Edmund S. "John Winthrop's 'Modell of Christian Charity' in a Wider Context." *Huntington Library Quarterly* 50 (Spring 1987): 145–51.

———. *The Puritan Dilemma: The Story of John Winthrop*. 2nd ed. New York: Addison Wesley Longman, 1999.

———. *Visible Saints: The History of a Puritan Idea.* Ithaca: Cornell University Press, 1963.

Morison, Samuel Eliot. *Builders of the Bay Colony.* Boston: Northeastern University Press, 1981 edition of 1930.

Morris, Edmund. *The Rise of Theodore Roosevelt.* New York: Modern Library, 2001.

Moseley, James G. *John Winthrop's World: History as a Story, The Story as History.* Madison: University of Wisconsin Press, 1992.

Myerson, Joel, ed. *The Selected Letters of Ralph Waldo Emerson.* New York: Columbia University Press, 1997.

Myrdal, Gunnar. *An American Dilemma: The Negro Problem and Modern Democracy.* New Brunswick: Transaction Publishers, 1996 edition of 1944 original.

Neilson, Francis. "Henry George, The Scholar." Commencement Address Delivered at the Henry George School of Social Science, June 3, 1940. www.cooperativeindividualism. org/neilson_on_henry_george.html.

Neustadt, Richard E. and Ernest R. May. *Thinking In Time: The Uses of History for Decision-makers.* New York: Free Press, 1986.

Nevins, Allan. *Ordeal of the Union, Volume I: Fruits of Manifest Destiny, 1847–1852.* New York: Charles Scribner's Sons, 1947.

Niebuhr, Richard, "The Idea of Covenant and American Democracy." *Church History*, no. 23 (June 1954): 126–35.

Novak, Barbara. *Nature and Culture: American Landscape and Painting, 1825–1875.* Revised Edition. New York: Oxford University Press, 1995.

Novick, Peter. *That Noble Dream: The 'Objectivity Question' and the American Historical Profession.* New York: Cambridge University Press, 1988.

Orosz, Joel J. *The Eagle That Is Forgotten: Pierre Eugène du Simitière, Founding Father of American Numismatics.* Wolfeboro, New Hampshire: Bowers & Merena Galleries, 1988.

———. "Pierre Eugène du Simitière: Museum Pioneer in America." *Museum Studies Journal*, 1 no. I (Spring 1985): 11–21.

Oser, Jacob. *Henry George.* New York: Twayne Publishers, 1974.

Osgood, Robert Endicott. *Ideals and Self-Interest in America's Foreign Relations: The Great Transformation of the Twentieth Century.* Chicago: University of Chicago Press, 1953.

O'Sullivan, John L. *United States Magazine and Democratic Review.* "The Democratic Principle," (October: 1837); "The Great Nation of Futurity," (November, 1839); "Emerson's Essays" (June 1845); "Annexation" (July–August 1845).

———. *New York Morning News.* [editorial] "The True Title" (December 27, 1845); [Letter] (January 5, 1846).

Paine, Thomas. *Collected Writings.* New York: Library of America, 1995.

———. *Common Sense.* New York: Penguin Books, 1976.

———, ed. *The Pennsylvania Magazine, or, American Monthly Museum.* Bound volumes I and II January 24, 1775–July, 1776 [ceased publication].

Palgrave, R. H. I. ed. *Dictionary of Political Economy.* London: Macmillan and Company, 1894–99.

Parrington, V. L. *Main Currents in American Thought.* New York: Harcourt, Brace, 1930.

———. *The Colonial Mind, 1620–1800.* New York: Harvest Books, 1927, 1954.

Parrish, Scott. "Soviet Reaction to the Marshall Plan: Opportunity or Threat?" *Problems of Post-Communism* 42, Issue 5 (September–October 1995).

Paterson, Thomas G. *Soviet-American Confrontation: Postwar Reconstruction and the Origins of the Cold War*. Baltimore: Johns Hopkins University Press, 1973.

Patterson, Richard S. and Richardson Dougall. *The Eagle and the Shield: A History of the Great Seal of the United States*. American Revolution Bicentennial Administration, Washington, D.C. 1976.

Paul, Sherman. *Emerson's Angle of Vision: Man and Nature in American Experience*. Cambridge: Harvard University Press, 1952.

Perry, Ralph Barton. *The Thought and Character of William James*. New paperback edition with an introduction by Charlene Haddock Seigfried. London: Vanderbilt University Press, 1948, 1996.

Peter Force Collection, *Papers of Pierre Eugène Du Simitière*. Five volumes. Library of Congress, Special Collections, Manuscript Reading Room.

Phillips, Kevin. *Wealth and Democracy*. New York: Broadway Books, 2002.

Pierre-Eugène du Simitière: His American Museum 200 Years After. Library Company of Philadelphia Exhibition Catalogue, July–October 1985.

Pletcher, David M. *The Diplomacy of Annexation: Texas, Oregon and the Mexican War*. Columbia: University of Missouri Press, 1973.

Pogue, Forrest C. *George C. Marshall: Statesman, 1945–1959*. New York: George C. Marshall Foundation/Penguin Books, 1989.

———. *George C. Marshall Interviews and Reminiscences*. George C. Marshall Foundation, Lexington, Virginia, 1996.

Potts, William John. "Du Simitière, Artist, Antiquary, and Naturalist, Projector of the First American Museum, with Some Extracts from His Notebook." *Pennsylvania Magazine of History and Biography* XIII, (1889): 341–75.

Pratt, Julius W. "John L. O'Sullivan and Manifest Destiny." *New York History* XIV, no. 3 (July 1933) 213–34.

———. "The Origin of 'Manifest Destiny.'" *American Historical Review* XXXII (1927): 795–98.

Price, Harry B. *The Marshall Plan and Its Meaning*. Ithaca, Cornell University Press, 1955.

Quaife, Milo Milton, ed. *Diary of James K. Polk During His Presidency, 1845–1849, Volumes I–IV*. Chicago: A. C. McClurg, 1910.

Quarles, Benjamin. "Black History's Diversified Clientele." In *Black Mosaic: Essays in Afro-American History and Historiography*. Amherst: University of Massachusetts Press, 1988.

Rader, Benjamin G. *The Academic Mind and Reform: The Influence of Richard T. Ely in American Life*. Lexington: University of Kentucky Press, 1966.

Ramonet, Ignacio. "Time for a New Marshall Plan." *Le Monde Diplomatique*, June 1997.

Rampersad, Arnold. *The Life of Langston Hughes, Volume 1, 1902–1941*. New York: Oxford University Press, 1986.

Reade, Winwood. *The Martyrdom of Man*. New York: A.K. Butts, 1874.

Reddick, Lawrence D. "As I Remember Woodson." *The Crisis* (February 1953); reprinted in *Negro History Bulletin* (November 1953).

———. "Twenty-Five Negro History Weeks." *Negro History Bulletin* (May 1950).

Ricks, Christopher, and William L. Vance, eds. *The Faber Book of America*. London and Boston: Faber & Faber, 1992.

Riis, Jacob. *How the other Half Lives: Studies Among the Tenements of New York*. Edited by Luc Sante. New York: Penguin Books, 1997.

Riley, Woodbridge. *American Thought from Puritanism to Pragmatism*. New York: Henry Holt, 1915.

Roberts, Geoffrey. "Moscow and the Marshall Plan: Politics, Ideology and the Onset of the Cold War, 1947." *Europe-Asia Studies* 46, Issue 8 (1994).

Rochelson, Meri-Jane. "Israel Zangwill and Children of the Ghetto." *Judaism*, Winter 1999.

Rose, Edward J. *Henry George*. New York: Twayne United States Authors Series, 1968.

Rostow, Walt. "Lessons of the Plan." *Foreign Affairs* 76, no. 3 (May–June 1997).

Roth, Samuel, and Israel Zangwill. *Now and Forever: A Conversation on the Jew and the Future*. New York: Robert M. McBride, 1925.

Rousseau, Jean-Jacques. Translated by Maurice Cranston. *The Social Contract*. New York: Penguin Books, 1968.

Rusk, Ralph L. *The Life of Ralph Waldo Emerson*. New York: Charles Scribner's Sons, 1949.

Ruskin, John. *The Political Economy of Art; Unto this Last; Sesame and Lilies; The Crown of Wild Olive*. London: Macmillan, 1912.

Russell, Annie. Papers. Manuscripts and Archives Division. New York Public Library. Correspondence from Edith Ayrton Zangwill and Israel Zangwill to Annie Russell, 1904–1914.

Rutman, Darrett B. *John Winthrop's Decision for America: 1629*. Philadelphia: J. B. Lippincott Company, 1975.

Salter, Arthur. *The Meaning of the Marshal Plan, Now and in 1952*. London: E. Benn, 1948.

Sampson, Robert D. *John L. O'Sullivan and His Times*. Kent, Ohio: Kent State University Press, 2003.

Sawyer, Rollin Alger. *Henry George and the Single Tax: A catalogue of the collection in The New York Public Library*. New York: The New York Public Library, 1926.

Scally, Sister Mary Anthony. *Carter G. Woodson: A Bio-Bibliography*. Westport, Connecticut: Greenwood Press, 1985.

———. "The Carter Woodson Letters in the Library of Congress." *Negro History Bulletin* (June–July 1975).

———. "The Philippine Challenge." *Negro History Bulletin* (January–March, 1981).

———. "Woodson and the Genesis of ASALH." *Negro History Bulletin* (January–February 1977).

Schain, Martin, ed., Introduction by Tony Judt. *The Marshall Plan: Fifty Years After*. New York: Palgrave, 2001.

Scharf, J. Thomas, and Thompson Westcott. *History of Philadelphia 1609–1884*. Philadelphia: 1884.

Scheiber, Jane L., and Robert C. Elliott, eds. *In Search of the American Dream*. New York: New American Library, 1974.

Schlesinger Jr., Arthur M. *The Age of Jackson*. Boston: Little, Brown, 1945.

Schultz, Rima Lunin, ed. *Urban Experience in Chicago: Hull-House and Its Neighborhoods, 1889–1963*. Chicago: University of Illinois at Chicago and Jane Addams Hull-House Museum: www.uic.edu/jaddams/hull/urbanexp.

Schumpeter, Joseph A. Edited from manuscript by Elizabeth Boody Schumpeter. *History of Economic Analysis*. Boston: George Allen & Unwin, 1954.

Schweninger, Lee. *John Winthrop*. Boston: Twayne Publishers, 1990.

Sellars, Charles G. *James K. Polk*. 2 vols. Princeton: Princeton University Press, 1966.

"Settlers in the City Wilderness." Atlantic Monthly Review of Hull-House Maps and Papers (January 1896).

Shapiro, Aharon H. "Moses: Henry George's Inspiration." *American Journal of Economics and Sociology* (December 2001).

Siegenthaler, John. *James K. Polk*. New York: Times Books/Henry Holt, 2003.

Siegfried, Charlene Haddock. "Socializing Democracy: Jane Addams and John Dewey." *Philosophy of the Social Sciences* XXIX, no. 2, June 1999, 207–30.

Sifton, Paul G. *Pierre-Eugène du Simitière: Collector in Revolutionary America* (Unpub. Diss., University of Pennsylvania, Graduate School of Arts and Sciences, 1960).

Sklar, Kathryn Kish. "Hull House in the 1890s: A Community of Women Reformers." *Signs* X, no. 4 (1985): 658–77.

Smith, Adam. *Wealth of Nations*. Amherst, New York: Prometheus Books Great Minds Series, 1991.

Smith, Henry Nash. *Virgin Land: The American West as Symbol and Myth*. Cambridge: Harvard University Press, 1950.

Smith, Page. *A New Age Now Begins: A People's History of the American Revolution*. New York: McGraw-Hill, 1976.

Sorin, Gerald. *The Jewish People in America, A Time for Building: The Third Migration, 1880–1920*. Johns Hopkins University Press, Baltimore and London, 1992.

Sowell, Thomas. *A Conflict of Visions*. New York: Basic Books, 2002.

Stamps, James, E. "Fifty Years Later." *Negro History Bulletin* (November 1965).

Steel, Ronald. "George Kennan at 100." *New York Review of Books*, April 29, 2004.

———. "Playing Loose with History," *New York Times*, May 26, 1997.

———. *Walter Lippmann and the American Century*. New York: Vintage Books, 1981.

Stember, Charles Herbert, ed. *Jews in the Mind of America*. New York: Basic Books, 1966.

Stephanson, Anders. *Manifest Destiny: American Expansion and the Empire of Right*. New York: Hill and Wang, 1995.

Stern, Susan. "The Marshall Plan 1947–1997, A German View." Germany Online. www.germany-info.org.

Stiglitz, Joseph. *Globalization and Its Discontents*. New York: W. W. Norton, 2002.

Stoler, Mark A. *George C. Marshall: Soldier-Statesman of the Twentieth Century*. New York: Twayne Publishers, 1989.

Szmyd, Jan. "War, Peace and Human Rights: On the Social-Legal and Philosophic Views of Thomas Paine." *Dialectics and Humanism*, no. 4 (1983): 207–23.

Teilhac, Ernest. Translated by E. A. J. Johnson. *Pioneers of American Economic Thought in the Nineteenth Century*. New York: Macmillan, 1936.

Tims, Margaret. Jane Addams of Hull House, 1860–1935: A Centenary Study. New York: Macmillan, 1961.

Tocqueville, Alexis de. Translated and edited by Harvey C. Mansfield and Delba Winthrop. *Democracy in America*. Chicago: University of Chicago Press, 2000.

Tolstoy, Leo. Translated by Aylmer Maude. *What Then Must We Do?* London: Oxford University Press, 1935.

Turner, Frederick Jackson. *The Frontier in American History*. New York: Dover Publications, 1996, reprint of Henry Holt and Company, 1920.

Tuveson, Ernest Lee. *Redeemer Nation: The Idea of America's Millennial Role*. Chicago: University of Chicago Press, 1968.

Udelson, Joseph H. *Dreamers of the Ghetto: The Life and Works of Israel Zangwill*. Tuscaloosa and London: University of Alabama Press, 1990.

Updike, John. "*O Beautiful for Spacious Skies.*" Review of the *American Sublime* Exhibition at the Pennsylvania Academy of Fine Arts, Philadelphia (June–August 2002), *New York Review of Books* (August 15, 2002).

Vandenberg Jr., Arthur H, and Joe Alex Morris. *The Private Papers of Senator Vandenberg*. Boston: Houghton Mifflin, 1952.

Van Doren, Carl. *Benjamin Franklin*. New York: Penguin Books, 1966.

Van Leer, David. *Emerson's Epistemology*. New York: Cambridge University Press, 1986.

von Ranke, Leopold. Roger Wines, ed. *The Secret of World History*. New York: Fordham University Press, 1981.

Weber, Max. *The Protestant Ethic and the 'Spirit' of Capitalism, and Other Writings*. Translated and edited by Peter Baehr and Gordon C. Wells. New York: Penguin Books, 2002.

Webster, William G., ed. *A Sequel to Webster's Elementary Spelling Book: or A Speller and Definer*. Philadelphia: J. B. Lippincott, July 1845.

Weinberg, Albert K. *Manifest Destiny: A Study of Nationalist Expansionism in American History*. Chicago: Quadrangle Books, 1963.

Wentholt, Wyger. *The Marshall Plan and Its Chance of Success*. Amsterdam, The Netherlands, 1947.

Wenzer, Kenneth C. *An Anthology of Henry George's Thought*. Rochester, N.Y.: University of Rochester Press, 1997.

Wesley, Charles H. "Carter G. Woodson—As a Scholar." *Journal of Negro History* XXXVI, no. 1 (January 1951).

Wexler, Imanuel. *The Marshall Plan Revisited: The European Recovery Program in Economic Perspective*. Westport: Greenwood Press, 1983.

Wheen, Francis. *Karl Marx: A Life*. New York: W. W. Norton, 2001.

Whicher, Stephen E., ed. *Selections from Ralph Waldo Emerson: An Organic Anthology*. Boston: Houghton Mifflin, 1960.

Whitaker, John K. "Henry George and Classical Growth Theory: A Significant Contribution to Modeling Scale Economies." *American Journal of Economics and Sociology* (January 2000).

White, Hayden. *Metahistory: The Historical Imagination in Nineteenth-Century Europe*. Baltimore: Johns Hopkins University Press, 1975.

Whiteside, Walker. "The Story of a Play." *Chicago Record Herald*, January 24, 1909.

Whitman, Walt. *Leaves of Grass*. Edited and with an introduction by Malcolm Cowley. New York and London: Penguin Books, 1959.

Widmer, Edward L. *Young America: The Flowering of Democracy in New York City*. New York: Oxford University Press, 1999.

Williams, Alvin L. *Carter G. Woodson: Scientific Historian of African-American History and Education*. Unpublished Ph.D. Dissertation. Loyola University of Chicago, 1994.

Williamson, Audrey. *Thomas Paine: His Life, Work and Times*. London: George Allen & Unwin, 1973.

Wilson, Edmund. "Hull-House in 1932," in *The American Earthquake*. New York: Farrar, Straus & Giroux, 1958.

Wilson, Jerome D., and William F. Ricketson. *Thomas Paine*. Boston: Twayne Publishers, 1989.

Wilson, Theodore A. *The Marshall Plan, 1947–1951*. New York: Foreign Policy Association, 1977.

Wilson, Woodrow. "The Ideals of America." *The Atlantic Monthly* XC (December 1902) 721–34.

Winston, Michael R. "Carter Godwin Woodson: Prophet of a Black Tradition." *Journal of Negro History*, LX no. 4 (October 1975).

Wistrich, Robert S. "Zionism and Myths of Assimilation." *Midstream* (August/September 1990).

Wohlgelerntner, Maurice. *Israel Zangwill*. New York: Columbia University Press, 1964.

Wolfe, Alan. *One Nation, After All*. New York: Penguin Books, 1998.

Wood, Allen W., editor and introduction. *Basic Writings of Kant*. New York: Modern Library, 2001.

Wood, Gordon S. *The American Revolution: A History*. New York: Modern Library, 2002.

Woodson, Carter G. "The Celebration of Negro History Week, 1927." *Journal of Negro History* XII, no. 2 (April 1927).

———. *A Century of Negro Migration*. ASNLH, 1918.

———. "Early Negro Education in West Virginia." *Journal of Negro History* VII, no. 1 (January 1922).

———. *The Education of the Negro Prior to 1861*. Washington, D.C.: Associated Publishers, 1919.

———. *The Mind of the Negro as Reflected in Letters Written During the Crisis*. ASNLH, 1926.

———. *The Mis-Education of the Negro*. Washington, D.C.: Associated Publishers, 1933; Trenton: Africa World Press, Tenth Printing, 1998.

———. "My Recollections of Veterans of the Civil War." *Negro History Bulletin* (February 1944).

———. "Negro History Week." *Journal of Negro History* XI, no. 2 (April 1926).

———. "The Negro in Literature and Art." *Journal of Negro History*, III, no. 3 (July 1918).

———. *The Negro in Our History*. Washington, D.C.: Associated Publishers, 1922. Eleventh edition, edited by Charles H. Wesley, 1966.

———. "Negro Life and History in Our Schools." *Journal of Negro History*, IV, no. 3 (July 1919).

———. *Negro Orators and Their Orations*. Washington, D.C.: Association for the Study of Negro Life and History, 1925.

———. "1924 Annual Report of the Director." *Journal of Negro History* IX, no. 4 (October 1924).

———. "1922–23 Annual Report of the Director of the Association for the Study of Negro Life and History." *Journal of Negro History* VIII, no. 4 (October 1923).

———. Review of the "The History of the Negro Church." *Journal of Negro History* VII, no. 2 (April 1922).

———. "Some Things Negroes Need to Do." *Southern Workman* 51 (January 1922).

Yolles, Melanie A. *A Guide to The Henry George Papers, 1840s–1950.* New York: Manuscripts and Archives Division, The New York Public Library, March 1996.

Young, John Russell. *Men and Memories: Personal Reminiscences.* Edited by his wife, May D. Russell Young. New York and London: F. T. Neeley, 1901.

Zangwill, Israel. *Blind Children: Poems.* New York: Funk & Wagnalls, 1903.

———. *Children of the Ghetto.* London: William Heinemann, 1892; London: White Lion Publishers, reprint 1972.

———. *Dreamers of the Ghetto.* New York and London: Harper & Brothers, 1899.

———. *A Land of Refuge.* London: Jewish Territorial Organization, 1907.

———. *Manifesto and Correspondence.* London: Jewish Territorial Organization, 1905.

———. *The Melting-Pot: Drama in Four Acts.* New York: Macmillan, editions of 1909, 1914, 1926.

———. *The Melting-Pot* (Typewritten prompt-book script with manuscript notes, 1908–9). The New York Public Library, Billy Rose Theatre Collection. Liebler & Co. Records Collection.

———. "The Position of Judaism." *North American Review,* 140:461 (April 1895), 425–39.

———. *Speeches, Articles and Letters of Israel Zangwill.* Selected and edited by Maurice Simon, with a Foreword by Edith Ayrton Zangwill. London: Soncino Press, 1937.

Zausmer, Otto. "The Marshall Plan: Goals and Gains." *Boston Daily Globe,* 1950.

Illustration Acknowledgments and Permissions

1. **Governor John Winthrop**. School of Van Dyke. Courtesy of the American Antiquarian Society.
2. **Thomas Paine**. By William Sharp, after George Romney, 1793. Courtesy of the National Portrait Gallery, London.
3. **Design for the Great Seal of the United States**. By Pierre Eugène Du Simitière. Courtesy of the Thomas Jefferson Papers, Manuscript Division, The Library of Congress.
4. **Ralph Waldo Emerson**. By J. J. Hawes. Courtesy of the Print Collection, Miriam and Ira D. Wallace Division of Art, Prints and Photographs, The New York Public Library, Astor, Lenox and Tilden Collections.
5. **John L. O'Sullivan**. *Harper's Weekly*, 1874. Collection of The New-York Historical Society, Negative #43507.
6. **Henry George**. Courtesy of the Henry George Papers, Manuscripts and Archives Division, The New York Public Library, Astor, Lenox and Tilden Foundations.
7. **Jane Addams**. Courtesy of the Swarthmore College Peace Collection.
8. **Israel Zangwill**. Courtesy of the Dorot Jewish Division, The New York Public Library, Astor, Lenox and Tilden Foundations.
9. **Carter G. Woodson**. Courtesy of the West Virginia State Archives, Ancella Bickley Collection.
10. **George C. Marshall**. Courtesy of the George C. Marshall Research Library, Lexington, Virginia. GCMRL #1094.